Reviews and Reader Comments

***** From the Author of "Sweet Comfity Tea"
Reviewed by: Betzi Abram (4/8/2005)
"An epic memoir of survival under Stalinist purges and Nazi enslavement during World War II. A magnificent family record. An excellent exciting story, which many should read, beautifully written full of emotion and intellect."

*****From the author of "Point of Honor" - latest "Dishonorable Few". Robert N. Macomber (6/8/05)
Anatole Kurdsjuk has written an engaging book about his youthful years in 1940's Russia as a prisoner of the commissars, prisoner of the Nazis, a displaced person after WW II, and finally as a new American citizen. His life sounds like an incredible Hollywood movie, but is amazingly true.

*****Admiration
Maria Marshal
I have just finished reading your book and know that I can never fully express my admiration and also my sadness as I read the saga of a little boy and his indomitable parents overcoming endless obstacles, traversing a continent and an ocean to find peace and freedom. My mind feels sadness that humans can treat each other with such brutality. That you witnessed this brutality as a child hurts my heart and I feel gratitude that my own babies did not suffer this.
You have told the story. You have been a witness. I hope many people will read it and feel as I do. I will never forget.

*****A story of human endurance
Reviewed by: V. Mac Baldwin
What a story of human endurance, perseverance and survival. It is a 20th century epic of man's inhumanity to man and God's hand in the life of a courageous family.
It must become a movie.

*****I have a new appreciation for freedom
Reviewed by: Craig N. Holland
Just finished reading the last chapter of your book again. What I
like about your book, is that it makes me value my American
freedom. I have a new hero to respect now, his name is Jacob
Kurdsjuk

*****Delightful
Reviewed by: Douglas Duggan
         I am delighted you wrote the story. It needs to be told
before the Soviet regime is totally forgotten by the younger generations. May your work endure through the ages.

*****This Should be Required Reading
Reviewed by: Pastor Tim McDaniel
Thank you for sharing the story of your family. It is a treasure that
will be required reading for my children. The darkness, sorrow, and
pain of evil serve to contrast God's love, grace and freedom. The
strength and dignity of your parents is an inspiration. You have
honored them and our Lord. Thank you again for giving of yourself in this way.

**** Mandatory Reading
Reviewed by: LMK (May 31, 2005)
Anatole Kurdsjuk splendidly and warmly describes the suffering of
his immediate family during Communism in Russia starting after
the fall of czarist regime, during the Nazi occupation and its labor
camps in Germany until liberation by the American Army, followed
by life in the Displaced Persons (DP) camps and immigration into
the USA. The suffering of the Russian people during these 40
years is incredibly cruel and often forgotten as it fell into the
shadows of the Holocaust. This book, by portraying truthfully the
miseries endured by the common people, is a warning against
Communism, Fascism and Totalitarianism. It should become
mandatory reading in schools to show our children what our
grandparent's generation experienced and suffered on the way to a
new and better future.

Don't forget to tell the children!

The Long Walk Home

Best Wishes

With Miracles Along The Way

Anotile 1/29/05

A Historical Memoir

ANATOLE KURDSJUK

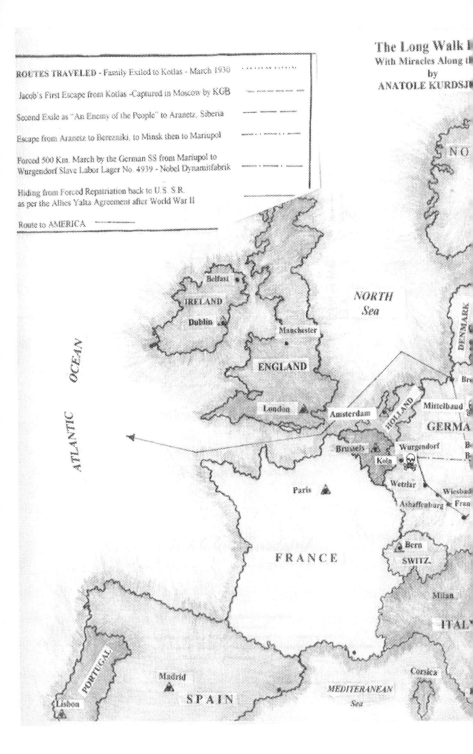

The Long Walk
With Miracles Along the
by
ANATOLE KURDSJI

ROUTES TRAVELED - Family Exiled to Kotlas - March 1930

Jacob's First Escape from Kotlas - Captured in Moscow by KGB

Second Exile as "An Enemy of the People" to Aranetz, Siberia

Escape from Aranetz to Berezniki, to Minsk then to Mariupol

Forced 500 Km. March by the German SS from Mariupol to
Wurgendorf Slave Labor Lager No. 4939 - Nobel Dynamitfabrik

Hiding from Forced Repatriation back to U.S.S.R.
as per the Allies Yalta Agreement after World War II

Route to AMERICA

NO

Belfast

IRELAND

Dublin

NORTH
Sea

Manchester

ENGLAND

DENMARK

Br

London

Amsterdam

Mittelbaud

HOLLAND

GERMA

ATLANTIC OCEAN

Brussels

Wurgendorf

B

Köln

B

Wetzlar

Wiesbad

Paris

Aschaffenburg

Fran

Bern

SWITZ.

FRANCE

Milan

ITAL

PORTUGAL

Madrid

Corsica

Lisbon

SPAIN

MEDITERANEAN
Sea

Front and Back covers designed by:
Terry@Keenan-Design.com

Ellis Island Immigrants (Photo E120) used with permission of the US National Parks Service.

ISBN 0-7414-2428-2

Order the book and contact the Author at:
www.thelongwalkhome.com

Published by:
Printing and Publications, Corp.
21 E. Cabot Blvd
Langhorne, PA 19047
www.printandpub.com
215-547-0700
Fax: 215-269-2532

Printed in the United States of America
Printed on Recycled Paper
Published June 2005

The Beginning

The wedding of Jacob and Olga Kurdsjuk
May 1923 on the Holy Orthodox Day of "Troitsa", Pentecost
in Bolshaya Sliva, Beloruss

Zachary Filipovich Kurdsjuk
In the Czar's Army World War I
1914 - 1916

Jacob's father Zachary served in Poland during WW I. where he was gassed and severly wounded in the trenches. Unable to continue in service, he was released from the army and walked home through Poland to Bolshaya Sliva, Beloruss.

Table of Contents

Dedication

In loving memory of Mama, Papa, my brothers Michael, Victor, Sergei and sister, Anastasia, together with Dedushka Zachary, Babushka Yelena and uncles Boris, Sergei and Alexei, but most of all to Grand Uncle Stephan, who was the first to recognize Papa's abilities and inspired in him a thirst for knowledge and truth.

From The Russian Orthodox Requiem Service

May their Memory be Eternal!
Vechnaya Pamyat!

Their souls shall rest with the righteous
And their rememberance will be from
generation to generation!

Amen

Preface

Jacob Alexander Zacharyevich and Olga Stepanovna Kurdsjuk were my parents. It was in October of 1972 that I made a promise to Papa on his deathbed.when I told him:

"Papa, I promise I will tell your story. I will put into words the tale of your and Mama's life. I will write of your struggles, agonies and pain, so that your grandchildren will know their heritage and of the legacy you have left."

Since that day, I have sat down to write the story many times. Just as often, I found merely that recalling the incidents of my parents' lives and those of my own, became so overwhelming that any progress was slow, if progress was made at all. As I entered into retirement, I realized that now was the time. The stories that have been told over countless meals and family gatherings now needed to be put on paper, if only in snatches of events, so that they would be preserved for my children and their children.

I began with simple facts and background, most of which I was still able to recall from conversations with my parents. What I could not recall directly, I was able to piece together from conversations with family friends and from photos and documents, all of which Papa somehow managed to preserve through the tumultuous events of their lives. The fact that I have them now is nothing short of miraculous, as they survived no less than exile to Stalinist Siberia, imprisonment in a Nazi Labor Camp during World War II, and the trip to America.

As I began sharing these written records with friends and family, I was surprised by the number of times I was told that "The story needs to be told to others" and that "this needs to be a book." You see I am not a writer, at least in the formal sense. I've written as part of my job and as part of normal communications, of course, but the thought of me being "an author" was one that would have never occured to me naturally. Yet, as friends and family persisted in their encouragement I caught the vision and accepted their challenge, and their help. After several years, and more than a few drafts, I am now ready to share Mama and Papa's story with you, and the rest of the world.

As you read their story, I hope that the emotions, anxiety, fear, stress, faith and, most of all, the unconditional forgiveness shown under the most arduous conditions are abundantly clear, despite the lack of my formal writing skills that may become evident as you read. You see, for while we Russians may be natural story tellers, or so I've been told, the gift of the written word is far less natural, as I've come to realize intimately over the course of this project.

Acknowledgments

Without the patience and spiritual support of my darling wife, Linda, this book could not have been written.

I am grateful to my sons, Jake and Tony, who encouraged me continually, providing computer, literary and photographic help, and their wives, Muriel and Jenny, who urged me to begin this project and prodded me in countless ways to start.

My cousin, Anne, who was my earliest advocate to write it.

The book is considerably different from my first draft, thanks mainly to the feedback from Anne, Betzi Abram, Doug Duggan, Ellen McLeod, Rev. Hans Jacobse, William English, and Lily Wadiak. I asked for their help, and their comments were exceedingly helpful; I am in their debt.

And to other members of our family and dearest friends, who heard our story many times, either in part or completely, and have inspired its creation, thank you!

Also my sincere gratitude to Daniel Krotov for his help in structuring the electronic version of the manuscript prior to publication, and to Terry Keenan for creating the cover artwork.

Thank You All

Papa always said: "If you think you have done everything. You haven't."

Mama and Papa this is your life as best I can recall.

Timeline

1903 -1929 The Khutor - BOLSHAYA SLIVA, BELORUSS
    Dedushka Zachary
    Meeting "The Love of my Life"
    World War I and Bolshevik Revolution of 1917
    Starting Life and The Kulak's Fate

1929 - 1930 THE SIBERIAN EXILE to KOTLAS
    The GULAGS on Severnaya Dvina
    Children Dying
    Attempts at Escape
    The Gold Buttons

1931- NOT QUITE GETTING AWAY
    The Lubyanka KGB Prisons in Moscow
    Permanent Exile
    The Second Escape

1931 -1932 Beloruss, Ural Mountains and Ukraine
    Running, Hiding and Surviving Without Papers
    Doctor Meyer Zelagin

1932 - 1943 MARIUPOL in the Ukraine
    The Sea Port
    Building Azov Stal
    Life on Cherry Lane and Dedushka Svyatoduchov
    World War II German Occupation

NACH WEST - September 7, 1943 to December 10, 1943
    The Forced 500 Kilometer March
    Pzemysl, Poland - Disinfecting Bath

1943 -1945 Alfred E. Nobel DYNAMITFABRIK
    Wurgendorf - Westfallen Deutches Reich
    Slave Labor Lager No. 4939

1945/46 - March 29, 1945 - RESCUED

Gen. George Patton and the Third Armored Division
Hiding from our rescuers and the forcible return to
    USSR
DP Camps - Wetzlar, Mainz/Kastel, Aschaffenburg
Searching for Aunt Mary in America
Immigration stumbling blocks - "Lost Visas"
Schweinfurt, Bremerhaffen - SS Gen. Black -
    March 29, 1949

AMERICA! AMERICA! - April 6, 1949

Chapter 1

The Khutor, World War I and the Russian Revolution

The GULAG in Aranets Siberia, just above the Arctic Circle, was considerably different from the camp in Kotlas to which Jacob and his family were initially exiled in 1930. He and Olga escaped from Kotlas only six months ago but, once again, Jacob was back in Siberia, even farther north than before.

During his first escape he was captured and imprisoned at the NKVD Secret Police Lubyanka prison in Moscow, where he endured a variety of persuasion techniques, beatings and tortures, including forty-five days in solitary, as his captors attempted to extract a confession. In accordance with "Article 58" of the Soviet Union's 1926 Legal Code, a prisoner's confession was a prerequisite before the accused could be labeled an "Enemy of The People" and sentenced. Jacob received twenty-five years at hard labor for "rehabilitation" in this Godforsaken part of the Soviet Union. Very few survived this exile, Jacob's prospects did not look any better.

At thirty he felt he could survive in this climate, but he also knew that sooner or later the *urki* or *blatnye* (thieves and cut-throats), who comprised the greater population of the camp, would finish him off for his boots or the warm coat. How long could he last? To stay here would be capitulating to the Soviet Regime which so unjustly destroyed his family. But, if he survived, there could be a chance to escape and possibly see Olga again. He decided to run at the first opportunity.

He was a desperate man, and desperate men accomplish things sane men would hardly consider.

When the exiles were brought to the camp, the guards began separating them into groups and distributing them into barracks. Jacob was shoved into the nearest building and told to find a place. These accommodations were not much different from the Stolypin railroad car cages in which he and the others were transported to the camp. At least here the air smelled clean.

1

One could take a breath without choking on human odors. Looking around, he did not see anyone and noticed an open door at the end of the hall. What did he have to lose? The guards were preoccupied with new prisoners, right now would be the best time to try his escape, at least from the barracks. What lay beyond the open door, only God knew.

As he crept toward the open door, chills and cold sweat ran down his back. Will he make it out? At any moment he anticipated a "HALT!" from a guard; if he didn't obey the command immediately, a rifle shot would follow. He pressed on toward the light. His mind was bombarded with fear and anxiety but the survival instinct in him was stronger and he concentrated only on the next step, while a persistent thought reverberated in his brain, "Will I hear the bullet screaming toward the back of my head?"

He glanced through the opening, there were no guards outside. Stepping out, he bolted toward the trees. Before him lay the Taiga; there was no need for a fence, the Taiga was a sufficient deterrent to anyone attempting an escape into its domain.

No shout to HALT! was heard as he plunged into the Siberian jungle. Branches and barbs tore at his hands and face while thick spider webs enveloped him, but he had only one thought. Get away, run! His legs were tangling in the undergrowth but he broke free, as the adrenalin urged him on.

Jacob did not know how long he had been running, when suddenly losing his footing, he stumbled over a log. Instinctively, he put his arms out to fend off the branches reaching for his face, but it was too late. His head struck the trunk of a tree as his chest smashed full force into a stump. He felt the ribs give way as a lightning bolt of pain pierced his brain. Just before smashing to the ground his hands felt something soft. As he lay there in a semi-conscious state, the aroma of the damp earth and vegetation penetrated his senses, transporting him back to the village of his youth, Bolshaya Sliva near Slutsk in Beloruss.

It was spring of 1913 and his father Zachary, was teaching him how to plow behind a horse, urging Jacob to hold on tightly to the plow handles while guiding the horse in a straight furrow. Behind them, a flock of birds were squabbling over the uncovered feast of bugs and worms in the newly turned earth as he proceeded toward the end of the field.

He was the first born of four sons in a family of serfs, to Zachary Filipovich and Yelena Fedorovna who worked for a *pomeshchik* (land owner) as did most of the peasants at the time. In the 1900's more than 75% of Russia's population was involved in agriculture. Serfs were considered property and could be bought and sold at a whim of the owner, just like a horse or a hut. Nikolai Gogol in his novel, "Dead Souls," tells of an enterprising swindler who sold a village, and to inflate its value in serfs, added the names of deceased villagers from head stones.

Serfs spent most of their time at tasks assigned by the *pomeshchik* for which they were compensated in produce grown on his land, such as wheat, corn, oats, and potatoes. Money was a scarce commodity. They were also allotted a piece of land called a *khutor,* on which they grew additional food. Some of the *pomeshchik's* land was designated "common ground" where the serfs brought their animals to graze. They were also permitted to use his forest to gather mushrooms and berries, a major portion of their diet. If you are interested in reading more about the origins of serfdom, I strongly recommend you investigatethe writings of Leo Tolstoy, Ivan Turgenev and Nikolai Gogol.

Growing up in such an environment provided the serf little time for education. The peasant children attended a village school for a maximum of four grades where they were taught to read, count and write their name. Higher education was reserved for the upper classes.

Winter is the longest season in Russia but it was a short one for the serfs and the only time available for schooling. The many chores in preparation for spring planting consumed all available time, but winter was also the only time to earn a few *rubles*. Many serfs, with the *pomeshchik's* permission, hired themselves out to merchants in town, leaving their families to fend for themselves until they returned for spring work. This privilege was not free, and the serf had to pay *obrok* (a surcharge) to the *pomeshchik* on the money he earned. Jacob's father Zachary did not want to leave his family and found an alternative way to earn the money. He became a woodcutter, harvesting ash trees in the forest. Ash was used to make wooden wagon wheels. Zachary cut, split, steamed and bent the wood into curves which he sold to the wheelwrights in town.

Jacob, being the oldest, had to help Zachary with this arduous work, but even in this task he found adventure and amusement. While driving a sledge into the forest over the frozen road, he noticed how ice sparks flew from the horse's hooves as they pounded their way on the icy path. One day he decided to see if he, too, could make the ice fly; he was eight at the time. Taking two horse shoes and some rawhide straps from the barn, he hid them in the straw of the sledge for the next trip. On the way to the cutting site, he tied the horseshoes to his feet, quietly slid off the sledge and started pounding his feet on the icy road. Alas, the sparks did not fly, Jacob flew off to the side of the road with a yelp and a thud. Zachary heard the scream and turned around just in time to see his son buried up to his neck in a bank of fluffy fresh snow. Halting the horses, he went to rescue Jacob, laughing so heartily that tears came to his eyes. Jacob did not think of it as a laughing matter. In the evening, when they got home, Zachary told the story to his wife and family as the older brother had to once more endure the humiliation.

Some landowners were kind to their serfs, while others frequently beat them with a horse whip for any infraction or disobeyed order. This was the standard punishment at the time, encouraged by local magistrates who often administered it. Russia was ruled by the Czar whose policies were forcefully carried out by the local authorities appointed by him and the *Dvorianie*. The Czar considered his power to be ordained by God, and since Russia was a very religious Orthodox country, the population trembled at the mention of his name, especially the downtrodden serfs. They called any male above them *batyushka* (father), inferring the power of the Heavenly Father, God. The Czar's edicts and woeful treatment of the population were some of the causes for the Russian Revolution.

In 1914, after assassination of the Grand Duke Ferdinand of Austria, Russia was preparing for war. Conscription of serfs for the army was in full force and Zachary was called to defend the Motherland, while Jacob, at the age of eleven, became the head of the household.

Jacob hated the farm, and at every available opportunity he would sneak away to read whatever he could lay his hands on. He had completed the four years of the village school but that only inspired his thirst for knowledge. He was blessed with a photographic memory and could recall paragraphs verbatim. He loved reading of new ways and lands, devouring every book on any subject that his Uncle Stephan brought him. Stephan, was his father's brother and one of the local elders who early recognized Jacob's abilities. He encouraged Zachary to have Jacob pursue higher education and offering to sponsor him but Zachary would not hear of it. Jacob was the eldest and soon it would be his responsibility to guide the family.

One evening Zachary found Jacob reading in the barn under a kerosene lamp. He went wild and beat him unmercifully. Zachary's main concern was the possibility of fire if Jacob fell asleep. In addition, Jacob was losing sleep, "wasting time reading" making him too tired for work the next day. The beatings did not divert Jacob from pursuing knowledge; just the opposite, he spent every available moment with a book.

Once, while hiding in the woods to read, he spied a pretty girl bringing her cows and sheep to pasture. She was so darling that he could not go back to the book but followed her at a distance, hiding behind the bushes. She also noticed him and was playing coy and shy, sneaking a peek from behind stacks of newly-mown wheat. This initial encounter was later to bloom into a full and passionate love. The girl's name was Olga, and their romance continued to grow as they met in the pasture or near the forest. However, such meetings were few since the farm and the animals came first. Olga's family were also serfs and lived in the

***Uncle Stephan Filipovich Kurdsjuk with his best friend
Nukolai Kuznetsow- After The Hunt - October 1, 1916.***

*Stephan insisted that Zachary allow Jacob to pursue higher
education, but Zachary would not permit it. Jacob's duty, as
the eldest son, was to care for the farm. Stephan encouraged
Jacob to read and brought him books on many subjects, all
of which Jacob devoured. This became the basis of his life
and future education. Jacob had a photographic memory.*

next village of Bondary. Her father Stephan was an ardent farmer, a woodcutter and a very religious person who often accompanied his grandfather on pilgrimages to the Holy Sites and monasteries in the region. This Orthodox religious fervor was transmitted to Olga and Stephan's family which consisted of five girls and two boys. Olga's mother Maria died during the birth of her last child. Being the oldest, Olga became the "mother" of the family at age of twelve, leaving little time for romance.

One morning when Stephan went into the barn to harness the horses for the day's work, they were gone. The stall was empty. Stephan knew that, the night before he had tied them to the post and closed the barn doors; therefore, they could not have wandered away. There was only one answer, someone had stolen them! To a farmer this was a catastrophe since his livelihood depended on the animals. Stephan cried an alarm, rousing his family and neighbors to start searching for the animals. The only evidence were tracks leading into the forest. The deeper they went into the forest, the more the tracks disappeared. What was he to do? How could he find out where they were or who stole them?

After a day of inquiries in the village and surrounding area without success, he decided that the only alternative was to go and see a soothsayer in the next village. This man was known for his craft and helped many with his advice; possibly he could find his horses. Stephan decided to give it a try and started getting ready. He picked up his walking stick and looked for his hatchet which he always stuck in his belt and never left the house without it. It also was nowhere to be found; this was not a good sign. But, he had no choice, without the horses he was lost and could not do his work. He went to the soothsayer.

Stephan explained his predicament and asked for help. Without waiting, the soothsayer asked Stephan if anything else was missing; Stephan could not immediately think of anything, including his hatchet. The soothsayer said: "Look for your favorite hatchet, whoever has the hatchet has your horses." Where does one look for a small ax? Stephan was perplexed. The soothsayer continued: "You will find your horses, but you have a more serious problem in your

7

house. When you get home, climb into the attic and check out the chimney above the stove there is a crack and if it t isn't fixed your house will burn down."

Stephan paid the soothsayer with a ham, some eggs and a bottle of vodka. Upon returning home he immediately climbed into the attic. Sure enough, there was a crack in the chimney where the bricks separated, large enough to place one's fist into.

Village homes and barns had thatched straw roofs and fire was always a potential danger not only for the owner but for the whole village since sparks could easily ignite other roofs. There were many incidents where whole villages were destroyed because one home burned. To prevent such happenings, buildings were separated by the largest distance possible. Fires were fought with bucket brigades using water hoisted from wells and cattle watering troughs. A disaster was averted and Stephan was grateful to the soothsayer, but there was still the matter of the horses. He went to the *pomeshchik* and borrowed two plow horses; for which he was charged real money.

A month later, on market day, while Stephan was wandering about the open market in Slutsk, he spied his missing hatchet on a wagon and waited for the owner to return. When he did, Stephan recognized him as a villager from a neighboring county. He got his boys and several neighbors together before confronting "the thief." They all confirmed that the hatchet really belonged to Stephan, since he rarely went anywhere without it, he always had it stuck in his belt. A policeman was summoned and they confronted the wagon owner. He stammered, vehemently denying that he had anything to do with the theft of the hatchet or horses. However several of the villagers confirmed that this man was a suspected horse thief because he always had horses to sell for which there rarely was a bill of sale. The whole entourage followed the accused to his home, and upon opening the barn doors found Stephan's horses in the stalls. The thief swore that he knew nothing about it, saying that someone was playing a dirty trick on him. The thief was arrested and Stephan got his horses and hatchet back.

Religious holidays were the only time young people could get together for fun and frolic. Such gatherings involved games, singing, dancing and often semi-superstitious activities. These were pursued mostly by young girls and usually had something to do with the selection of a future mate, or at least an attempt to find out who "he" might be. Village life had many superstitions, thoroughly believed in, even though they were contrary to the strict teaching of the Orthodox faith. There were soothsayers, babushki and gypsies who plied this trade and quite often were good in foretelling fortunes.

The holiday of Yanka Kupala, a mythical Spirit, celebrated in early June, was the special day on which young girls attempted to learn of their prospective mate. To find this out, a special ritual was performed just before sunset. At dusk, young girls went to the edge of the forest where wild flowers grew. While repeating an incantation, they picked the flowers with their teeth, placing them in the fold of their apron. The process continued until it was almost dark, at which time they would weave a crown from the flowers placing it on their head, and return to the village. It was said that the first young male the girl saw would be her husband. Young men knew of this practice, and if they were sincerely interested in a girl, they would follow her and position themselves to be seen first. Olga was pretty certain that she would marry Jacob, but an assurance from the Spirit of Yanka Kupala would make it that more certain. She picked the flowers with her teeth, while intoning the special words, and thought of no one else but Jacob. At dusk, she started walking toward the village when suddenly, something grabbed her from behind. She screamed, thinking it was "A Spirit," but to her delight it was Jacob. She was assured in her heart that the love of her youth would marry her someday.

Olga was fifteen at the time.

Stephan Makarenko - Olga's father

With children of his son Dennis who perished during the Russo-Japanese War. It was said that Dennis was taken by a Siberian tiger during the platoon's march to the front, and never seen again.

Chapter 2

The Steam Mill in the Swamp

Much has been written about the Russian Revolution and to recount its history would require volumes. I will primarily speak of the impact it had on our family and serfs like Grandfather Zachary.

Land reforms were attempted by some of the czars. Czar Alexander II, known as "The Liberator," appeared to have had one of the most promising concepts. His reform would have given the serfs not only land of their own but certain privileges which had been long denied them. Alexander II however was unable to implement it; he was assassinated by a "revolutionary." It is believed by many that his death was instigated by the *Dvoriane* and landowners who would have lost a great deal under the proposed reforms, had they been implemented. Instead of more freedom, the serfs became more downtrodden; they were forced to work in factories and mills; thus came the beginning of Russia's industrial revolution.

The communist state under Lenin passed many storms after October 1917, and the Civil War which followed sank the country into a great affliction; terror became the main weapon of the revolutionaries. Those in power established the most "legalized" terror history has ever known. It is estimated that at least ten million Russians lost their lives in the first three years which followed Lenin's dominance. "As a 'lawful' weapon of state, terror became status quo in Communist Russia." *(Kannelopolus, P., Twentieth Century,* Athens, 1956)

The working conditions in factories and mines, which supplied the raw materials for the mills were primitive. Serfs, who were used to the hard labor in the fields, now became factory workers and city dwellers. However, those who could choose, continued to stay on the land, which they knew, and had been accustomed to working on for generations.

"Three years after the revolution, the first workers' state was at the brink of collapse. Industrial production was at 20% of

11

pre-war levels. The production of iron had fallen to 1.6% and steel to 2.4% of pre-revolutionary times. In 1920 the cost of a workers necessities was two-and-a-half to three times greater than his pay. By 1923, the Russian industry was in complete disarray." (*Working Opposition, Athens:* Vergos Pub., 1975)

After his stroke, Lenin began to lose ground as internal oppositions arose. Political differences, and personal ambitions, undermined the coalition. Someone was eagerly waiting. Stalin was preparing. Lenin recognized the trap but was unable to react in time. Finally, in January of 1924, he died. Stalin was elected as the General Secretary of the Communist Party and dominated the situation, casting aside and annihilating everyone in his way. Russia was entering an even more tragic era.

In 1926, a legal code was implemented, in part as a class weapon against those who opposed Stalin's power. It instituted a wholesale extermination in the Bolshevik state.
"Article 58" of the Code foresaw sanctions for whoever was suspected of endangering Bolshevism. Certain regulations legalized capture and condemnation of people who had committed no crime at all against the state, and the law became an instrument of political terror.." (*Imprisoned Heroes and Martyrs of the USSR, p.25*)

Stalin's life was a chain of crimes. His "comrade" and fellow struggler Trotsky, whose life came to a dreadful end at Stalin's hands wrote: "Stalin admitted he found that the greatest joy in his life was to closely observe some enemy of his and, then painstakingly preparing each step, take merciless revenge on him, and then go peacefully to sleep."

Later in life, Jacob had the pleasure of discussing Stalin's early escapades in crime with Nikolai Ivanovich P. who had been a railroad policeman in the province of Georgia during the czar's time. He recalls the day he arrested Stalin after a train robbery in Tiblisi. Even then, he felt the sinister character of this individual.

"Article 58" was responsible for the exile, torture and annihilation of millions of Russian people. However, before Lenin's death, the Bolshevik Revolutionary Government attempted to implement some of the propaganda slogans coined by him which helped to win people to his cause. "Land to the farmer, factories to the worker!" was one of the more prevalent and popular cries with the masses. Without it, the Bolshevik Revolution would certainly have failed.

Under a New Economic Policy (NEP) developed by the Duma (Senate), land owned by the *pomeshchiks* was confiscated and began to be distributed to Soviet Citizens based on the old European feudal concept of "sons", or on the "number of mouths" the family had to feed. The more mouths one had to feed, the more land was assigned.

The land initially was "given free" with the proviso that future low taxes would be used to repay the price to the government. In Russia land is measured in *desiatynas*, one *desiatyna* equals approximately 2.7 acres. For each mouth he had to feed, the serf received one desiatyna of land plus three desiatynas for himself. Zachary received fifteen and a half acres. There were options as to the type of land one could select or exchange for. Most desirable was land ready for planting. Forest, pasture or lowland consisting primarily of swamps but having access to water, was least favored. Exchange formulae were established, with lowland being the least desirable. Grandfather Zachary chose to exchange most of the land offered to him for a swamp near Bolshaya Sliva, where he was born and lived. He was familiar with the land and had ideas for it.

Most of his neighbors thought that Zachary was "off his rocker"'due to the concussion and gassing he received during World War I. They commiserated with his wife Yelena and the children. He kept only two *desiatynas* for planting and three of forest for harvesting ash trees.

When the land was officially assigned, he immediately began the exhaustive effort of draining the swamp. It had been there for as long as anyone could remember, and it was said that at one time it protected a nobleman's castle. This was substantiated when every so often huge beams would pop out of the ground. Zachary gathered them, dried and sold the wood to furniture makers. After cutting, and finishing, the items manufactured showed wood patterns of exquisite beauty, demanding a high price.

Zachary had two horses and four sons, when he began to cut drainage ditches in the swamp which emptied into a nearby stream. He and his boys worked hard and completed the project in four months, just before the winter set in. They planted winter wheat on the arable acreage. During the winter, they felled ash trees in the forest and prepared the wood for wheelwrights. It was a difficult first year and Zachary had to borrow money from his brothers to survive.

When spring arrived, their efforts of the previous year began to bear fruit. The thaw began to drain the swamp leaving mounds of peat which Zachary cut, dry and sell to his neighbors for fuel. Peat was easier to manage than wood and produced more heat with less ash. After the peat was removed, the dark rich soil underneath was full of nutrients for planting. Their initial planting of potatoes and sugar beets on this reclaimed land produced one of the best harvests anyone had ever seen. Not only did they have enough for their own use but sold the excess to pay off a portion of the family debts from the previous year. Within two years they were debt free, with money left over.

That winter Zachary outlined his plans to the family of what he had in mind when he chose the swamp. It had already proven its value in peat and potato harvest, and now was to begin the next phase of growth. He told them of the steam mill he had seen in Poland, and said that he had already ordered the steam engine, which should arrive in the spring.

There was a windmill near Bolshaya Sliva, the only one within a reasonable distance, but it operated only when the winds were favorable. His steam mill would run whenever it was needed since there was plenty of water and peat for fuel. The building, to house the mill would be inexpensive to build, and consisted primarily of a roof over the engine and enough storage area to keep the elements off the grain to be milled.

His younger sons were skeptical of the proposal since they could not relate to the steam engine and its operation, but Jacob, his eldest, said it was a great idea because he had read about the process in one of the books Uncle Stephan had brought him.

Next day, Jacob went to visit Uncle Stephan and brought the book home. That evening and on successive nights he read and explained the process to his father and brothers. The book also contained complete plans for a steam mill, its construction, water supply and operation. Zachary knew he had made the right choice and God had given him a smart son. Nothing was ever mentioned of the beatings Jacob received because he was caught reading, and of course there was no apology. It was the eldest son's duty to do his father's bidding!

The arrival of the steam engine was a major event in Bolshaya Sliva. It was delivered on a large wagon drawn by two matched Belgian horses accompanied by a Polish engineer who would install it. The engineer spoke Russian and was very pleased to learn that Jacob was familiar with the process from reading the book. They discussed the procedure and immediately began laying a foundation for the steam engine and the building which would house the mill. Many of Zachary's neighbors were skeptical, not believing that the process would work, nicknaming him "Crazy Zachary".

The building was completed in record time, the steam engine installed and the magic day to begin operation arrived. Zachary invited his neighbors to the event, asking all of them to bring two sacks of grain to be milled, for free. Two sacks was a small price to pay to see the steam-powered mill and to prove that Zachary was really 'touched'. Unlike the windmill, the metal grinding gears in Zachary's mill could be changed quickly; thereby offering various grades of flour. The wind mill offered only one grade, that is if the wind was up.

God blessed the efforts of Zachary and his sons. The event went off without a hitch and the Bolshaya Sliva skeptics became believers. When the demonstration was over, the engineer unveiled a special gift for Zachary. He had installed a steam whistle which announced the mill's operation, and its sound became a call sign for Bolshaya Sliva.

Since money was a scarce commodity for the serfs, Zachary's

15

charge for milling the grain was in barter fashion, for every ten sacks of grain milled, he received a sack of grain, an acceptable exchange for the farmers. Soon, not only the villagers of Bolshaya Sliva but others from the surrounding area drove the extra distance to bring their grain to his mill, to be milled by 'the new-fangled machine' and, they didn't have to wait for the wind! "Crazy Zachary" was gaining respect from his neighbors and began to prosper.

By this time his eldest son was very seriously courting the love of his young life, Olga Stepanovna Makarenko, and anxious to be married. However, Olga's father had received numerous proposals from other suitors for his daughter's hand, some were from town merchants from town. Olga was a beautiful young woman skillful in everything she did. Even the *pomeshchik* recognized her skills and paid her an adult's wage for the work in the fields. Such a skillful girl was worth a great deal, and required minimal dowry. Jacob and Olga had vowed to marry while still in their early teens and waited for the right moment. Now they were nineteen, and it was time.

In Russia of old, marriages were arranged by the parents of the young people, utilizing go-betweens called *swaty*. These usually were the more respected members of the village or relatives from the bridegroom's side. The process was quite elaborate and imbedded with village traditions. The elders came to the house of the bride girded with fancy embroidered linen towels, thus signifying that the process was in earnest and that the towels would "bind the couple together." The father of the bride would discuss the terms with them, agreeing upon the dowry and date of marriage. Once the agreement was reached the potential bride was informed. Her refusal to accept the proposed arrangement was considered a disgrace to her family, a slap in the face to her father and a serious breach of the village honor. Jacob was aware of the potential suitors for Olga's hand and prepared to dissuade all comers by any and all available means.

One such suitor, from town, came to Olga's father with a proposal of marriage, bringing Stephan a substantial gift of gold money. It was winter and he arrived in a sleigh drawn by a *troika* of matched horses with bells ringing from the harness. Such an appearance indicated that the suitor had substantial wealth and was a "catch" even if the bride was not in love with him or possibly had never even seen him. Jacob and his friends heard the bells and began preparations to meet the suitor outside the village.

Jacob with his three brothers and several cousins had anticipated such an occasion and planned an ambush by the side of the road. He and Olga had agreed that if there was an agreement for her to marry anyone else they would commit suicide, rather than comply. Olga had conveyed these thoughts to her father and he promised that he would not make the final decision without first letting her know. Jacob knew what was happening because he had an ally in Olga's younger brother Yesip, and relied on him for the latest news.

When the suitor and his *swaty* were ready to leave, Yesip ran to the pre-arranged place where he knew Jacob and his friends were waiting. As soon as the *troika* rounded the curve in the road, Jacob and his pals jumped into the horse's path screaming and yelling, causing them to bolt. Some of the youths grabbed the reins and brought the sleigh to a halt while Jacob and several others dragged the unsuspecting suitor and his *swaty* out of the sleigh. Fists flew and met their mark, with the accompanying comments, "Aha! The town girls are not good enough for you! So, you came to steal ours! We'll show you! Tell the others like you not to show their faces in our village or they will get more of the same!"

They threw the bruised men into the sleigh, smacked the horses on the rump, and sent them galloping into the night. Next day the news of the incident spread throughout the village. After that there were no more "town" suitors for the girls of Bondary. Of course everyone knew who "did the deed" but the honor of the village was at stake and no one would identify the perpetrators.

The incident soon faded from conversation and Zachary sent his own swaty to Stephan. These were greeted with love and warmth; after consuming several bottles of vodka, provided by the future father-in-law, it was joyously announced that the wedding would take place in May of 1923 on the Orthodox Holy Day of *Troitsa*, Pentecost.

In the Orthodox Faith, *Troitsa* is considered the most sacred Holy Day after *Pascha*/Easter. It is the day on which, according to Biblical scripture in Acts Chapter 2, the Holy Spirit descended on the Apostles as they awaited His arrival in the upper room in Jerusalem, forty days after Christ's Resurrection. Only a few months were left before the wedding date and preparations had to be started in earnest, considering the spring work which had to be done before the celebration.

Village Orthodox weddings are protracted affairs lasting anywhere from three days to a week and the entire village was invited. It begins with the groom's friends "stealing the bride" from her home, then coming to him demanding a "ransom" to get her back. This usually occurres on the day before the wedding, while friends of the bride tried to "steal her back," resulting in a great party at which the bride and groom are kept apart by whatever means possible. The revelry usually lasted through the night; then the friends of the couple spirited them away locking them up in separate sheds built for this purpose. A guard was posted, since it was considered a bad omen for the groom to see the bride on the wedding day until they met in church.

Zachary began preparations for the event by buying up empty bottles for the vodka he and his sons would brew to host the wedding. He had plenty of corn and other grain at the mill; therefore, the ingredients were not a problem. The deterrent was how to keep the production process secret, since brewing vodka was the prerogative of the government and it heavily taxed anything "home brewed." A still was built in a very inaccessible part of the swamp, where inspectors would have difficulty locating it, and the "aroma" of the sour mash could not be easily detected. Production began as soon as it was possible to make the sour mash without it freezing. It was an around-the-clock process. Vodka was brewed and bottles were filled, corked and sealed with bee's wax. To prevent the possibility of the government men finding the vodka, it was hidden throughout the swamp. Jacob and Zachary lost count of the bottles and had to prepare a detailed map showing locations of each cache.

On the wedding day, as the bride was getting ready, the groom sent musicians to her house to play for the gathering while the wedding party decorated the wagon and horses with garlands of wild flowers. Then, the bride was placed in the wagon and the procession to the church began. It was led by the *swaty* who "arranged" for the marriage. They were girded with the same decorated linen towels which they wore during the wedding arrangement process and carried a huge candle to the church. The *swaty* were followed by musicians and the bridesmaids who lamented mournfully because their friend was leaving them and would now become a "woman." The candle was the bride and groom's first gift to the Lord, asking Him to bless and shine on the marriage. It was placed in the church next to the altar and lighted at the start of the ceremony where it burned throughout the week of festivities. The *swaty* were followed by musicians, then parents and relatives of the couple. The rest of the village followed.

Meanwhile, the groom dressed in his 'Sunday best' and, accompanied by the best man, either rode his horse or walked to the church to await the bride.

The Orthodox wedding ceremony is very ornate with many beautiful hymns sung by the choir and extensive prayers intoned by the priest for the success and bounty of the marriage. On that day, the bride and groom are considered to be king and queen. To symbolize this, the groom's ushers, during most of the one-hour-long ceremony, hold gold crowns over the couple's heads. Holding the crown aloft without touching the heads of the bride and groom for that period of time is not an easy task; therefore, the groom selects his strongest and tallest friends as ushers. As one holds the crown aloft the blood drains from the arm, and it is a testimony to the groom's strength when his ushers hold the crown up without switching hands. Only a few were capable of performing this feat. After the ceremony many of the ushers are unable to bend their arm for hours, and have to drink the toasts with the help of the bridesmaids, which really starts the fun.

The wedding feast begins at the bride's home, then moves on to the groom's house, thereafter moving to other relatives' homes. After three-to-five days, or when vodka and food run out, whichever comes first, the wedding feast is over. Jacob and Olga's wedding lasted six days. Zachary and his boys made numerous trips to the swamp to locate the cache of vodka. It never ran out. As a matter of fact, it is said that for many years thereafter bottles kept popping up in the swamp, to the delight of hunters and berry gatherers.

After the wedding, while their house was being built, Jacob and Olga moved in with Zachary and Yelena. Yelena found her new daughter-in-law to be a wonderful wife for her son and a great help to her with everything in the house. There wasn't anything she could not do, either in the home, the barn or the field. Yelena felt greatly blessed and became more than a mother-in-law to Olga, they became friends.

Jacob selected a beautiful parcel of land between the mill and Zachary's house. It was cleared, lumber purchased, and by the fall of 1924 they moved into their own quarters. Olga was overjoyed and put all of her efforts into making it her own little haven. It was her own house and she would make it a dream-home. The four-room bungalow was constructed of sturdy pine beams in the form of a log-house. The interior walls were plastered and whitewashed to make the rooms brighter and to provide more insulation. The standard Russian stove was built in the center of the house and served as the cooking, baking and heating source for the home.

Jacob and Olga's first child, Michael, was born just before their house was finished. A pathway from the front door led to the main road along which Jacob planted birch trees on both sides, creating an alley. It was a beautiful home, ringing with Michael's laughter. Jacob was overjoyed to have a son and Olga worked hard to make the home a special one for her new family. She put all of her heart into everything she did.

In the village a woman's lot was a difficult one. Not only did she have to care for the family but a great deal of other farm work fell to her. Much of the planting, weeding and gathering of crops was on her shoulders including the care of domestic animals. It was a sunup to sunset day! The evenings were devoted to spinning yarn or weaving cloth. Most of the serf's day-to-day clothing was made from homespun cloth and only "Sunday clothes" were purchased, or made from store bought fabric.

It was a hard but satisfying life. While Jacob worked at the mill, Olga cared for the home. She was so happy! She didn't have to go far for anything she needed. The forest was just outside the door where berries and mushrooms were abundant. Mushrooms were a substantial staple of the peasant's diet. Many varieties were gathered and dried, the favorite was *borovik.,* which grew under oak trees on mossy ground. It was the tastiest of all mushrooms, prized by the gatherers. Fried or cooked fresh the borovik produced an aroma and taste equal to that of truffles. These mushrooms were also strung and dried in an oven to be used in soup or *kasha* during winter. Just several slices made all the difference in flavor and aroma, and they were plentiful in the forest, right next to Jacob and Olga's home.

Grandfather Zachary was a frequent visitor and loved playing with his new grandson marching him around the room, counting cadence he learned in the military. "Hut, two, three, about march" echoed round through the room as he spun his grandson round and round making him giggle and laugh. He could not wait until Michael started walking so that he could teach him all kinds of things.

This idyllic environment was cut short as Michael contracted pneumonia and died very suddenly. Jacob and Olga were devastated, but during those years many children died due to lack of medical help. Remedies for most illnesses were home-brewed herbs. Many times the only human help was provided by the services of a "*babushka*" (a healer). Doctors were available only for the city people.

They mourned the loss of their first child, but were confident that God would send them more children. He did not disappoint them. Within a year a beautiful daughter was born whom they named

21

Jacob and Olga's brother Yesip - 1925
Best Friends. On Market Day in Slutsk

Anastasia, in honor of the youngest daughter of Czar
Nikolai II.

Chapter 3

Building a Life

Jacob and Olga's life was becoming a pleasant daily routine. The mill was running well, without many problems. Peat was cut and sold to the villagers, some of it was even being delivered to the neighboring towns. The income was growing and Zachary began to acquire additional horses and livestock.

Boris, Zachary's second son born in 1905, was infatuated with livestock and spent all of his spare time at the family *khutor*. It was getting difficult to get him to work at the mill. He still lived at home with Zachary and his younger brothers, Sergei and Alexei, and was anxious to get a place of his own. However he was still single and would have to wait. He doted on every animal. If a cow or a pig would not eat, he would stand and cry. Boris desperately wanted to have an animal of his own, not owned by his father.

Time came for one of the cows to be bred. Boris had heard of a bull several villages away that was said to be something special and begged his father to have the cow bred with him. Zachary, seeing Boris so intent, relented and permitted the breeding. Boris walked the cow to the village staying there until the breeding process was completed. When he brought the cow home, he made a special place for her in the barn, and only he was allowed to feed, milk and water her. He also took her to pasture where the grass was the best. His younger brothers started teasing him saying that he was in love with the cow and that was why girls didn't interest him. Boris just shrugged it off and continued his vigil.

When the time came for the calf to arrive, Boris got the veterinarian nothing was going to go wrong with this birth, it was his calf. It was born without any complications, had a beautiful coat the color of coffee and cream. Boris named it Hero and moved into the barn to keep an eye on his calf and its mother, all the time stroking Hero and quietly talking to him.

It was the custom for male cattle to be neutered several weeks after birth, Boris would not hear of it and announced: "This is going to be a prime breeding bull"and threatened everyone with death if an attempt was made to harm Hero. He was overjoyed to finally have a calf of his own.

At this time the Communist Regime was entrenching itself. Visits to the *khutors* of the more prosperous peasants by the New Ruling Committee of the area were becoming more frequent as they preached the Proletariat's way of life. Some young people, influenced by the propaganda jumped at the opportunity to leave the villages and help the Revolution prosper. Soon they returned with banners and placards extolling the Communist way.

Stalin began to issue dictums which affected the development of the whole nation. His whims became the mode by which USSR was going to grow. He desperately tried to show the rest of the world that the Union of Soviet Socialist Republics could become equal to or better than any nation in the world and set his sights on getting it accomplished. However, there were many stumbling blocks along the way.

Russia is a land rich in minerals, grain and timber. Stalin decided to exploit these resources to break into the world export market and the quickest way was to utilize the resources of the land. The first would be the abundant harvests from the land, rivers and seas. To speed up production, villages were organized into collectives, with each citizen contributing to the whole. Everyone was going to put everything they produced into one pot and, supposedly all would share equally in the work and profit of the collective.

This eliminated private ownership and everyone had to place all they owned into the "Collective" pot. Initially, it was voluntary; later it was mandated by a government edict. Not many were ready to give up private ownership, since the serfs had just acquired the land after the Revolution. The concept was not working. Stalin, to show that this was his way to catapult the Soviet Union into the world markets, implemented "The Five Year Plan." It was developed by the Politburo, which was totally under his control consisting of handpicked sidekicks. "The Plan" defined production quotas for every industry and was based on empirical formulae developed by the new economists and supported only by a few insiders. It was Stalin's grandiose plan and his inner circle tried to out-promise each other in an attempt to gain Stalin's favor. It was a pipe dream bound to fail, and it did!

However, before it collapsed, numerous alternatives were attempted which did nothing more than to try to forcibly "make it happen," at the expense of the population. The collective or *Kolhoz*, as it was called, had the greatest impact on the industrious farmers like Zachary, Jacob and his family; millions starved to death.

Implementation of the plan was slow, and many of the villagers who were not as successful as their neighbors or basically lazy, became its greatest proponents. These rules were likewise embraced by the local party committees who were responsible for its success. Jealousy and hatred began to rear their ugly heads and informing on one's neighbor became the rule of the day. Anything spoken or done which seemed even remotely non-compliant with "The Plan" or growth of Bolshevism was reported by these individuals to the local Party Committee, which had complete power to "rehabilitate" the individual.

It was becoming evident that 'The Party' was determined to make the communist way work. Farmers, who had a little more than their neighbors, were labeled *Kulaks*. It was said that *kulaks* were holding the worker in their fist for their own profits, preventing the growth of the Soviet Republic. In the eyes of some of his neighbors, Zachary met the criteria of a *kulak*. It did not matter that he and his family had worked day and night to achieve their dreams. Zachary recognized that the future of his mill and family were in perill and began to slowly sell off some of the assets. The first to go was Boris' bull, Hero. Boris cried when he heard of the decision, and even though it was his animal, he understood the potential impact on the family if it was not sold. It would most likely be slaughtered if taken by the collective farm. That fate for Hero, Boris could not accept.

Hero had grown into a huge animal, over 1200 pounds. It was a gorgeous beast with a hint of the Brahman breed. It had a hump on its back and horns so large that their size at the base of the scull measured twelve inches in circumference. Everyone was frightened by its size, but Boris led Hero around by a ring in its nose as if it were a puppy, and Hero wanted to follow Boris everywhere.

When the time came to sell Hero, Boris cried like a five-year old, but dutifully tied a thin rope around Hero's horns and led him to the market. The sale was already prearranged with a person in Slutsk. To throw off suspicion that Zachary was selling off his assets, the Bolshaya Sliva villagers were told that Hero was being sent for a month to a *Kolhoz* for breeding purposes.

The buyer was waiting at the market when Boris and Hero arrived. He brought a huge wagon to which Hero was to be tied for the return trip to the buyer's village. He gave Boris a thick rope to tie around Hero's neck while the other end was tied to the wagon. Boris gave Hero an armload of fresh hay and went wandering in the market place, he could not take the parting. Hero was quiet and calm, but after an hour or so Boris heard loud shouts and screams as people scattered everywhere. He didn't know what the commotion was about, but soon heard Hero's bellowing as the bull rampaged through the market, dragging part of a demolished wagon behind him. Hero was looking for Boris. When he saw him, he stopped and gently nuzzled Boris. Hero had found his friend. The devastation at the market place was considerable. Luckily no one was killed, but there were many injuries as the almost demolished wagon sideswiped people and animals. The buyer wanted to get away from the market as fast as possible, before he was arrested, and Boris had to agree to take the beast to the buyer's barn where a strong stall was waiting for him. After delivering Hero to the buyer's village, Boris drowned his sorrows in vodka, and didn't come home until several days later.

Olga had found her ultimate happiness in life. Anastasia, her new daughter, was growing and a joy of the family. When she was two years old Olga once again became pregnant and their second son Sergei arrived on schedule. She now had the true beginning of a family. Yelena worshipped the ground Olga walked on, and told everyone of her son's good fortune. Zachary had a grandson, Yelena had a granddaughter and their eldest son Jacob loved his wife with all his heart. Their home was a place of love and happiness. Olga's brothers and sisters visited often, marveling at her wonderful life. Yes, she worked hard, but she knew that every hour spent was building a better life for her husband, children and family.

For Anastasia's third birthday Zachary made her a child's bed. She had outgrown the crib and Sergei needed it. Babushka Yelena knitted a special blanket for her and Nastia felt like a big girl in her own special place. Mother was allowing her to hold Sergei and, sometimes, she even fed him milk *kasha*. She loved her little brother and could not do enough for him. It was an idyllic home.

One day the *Commissar* of the District arrived at the mill and insisted that Zachary and Jacob join the Collective. Jacob said that he was contributing more through taxes, grain and flour he gave from the mill. That did not satisfy the committee or the *Commissar* who said he would return in a few days to follow-up on his demands. Perhaps by then Zachary and Jacob would have changed their minds.

Jacob had heard of several families in other villages who refused to join the Collective voluntarily and were forced to join. Their property was confiscated and those who resisted were exiled. He knew that his father was not going to give up the farm, the mill or anything he had worked so hard for; therefore, it would be exile that awaited them in the coming weeks.

He got his brothers together and told them to run away before the Communists came to take them by force. Sergei and Alexei, the youngest of the four, were not certain where they should go and what they would do when they got "there." Sergei was eighteen and Alexei sixteen. Boris however was only two years younger than Jacob and was ready to listen to reason. Jacob got the money they received from the sale of Hero and gave it to Boris, telling him to run to the Ural Mountains where there was still some freedom. That night Boris, after tearful good-byes left, promising that he would let Jacob know where he finally settled. Zachary was completely shaken by the demands of the party committee and became ill, his wife was getting on in years and would need help if anything happened. Therefore it was decided that Sergei and Alexei would stay with the family to await the future.

It wasn't long before one of the neighbors, who became an ardent member of the Communist party, came by and started looking over the mill and Zachary's farm. The way he was walking about and his demeanor indicated that he would be the person "who would do the deed." He was a good-for-nothing, a third cousin of Zachary's wife.

Jacob began to prepare for what seemed like the inevitable. He took thirty ten-ruble gold coins and told Olga to sew them into the hem of his jacket and to also wrap several coins in cloth making buttons which were sewn onto the coat. These coins would be used in case of real emergencies. Inflation was rampant at the time and paper money had no value. A loaf of bread cost a thousand rubles, a stamp to mail a letter ten thousand rubles. Gold was the only medium which could buy anything. They sold two of their best horses, but the buyers already knew that Zachary was a man marked for exile and offered minimal price. In fact, they were almost stealing them for what they paid. They knew that in a few days they would be able to come and help themselves to Jacob's and Zachary's goods. The *Kolhoz* would take over the mill and the remaining personal property would be there "for the taking."

Jacob and Olga began to prepare by gathering and packing food and clothing for "the trip." Who knew where they would be exiled to? Most likely it would be to Siberia, but wherever they were sent, they felt they could establish a new life for themselves and their children. They were young, strong and could overcome any adversity. Olga's sisters begged her to leave the children with them, but how could she part with them. They were her life and come what may, she and Jacob could take care of them.

Chapter 4

The Kulak's Fate

What is a *kulak*? The best description is provided by the chronicler of this misery in the Soviet Union, Alexander Solzhenitsyn...

"In Russian, a *kulak* was a miserly, dishonest rural trader who grows rich not by his own labor but through someone else's, usually by usury operating as a middleman. In every locality, even before the revolution, such *kulaks* could be numbered on one's fingers. And the Revolution totally destroyed their basis of activity. Subsequently, after 1917, by a transfer of meaning, the name *kulak* began to be applied (in official propaganda literature, whence it moved into general use) to all those who in any way hired workers even if it was only when they were temporarily short of working hands in their own families. But the inflation of this scathing term *kulak* proceeded relentlessly, and by 1930 all strong peasants in general were being so called - all peasants strong in management, strong in work, or merely strong in convictions. The term *kulak* was used to smash the strength of the peasantry. But wasn't it most often a matter of hard work and persistence and now these peasants, who had fed Russia in 1928, were hastily uprooted by the local good-for-nothings and city people sent in from the outside."

Like raging beasts, abandoning every concept of humanity and humane principles, which had evolved through millennia, they began to round up every one of the best farmers and their families ,driving them naked, stripped of their possessions, into the northern wastes of the tundra and taiga. Such was the fate of Zachary, Jacob and their families.

On March 8, 1930, a rainy and dreary day, the Commissar

31

and his followers arrived at the mill. Roads were muddy and they had a problem getting their wagon to the mill and Zachary's property. A group of party members and Zachary's neighbors, who were always jealous of Zachary and his family's life, accompanied the mob. Red banners and placards were flying, praising the Bolshevik Revolution and denouncing the *Kulak* who was undermining the *Proletariat.* It was an ugly mob. The leader of the group was a fellow dressed in a black leather jacket, high boots and a leather cap brandishing a red star. His face was pockmarked with the remnants of chicken pox, which lent an even meaner look to his countenance.

He proceeded to outline the "sins" Zachary and his family committed against the Bolshevik System, and how vehemently they exploited the village people at their mill. The night watchman was the only worker they hired to work part-time. He was crippled during the war and could not get any work. When Zachary tried to say a few words in his own defense, he was shouted down with,"Enemy of Bolshevism! Exploiter of the Workers! Kulak, Kulak!"

There was no possibility of being heard and even less of a chance that the mob could be stopped. When Zachary recognized some of his neighbors in the crowd, whom he helped in many ways, and who were now shouting obscenities at him, he hung his head and cried.

The man in the leather coat stepped in front of the mob and shouted, *"Tovarishchy*! Comrades! We know how to deal with these provocateurs! Let us take them to Slutsk, where they will be examined more thoroughly by the *comendatura*!"

This was what the mob needed to hear. They bodily threw Zachary into the wagon and proceeded to his house, where Yelena was praying on her knees and begging the mob to leave them alone. The commissar gave them only minutes to collect what they could of their belongings before tossing them into the wagon! Sergei and Alexei tried to fight off the mob but were beaten down by the crowd and thrown into the wagon. Four of the party members, with red bandannas on their sleeves and brandishing revolvers, jumped up on the back of the wagon blocking any possibility of escape.

As they passed Jacob and Olga's house, the crowd was becoming more boisterous and ugly. Jacob was ready for them, and stepped out on the porch hailing some of the neighbors in an attempt to change the situation. It was futile. Olga was holding Sergei in her arms while Anastasia, her eyes filled with terror, was hanging on to Olga's skirts. They had never seen such a mob or been in a similar situation. There was venom in the mob's voices and hatred in their eyes. Several of them ran into the house and in a few moments one came out dragging the bed Zachary made for Anastasia which was still covered by the blanket Yelena made. Anastasia left her mother's side and ran towards the thief falling on the bed screaming, "It is mine! It is mine!"

The thief brushed her off the bed, but she was able to hold on to the blanket. Jacob and Olga grabbed a few of their belongings and joined Zachary and Yelena on the wagon. Everyone was crying. Olga and Yelena wept from grief but Zachary and Jacob out of rage since there was nothing they could do to stop this outrage. It was like a scene out of one of the French Revolution films when the victims were being driven to the guillotine.

As they were driven through the village, many of the neighbors ran up to the wagon, saying good-bye and offering prayers. Others however, stood either silently by the side of the road waving their fists at the occupants in the wagon. Little did many of them know, soon it would be their turn.

The day started gray and rainy, foreshadowing the terrible days that lay ahead for this innocent family. When they reached Slutsk, the wagons stopped at the police yard. Several other wagons were already there with occupants similar to Zachary's family. A uniformed person wearing a "*Budienovka*" hat, the symbol of the Bolshevik Revolution with a huge red star on it, was shouting at the occupants of the yard. The clatter of horses hooves' bringing Zachary's family stopped his oration. He came running over and yelled, "Aha! Now we have all of the *Kulaks* together. Take them to the train!"

It became apparent that all of this had been planned, ahead of time. The train station was only one kilometer from the police yard, but it took quite a while to get the wagons lined up and moving. Night fell. The only light came from lanterns hanging on the wagons or carried by the policemen guarding the convoy. When they arrived at the station a train was waiting at the siding. Several third-class coaches were at the front while the remainder were freight cars. As the wagons pulled alongside the train, the doors of the freight cars slid open and all were ordered to get in. Straw covered the box car floor and along the walls were wooden plank shelves, three tiers high, called '*nary.*' They were told to occupy the *nary*, three people to a shelf. Jacob put Olga and the children in the middle while he settled Zachary and Yelena on the lower shelf. Sergei jumped up on the top shelf, while at the same time trying to hang on to the few belongings they brought. They were only in the cars a short time when, without a word to the occupants, the doors were suddenly slammed shut and locked. Shouts came from all cars as the people panicked, not knowing where they were being taken, and what would happen to them. The only answer from the guards, outside the cars was, "*Zamolchi!*" (Shut up!)

The train lurched forward, causing many of the occupants to stumble and fall since they did not expect the sudden jolt. As the train started moving, the engineer gave a whistle and the journey to "Where?" Began.

The only light came from a kerosene lamp hanging on the ceiling in the middle of the freight car, visibility was minimal. Women and children were crying and there was a feeling of horror and desperation in the air. The clickety-clack of the wheels on the rails droned on monotonously, and soon it became quiet. A man's voice spoke above the noise saying: "It looks like we will be together for a while, and we must establish order!"

There were about thirty people in the car, mostly adults, but several children could be heard crying as the man continued: "We have no sanitary facilities in the wagon, only a barrel in the corner, those who have need should use it. Do not urinate on the floor! Remember, we do not know how long we will be inside."

He continued with several more admonitions and directions. It turned out that the speaker was a former officer in the Czar's army and was used to dealing with unexpected situations. Zachary recognized the tone of the commands and at the first opportunity presented himself to the officer as a former soldier.

Exhausted, shocked and amazed at what had just happened to them, the people soon began to fall asleep. Thank God there was enough space on the *nary* for almost everyone. One man sat huddled in the corner, next to the barrel, staring into space, unaware of what was happening around him. The only windows were four grated openings at the sides of the car, too high to be able to look out. Someone boosted another person up as the train was slowing down and in a minute there was a shout, "We are in Minsk", the capital of Beloruss. It was early morning, the dawn was just graying and it was still raining.

The train stopped outside the station and guards' voices were heard shouting commands, "Open the cars! Let them take out the barrel! Shoot anyone who runs!"

The former officer called for Zachary and got two other men to take out the barrel. They carefully moved it across the floor trying not to spill its contents. At the door they were ordered to jump down and carry it to the side of the tracks, where it was dumped. The barrel was returned to the car and the men pushed it inside. During the stop several shots were heard. No one knew why but surmised that the guards' earlier admonition to shoot runaways was the cause. It was later confirmed that two young men ran, and were shot. The former officer, who became the leader of the car's occupants, shouted to one of the guards, "The children need water!"

The guard replied, "Let them sweat a while, you will get water at the next stop!"

Similar requests were coming from the other cars, and soon a cart with several barrels of water was brought to the open doors. People scrambled to fill any container they could, but were not allowed to leave the car, and the guards ignored their requests for help. People were begging the guards, "Where are you taking us?",

35

to which they received a curt reply, "You will know when you get there".

Thus began the horrendous seven day journey to Kotlas, Siberia next to the Arctic Circle. The remaining days were similar to the first, except that the children were getting exhausted and hungry. No food was provided, and the occupants had to rely on what they brought with them. On the second day a modification was made to the corner barrel facilities. Someone hung a sheet around the barrel, and a bucket of water was placed next to it to be used for rinsing diapers of the infants on board. At several locations, where the train stopped, local residents came up asking what was inside. The only answer was, "Stay away! We are carrying the plague of the Revolution to where it will not infect the *Proletariat!*"

From 1929 - 1932 millions of dispossessed *kulaks* were exiled to the north to build a new "Motherland." In this manner Stalin disposed of complete families, and watched zealously that none of the children got away. It was the first such massive experiment - at least in modern history! Subsequently it was repeated by Hitler with the Jews, and other nationalities who were transported to the slave labor and concentration camps of Germany. Then again by Stalin after World War II, with nationalities and persons whom he considered "disloyal" to him or who were suspected to be infused with democratic ideals and views from the West.

Chapter 5

Kotlas, Siberia - Just Below the Arctic Circle

It is estimated that fifteen million or more peasants were exiled to the Arctic regions of Siberia during Stalin's *kulak* purges of 1929-1932. Kotlas was one of these dumping grounds. It is located just below the Arctic Circle on the Severnaya Dvina River, and the area to which Zachary and his family were "resettled."

When their train left Slutsk it was the beginning of spring. Snow was melting and crocuses were popping their heads out of their snowy prison, beginning to bloom. The temperature was climbing to forty degrees and the farmers were getting ready to plow their fields. When they arrived in Kotlas on March 15, 1930 winter was still in full force. Fields were covered with ice and snow and gale force March winds were sweeping the area; the sun was just above the horizon. It was freezing.

The freight car doors opened and occupants were ordered out. It was the first time they had been allowed out since leaving Slutsk, more than a week ago. Cold or not, everyone was ready for some fresh air, wanting to stretch their legs. Whatever belongings they brought were thrown on the snow as families gathered around them, huddling against the cold. Soon they were formed into a column and marched to a compound surrounded by barbed wire. The buildings in the compound looked like they had recently been thrown together. Only a window here and there broke up the long stretch of the walls. As they came closer to the buildings, cracks the width of a finger, were visible between the boards. These structures looked worse than the barns they left behind in their villages.

Families were just shoved into these barracks. The inside seemed colder than the outside. A single potbellied stove stood in the middle of the structure but, it was ice cold; there was no fire in it. The familiar *nary* which they just left on the train were aligned along the walls of the building; however, these were only two tiers high. Jacob proceeded to the center of the barracks and grabbed a *nary* nearest the stove, telling Olga to hold the space while he went to get his father and mother. They were nowhere to be seen. Apparently, they were put into another barracks. As he tried to go to the next building , he was stopped by a guard and told to return to his own place. He tried to explain that he was trying to find his elderly mother and father, instead of an answer he got a butt of the rifle in his back. He knew his parents were in the camp and he would try to locate them later. Anyway, Zachary was still strong, as was Yelena, and Jacob was certain that Sergei would make sure the parents were looked after. He turned to go to Olga and the children, but before he could say anything to her there was a call for all men to form a line outside the barracks. Just to make sure the order was obeyed, two sturdy guards with rifles at the ready came and 'helped' the men along.

Olga and the children huddled on the *nary* trying to keep warm. She wrapped Anastasia and Sergei in the blanket babushka Yelena made. It was cold, but at least there were no cracks in this part of the wall and the wind was not blowing. She had no idea where the men were taken and hoped they would come back soon. If they don't return what will she do? Other mothers were trying to keep their children quiet, but the same fright and panic was visible on their faces.

The men were formed into a column and marched to the other side of the camp where they were handed saws and axes and told to go cut firewood for the stoves. It looked as if the camp had only recently been cut out of a primeval forest, because outside the fence lay impenetrable brush, the *Taiga*. On the other side flowed a river, Severnaya Dvina/Northern Dvina. Soon men returned with arms full of wood and a fire was started in the potbellied stove. There was no insulation in the walls and, only a single ply of wood and earth piled half way up the walls separated them from the outside. Heating the building would be an impossible task. Even if the stove was fired twenty-four hours a day, it could not create tolerable temperature inside. Thank God , Jacob picked the nary closest to the stove. It was getting warmer but they had no water to drink. The snow on the ground was dirty gray and if melted would not be suitable for drinking, the only acceptable supply was from the river.

Jacob took a pail and proceeded to the river. The banks were steep and slippery. When he got to the river's edge, he saw that it was still frozen. The only way to reach water was to chop a hole in the ice. Other men were already at work using their axes to cut the ice, which was over a foot thick. He offered to help the man nearest to him and together they reached running water in a few minutes. The water was crystal clear and seemed suitable for drinking. The climb up the hill was even more treacherous than the descent, but he made it up. When he brought the pail into the barracks, others were already crowding the stove to heat the water for tea. Everyone wanted to put their pot on the stove first, but the top was only large enough for two or three pots at a time, depending on their size. Arguments arose as to who was there first and to prevent fist fights, a sequence was established. Eventually, Jacob was able to get their pot on the stove, and boil the water. It was their first meal in Kotlas, some mint tea and food they brought with them from home.

This place was a nightmare. How would they survive in this wilderness, especially with the children? Sergei was still in diapers and keeping him clean was a real problem. His bottom was already red and the corn starch Olga was using to prevent diaper rash was running out. Everything was running out and no one had even mentioned where their food would come from. They were in a camp surrounded by barbed wire and there was no town or village visible where they could possibly buy or trade for some food. But will they be allowed to leave the camp? To whom could they turn for help? Would anyone help? They were so far from home that they could not expect anyone to come to their aid. In any case, there was no one left of the immediate family back home to help, all were here in Kotlas or on the run.

Jacob did not know where Boris had settled, or if he was still on the run. Their only help would come from God! And He seemed nowhere to be found.

Several days after arrival, guards gathered the men and marched them off into the forest to "clear the land." What were they clearing it for? It seemed that with the cold weather little could be grown here. Since most of the people in the camp were farmers, tilling the land was what they knew. Clearing, plowing and planting was on their minds, but the intent of Stalin was to exterminate, not grow.

Jacob searched for his parents and brother in the camp, but could not locate them. Later he learned that because the Kotlas camp was overcrowded, Zachary and his family were taken to another nearby camp, but he was not allowed to go there. He prayed that Sergei was able to look after and help them.

Every morning the men were assembled into columns and marched off into the forest to clear the land and fell trees, returning in the evening, cold wet and exhausted. After several days the guards decided that due to the short daylight and the long trek to the cutting site, it was better to keep the men at the logging area in order to achieve their daily quotas. Similar lean-to barracks were thrown together and the men endured under those conditions all week long.

Conditions at the main camp were worsening with every passing day, especially for the young and the very old. Colds, pneumonia and other diseases were rampant. Children began dying. A gang of men was set aside to build coffins and dig graves in a spot just outside the barbed wire gates. The daily burrial procession of coffins continued from sunup to sunset. Men remained at the cutting site returning to the main camp only at the end of the week. Olga was left alone to fend for her children.

Three weeks after they arrived in Kotlas, Anastasia began running a fever; it was pneumonia. No medication or medical help was available and *banki* (cupping glass) was the only available means to possibly reduce the fever. The procedure involved making a cotton wick, wrapping it on a stick, dipping the wick in alcohol, lighting it and quickly inserting the burning wick into the open end of the *banki*. The flame consumed the air inside, creating a vacuum. At that moment, the banka was quickly pressed onto the flesh. The vacuum drew the flesh in thereby bringing extra blood to the area, aiding in the healing process.

The *banki* application helped for several days, but soon the fever returned. Olga was at her wits end. Her husband was away somewhere in the *taiga,* her in-laws were in another camp and there was no one to help. She persuaded a guard who daily went to the cutting site to take a message to Jacob. "Anastasia is very ill and almost near death, Sergei has a bad cough, come back if you can!"

This guard still had some compassion for these miserable poor people and delivered the message. That evening Jacob ran from the cutting site. It was dangerous traveling through the forest at any time but, by night it was horrendous. The log road, or what was visible of it, was treacherous. There were wolves, bears and possibly even tigers in the area. He heard the wolves baying at the moon every night. Thank God for the moon. He stumbled all through the night arriving in Kotlas on the following morning, exhausted. The guard at the gate recognized Jacob and let him in.

When he got to their *nary,* Olga was hysterical, clutching Anastasia to her bosom. All he was able to make out, between Olga's sobs and cries was, "Oh, My God, Nastia is dead!!!"

He tried to take Anastasia out of Olga's arms but she would not let go of her daughter. Finally, embracing both of them in his arms for what seemed like hours, Olga quieted down and Jacob was able to get Anastasia out of her embrace. There was no pulse but her body was still warm. Apparently death came only minutes ago, just as he arrived in the barracks. He held her in his arms not believing what was happening and would probably have stayed that way for a long time, when he heard Sergei's cry. The woman in the next *nary* was holding him and sobbing.

He laid Anastasia down on the nary and covered her with Yelena's blanket, then took Sergei from the woman's arms sobbing and clutching him to his breast. Anastasia died on April 13, 1930, less than a month after they arrived in Kotlas, but his son was still alive.

When Olga was finally able to speak, she told Jacob of Anastasia's last minutes. Nastia's fever was very high and Olga was applying compresses to her head. The child had not opened her eyes for quite some time, neither whimpered or cried, then suddenly opening her eyes she said, "Mama, can I have a cherry. I would be all better if I had one."

A cherry! It is winter, where do I get a cherry? Then she remembered that one woman in the barracks had some cherry preserves which she put in her tea. Still clutching Nastia, she ran to the nary where the woman sat and begged her for a cherry. The woman saw the state Olga was in, and taking the jar selected one cherry with a teaspoon and gave it to Anastasia. The child took it in her mouth and said, "That is so good!" Then smiling said, "Now I will be all better."

Sergei was crying, he was hungry and it was time for him to be changed. Olga thanked the kind woman for the cherry and returned to her own area. She asked her neighbor to hold Anastasia while she fed Sergei, but Anastasia said, "*Mamochka*, I want you to hold me." Sergei was screaming. Olga said, "Darling, let me feed Sergei and then I will hold you for as long as you want me to." Giving Anastasia to her neighbor, she began to feed Sergei. Anastasia, nestled in the woman's arms, took a deep breath and closed her eyes. After she finished feeding Sergei, Olga put him down and turning to the woman saw tears running down her cheeks. The woman said, "She is gone."

Olga snatched Anastatsia out of the woman's arms kissing her daughter's face and lips in an attempt to awaken her. As she kissed Anastasia's lips she tasted the cherry; it was still in Nastia's mouth, and she realized that her daughter was really gone. Just then Jacob came into the barracks.

For the rest of her life, Olga never forgave herself for not holding Anastasia during the last moments of her life.

Jacob was in shock. The only thing he could think of was to find some boards and make a coffin for Anastasia. Although there was plenty of wood in the area, boards were hard to come by, so many were dying. Walking to the carpenter shop, set up to make caskets, he ripped off one of the buttons from his coat, removed the cloth covering it and gave the ten ruble gold piece to a carpenter for the boards to build a coffin. The carpenter offered to build it for him, but Jacob refused, saying, "No! It is for my daughter, I will make it".

Returning to the barracks he carried the coffin with him. It was the first death in their barracks and everyone was standing around their *nary*. Olga was still clutching Anastasia, while Sergei was watching all the people. Jacob asked the people to move away so that he and his wife could share their grief together. He and Olga sat in silence for a long time, then both, as if signaled, started preparing Anastasia's body for burial. The finality of her death settled in their hearts, and they knew that there was still a son to care for.

Anastasia was wrapped in Babushka Yelena's blanket as Olga placed her in the coffin. When Jacob lowered the lid of the coffin, Olga exclaimed, "It is too shallow, her face will be crushed!"

But Jacob had already said farewell to his daughter and would not lift the lid, and began nailing it shut. Anastasia's coffin became part of the next morning's burial procession to the makeshift cemetery. Jacob carried the coffin and would not let anyone touch it. She was placed into the frozen earth and covered with soil mixed with permafrost.

Jacob was not permitted to remain at the camp and was marched back to the logging area the next morning. He gave a message to the guard who traveled between camps for Zachary and Yelena about Anastasia, but was not sure whether it would be delivered.

Sergei seemed to be getting better. His cough had subsided and his temperature returned to normal. Before returning to the logging area, Jacob wrote a quick letter to Olga's brother Yesip, in Bondary, begging him to come and get Olga and Sergei out of Kotlas. He also wrote another letter to his cousin Mary in America, once more asking for her help. He ripped off another button from the coat and gave it to the guard, hoping that the letters would be mailed.

After working a week at the logging site he received another note from Olga. "Sergei is very sick. Please come quickly!"

One more button from his jacket got the guard at the cutting site to look the other way and assurance that Jacob would not be missed during the next morning's count. The road was more familiar to him, and although there was no moon, he got to the camp without being attacked by wolves. He was allowed in and as he walked to their *nary* in the barracks, he saw Olga feeding Sergei. He was not too late!

During the night Sergei's fever rose, *banki* were applied and he fell asleep. Jacob was permitted to stay the night, but was told he had to return to the cutting site the next morning.

That night the little family huddled together on one *nary* with Sergei between them. Toward the morning he started fussing. Olga changed and fed him. Jacob could not sleep and began walking Sergei up and down the barracks' hall. After walking Sergei for some time he realized that he was not moving. His son was asleep forever. Olga was also in a deep sleep, she needed her rest. What would waking her now accomplish? So, he let her sleep and continued holding his son. He didn't know if they could survive this second tragedy, it was only little more than a week since Anastasia died. Could they remain sane?

For another gold button, Jacob was able to get the materials to build a coffin for his son. He and Olga were in a trance and just went through the motions as the next day they buried Sergei beside his sister. The ground was thawing and the soil was softer now.

That day Jacob decided that the only possibility for them to survive was to escape. If they didn't, they would go out of their minds. There was nothing left for them now, only Zachary, Yelena and his brother Sergei.. They hadn't heard from them for quite a while. Were they still alive?

The buttons from the front of his coat were gone but, the hem of his jacket held several more.

Chapter 6

Escape - Into the Hands of the KGB
At The Lubianka Prison

After Sergei's death, Jacob was permitted to visit his parents at the Toymushka GULAG. A group of exiles was being transferred under guard and he was allowed to make the trek with them.

Arriving at the camp he located the barracks where his parents were housed. As he approached, he recognized his father Zachary sitting in a sunny spot on a log, leaning against the building. Zachary had a Bible in his hands. Jacob could not remember his father ever reading the bible. He called out, "Papa!", but Zachary didn't even look up. His lips were moving and Jacob thought he was in prayer. After waiting a few moments he once more called out, "PAPA!"

Zachary lifted up his head and looking at Jacob said, "Oh, it's you. Go see your mother inside."

His demeanor was still the "old Zachary" but his face belied the thoughts. He looked gaunt, pale and gray. His hands shook. He had no boots on and his feet were wrapped in *partianky* (cloth wraps). Without giving his son a second look, Zachary bent his head and continued looking at the book as Jacob went inside to look for his mother. He found her in the far corner of the barracks, huddled on the *nary* rocking back and forth. Her face and hands were swollen and she could hardly open her eyes. Recognizing Jacob she stretched her hands for an embrace but did not have the strength to reach him. Jacob saw the now familiar signs of malnutrition and hunger; her body was swollen with edema. Yelena said, "We don't get enough to eat. Sergei tries but since he is in the forest, we don't get our full portion. Did you bring anything to eat?"

When Jacob left Kotlas, he did not know how long he was going to be away. On the way out grabbed a piece of bread and salted pork which he stuffed in his pocket. He gave it to his mother who took it with trembling hands and hungrily devoured it. Jacob's heart ached, seeing his parents in this state. How could they have gone down hill so fast? It had been only a month since they left Bolshaya Sliva! They had brought food with them. He saw it on the train. Then, his mother began to tell him their tale of woe.

Several days after arriving at Toymushka, their food bag was stolen while Sergei was in the forest. Try as they might, they could not find it. This camp, unlike the one in Kotlas, contained a large number of the criminal element. Primarily, robbers, rapists and *urki* (petty thieves), who began preying on the defenseless elderly as soon as they arrived. When Sergei returned from the forest he began to search for the thieves. At one point he saw several urki eating some of the stolen food and went to report it to the guards. The way the guards treated him it was obvious that they were in league with the thieves and it would be futile to protest. On the return trip to the barracks, he was pounced upon by a mob of *urki* and beaten severely. One of them grabbed Sergei by the throat, and flashing a knife, sliced Sergei's ear as he hissed, "If you don't want to lose your life, keep your mouth shut!"

There was no one to help them and they attempted to survive, as best they could, on gruel and hot water.

Yelena said that after the incident, Zachary stopped talking to everyone and just kept his nose in the Bible, seldom even eating the gruel or sleeping on the *nary*. He just crouched in a corner, mumbling to himself. Here was a man who only a few months ago ran a prosperous mill business; it was unbelievable how man's inhumanity to man can destroy a person in such a short time. Cold, starvation and fear transformed Zachary into a trembling hulk.

Jacob attempted to get permission to have his parents and brother transferred to Kotlas but was rebuffed by the administrator who said, "This is where the Soviet has put them, and here they will stay until they die!"

Jacob dug out another gold piece from the fold of his jacket and bought some food for his parents from one of the *urki*. The thieves tried to force him to give up his jacket but Jacob fought them off. One of the *urki* called after him, "We have time. We will get you later."

He brought the food to Yelena, hugged his father and, knowing that there was nothing more he could do, returned to Olga in Kotlas. When he returned to the camp and told Olga of his parent's condition, they cried and prayed that God would keep them safe and somehow provide more food. On the following day Jacob was returned to the logging area in the taiga and Olga was left all alone.

Try as she might, she could not stop crying and asking God, "Why?" But it seemed that He was nowhere to be found. After many prayers, which unburdened her heart, she calmed down and knew that there was a reason for all of this suffering and God would some day tell her. The only words that filled her mind were: "Forgive, Forgive!"

Next day two letters arrived. One was from her brother, Yesip, and one from Jacob's brother, Boris. Boris wrote that he was in the Ural Mountains living in a communal worker's home and working as a laborer in a tin mine. The work was very hard but he was surviving on what he earned. As long as he had the job, he was planning to remain there, unless or until there was a reason for him to run again.

Yesip's letter said that he was coming to Kotlas and hoped that he would somehow be able to take Olga home. Also he would bring as much food and bacon as he could. She shared the letters with Jacob, when he returned from the logging area. A glimmer of hope was reignited and they began to talk about a way to escape.

Several weeks later, Yesip arrived and brought Olga's sister Irina's papers, they would provide an identity under which Olga could travel. The food he brought was given to Zachary and Yelena when Yesip was allowed to visit them. They fervently prayed that the urki would not steal it again. By this time Jacob knew which guards could be 'bought' and who would look the other way when it was necessary. Once more he searched into the fold of his jacket to make sure there were still some gold coins in the fold. They would be needed for Olga's getaway. Some were still there, but they were disappearing fast.

After returning from Zachary's camp, Yesip bought Olga a ticket to Beloruss. Jacob, having no papers, could not travel with them since he could possibly jeopardize Olga's escape. It was decided that he would have to run on his own and get back to the village as best he could. On the return trip, Olga would assume the identity of Yesip's wife. That night Olga and Jacob said their goodbyes promising each other that they would do everything in their power to be together again. The "friendly guard" took the gold rubles and looked the other way as Olga and Yesip walked out of the camp early the next morning.

By bribing a railroad worker, Yesip was able to get several train schedules which outlined train movements to points south. The trains almost never ran on schedule, but at least it would give Jacob an idea of where the trains stopped. After Olga and Yesip left; Jacob ran from the camp to the nearest point where he could jump on a train. He knew that he would have to use only freight trains, but most trains had freight cars attached, and he was sure he could scramble aboard without being spotted. This was his plan, but how it would be accomplished was in the hands of God.

Kotlas was about eight hundred kilometers from Moscow, that is "as the crow flies." From Moscow to Minsk was another six hundred. The journey would be an arduous one, but Jacob was young and hoped that Olga would still be waiting for him at the end of the run, that is, if she and Yesip made it home without being arrested.

The first train he jumped brought him to Vologda, four hundred kilometers south. He was glad he brought some bread and *kolbasy* with him from the stash Yesip provided. Water was another problem but he was able to jump off and get a drink at the stops when the locomotive tender was being filled. Thirst was a bigger problem than food. Catching drips from the roof of the railroad car was a tough way to get a drink.

From Vologda he hopped a freight carrying logs to Ivanovo and wondered if some of them were those he had cut in the *taiga*? Thank God it didn't rain much and it was getting warmer as the train headed south. His jacket did not provide much warmth, especially when it was wet, but it was his lifeline inasmuch as he still had a few gold rubles in its fold. Ivanovo to Moscow proved to be a more difficult task. It was a smaller town and only a few trains passed through it. He waited two days, hiding in empty freight cars until a freight train carrying ore was heading to Moscow. Once on the train, he huddled between two cars and tying himself to the rail handle with his belt, fell asleep.

When the train pulled into the rail yard in Moscow he jumped off. He was hungry, thirsty and dirty from the cinders and smoke of the locomotive and the dust from the tracks. Almost more than food, he needed a bath and decided to look for a *banja*.

Banjas (bath houses), are facilities where the average worker could avail himself of a bath. These were primitive structures, no more than a sturdy insulated hut with heated rocks upon which water was poured to create steam. Buckets of cold and hot water were set inside for bathing. The bathing ritual included whipping oneself with a *venik* (small broom made of birch branches) creating improved blood flow, and soothing the tingling nerves. Several levels of wooden shelves provided space for a steam bath. *Banjas* were found in working districts or next to industrial sites. Jacob located one close to the railroad station, and availed himself of a bath on the money Yesip gave him. While in the bath, his underwear and shirt were laundered and dried by the female attendant. After the bath he felt like a man reborn, and decided to get breakfast at the rail station counter. As he finished eating, he was approached by a uniformed railroad official who demanded Jacob's travel papers. Jacob didn't have any and knew that it would be difficult to get out of the situation. He concocted a story that he was robbed and his papers stolen, but the official did not buy it and called a policeman. Jacob was arrested. Apparently this official's duty was to look for people like Jacob. When the police arrived, Jacob joined three other men who were also under arrest. This became an *etap* (a prisoner column) marched to prison. They were taken down the center of the main streets of Moscow to the GPU/KGB Lubyanka prison. It was the headquarters of the secret police where "criminals" were interrogated and where their fate was decided.

Alexander Solzenitsyn, in "The GULAG Archipelago," describes what it was like to enter the Lubyanka prison.

"We approach Novoslobod-skaya and disembark-and for the first time I see Lubyanka Prison from the outside. Oh, what a grim, high wall stretched there for two blocks! The hearts of Muscovites shiver when they see the steel maw of its gates slide open. I have been here before and can draw the interior of the prison from memory. I enter the tower of the guard house. I smile at the first court-yard and recognize the familiar main doors of carved wood. And it is nothing at all that they are now going to make me face the wall, and ask me: "Last Name? Given name and patronymic, year of birth?" And after several hours of inevitable processing of my body, confinement in a box, search, issuing of receipts, filling out an admission card, after the roster and a bath-I shall be taken to a cell with two domes, with a hanging arch in the middle (all cells are like that), with two large windows and a long combination table and cupboard. And I shall be greeted by strangers who are certain to be intelligent, interesting, friendly people, and they will begin to tell me their stories, and I will begin to tell them mine, and by night we will not even feel like going to sleep right away. Life in prison was monotonous and melancholic, except for the interrogations. One hundred and forty prisoners would be packed in a cell intended for twenty-five, and prisoners would have to lie on an asphalt floor. There was 'permanent twilight' due to the frosted glass and muzzle over the windows." (Solzenitsyn" GULAG Archipelago," pp 594-5; Ibid., pp. 124-5, 479-80).

Strict rules of behavior were enforced and for any infraction the prisoner received "X" days in solitary and deprived of the fifteen minute daily exercise. Most prisoners lost their privileges immediately. This was Jacob's new environment as he wondered what fate had in store for him. His cell was full of local thieves, *urki*, drunks and other undesirable elements. As soon as he was brought in, he was given the "once over" by the occupants to see what they could steal or in what other manner they could relieve the *novushka* (newcomer) of his possessions. Jacob's six-foot-two figure and muscles visible under his shirt initially kept them at bay. That first day he "slept with one eye open;" in the evening he was summoned for his first interrogation.

Interrogation of prisoners usually occurred at night. Basically, it was the deprivation of sleep, when the body's natural tendencies to relax were at their height that gave the interrogators an advantage over the prisoner. The interrogation room contained a large table, behind which sat the interrogator, with the prisoner's file on the table, next to which lay a revolver. On the side stood a guard with a pistol at the ready. The prisoner was told to stand at attention in front of the desk until given permission to sit down or relax. Initial questions probed the prisoners on origin, education and last place of residence, asked in a matter-of-fact manner. Depending on the answers, the mood changed. Next, the "charges" either real or fabricated, were read from the file and the prisoner was asked if he agreed with them. Jacob disagreed with everything that was read. At that moment, the interrogator motioned to the guard, who struck Jacob on the face with the butt of the revolver. Pain reverberated through his head and the salty taste of blood filled his mouth. The interrogator shouted, "Don't lie, you know you are guilty! You have disobeyed the directives of the Supreme Soviet! The more truthful you are the easier it will go on you! And, we don't really want to hurt you."

Interrogation continued for the next six hours questions being repeated, threats implied and incentives for cooperation explained. Jacob gave only one answer: "I have not committed any crimes against the State. I have always obeyed the rules of the Soviet and paid my taxes. I shared the mill with the *Kolhoz* and gave free service when requested. You have killed my children and parents in the North, and I have lost my wife."

During the questioning the interrogator continually wrote in the file. After six hours he gave Jacob a sheet to sign which outlined his crimes against the State. These ranged from disobeying direc-

Jacob with younger brother Sergei - Toymushka, Siberia

The GULAG to which Sergei, Zachary and Yelena were sent when they were exiled as "Kulaks."

tives to speculation, *kulak* activities, and antigovernment propaganda, and other fabrications. Jacob refused to sign and was taken back to the cell with an admonition, "Think about it, and we will see you again soon! You are not truthful in your testimony therefore, we may have to use other persuasions to help you remember."

He was taken out of the interrogation room, pushed into a closet-sized space and the door locked. The interior was painted bright white and in the ceiling burned a very bright light. There was only enough room to stand, and when he leaned against the wall, he got an electric shock. Initially the shocks were mild but became stronger as his body weakened and he leaned more against the wall. The light just above his head was so bright that even when he closed his eyes, the eyelids could not shut out the light. Every time he closed them and relaxed, there was another shock. The cell was extremely cold since there was an inch of water covering the floor. Sleep deprivation was one of the most effective methods for reducing the prisoner's resistance during questioning.

Jacob did not know how long he had been in the closet, but when the door opened he was dragged and kicked to the general cell. To him it looked like home. Immediately, he collapsed on the floor and fell asleep. However, as soon as he closed his eyes, he was kicked, jerked up and once more marched to the interrogation room. When they got there, he was told to stand at attention and await his turn; he was forbidden to lean against the wall. If his back rested on the wall, the guard opposite him immediately kicked him in the shins or ribs forcing Jacob to stand erect. The wait was a long one. Since coming to the prison , he had not been given either food or water.

Finally the interrogation room door opened and he was thrown in. The interrogator behind the desk, seeming to show compassion, admonished the guard for treating the prisoner so roughly and invited Jacob to sit down on a chair in front of the desk. Jacob collapsed into the chair but was quickly told to sit up straight and not lean against the back. The minute he leaned back the guard smacked him across the face. This interrogator began with a new persuasion technique, "My friend who spoke to you yesterday told me that you were not very cooperative. You know you are guilty and will get a prison term, whatever happens, cooperate and things will go easy with you. If you resist you will get more of what you already experienced, and much more. So, why not sign right now and avoid *future difficulties*?"

Jacob asked for a sheet of paper and said he would write his confession. This seemed to please the interrogator and he complied. After giving him a few minutes to write the interrogator came over and took the sheet from his hands, telling Jacob to move forward to the edge of the chair so that he could hear him better, and returned to his desk. Two more hours passed before a word was spoken. Jacob's back was in excruciating pain. Again, the minute he leaned back he was hit by the guard.

Have you ever sat at the edge of a chair with your back in the 'attention' position without leaning back for any period of time? If you have not, try it, before long you experience excruciating pain. Then suddenly, the interrogator exploded out of his chair and grabbing the pistol shoved it under Jacob's chin shouting, as saliva spewed from his mouth, "You bastard! I have treated you fairly, and what you have written is an insult to me and the Supreme Soviet. Maybe I should put a bullet in your head right now and save myself and the government trouble and aggravation!"

He cocked the trigger as Jacob awaited the inevitable. But soon, the pressure under his chin lessened and the interrogator sat down again.

Sleep deprivation, hunger, thirst, intimidation, threats, standing at attention and beatings continued for many days with brief moments of time in the closet. Jacob still would not confess or sign anything, but he didn't know how long he could hold out. He could not remember when he last ate or slept. He remembered tasting bread, but it seemed so long ago and his mouth, tongue and throat felt like a dust bowl, there was almost no saliva.

The next time he was brought to the interrogation room there were two additional guards and the interrogator began, "Since our previous methods don't seem to convince you, I have asked some of my friends to help me."

Both of the guards were built like wrestlers. They proceeded to rip the shirt off Jacob's back and removing their pistols from the holsters shoved them under his armpits. The triggers were cocked as they proceeded to raise him off the floor. Suspended on the gun barrels, pain cascaded through his back and shoulders. The interrogator asked, "Doesn't that feel fine?"

Jacob couldn't answer because his breath was caught in his throat and his lungs were bursting. After several up and down movements, he lost consciousness.

How long he was out he didn't know, when suddenly a torrent of water enveloped his body. It was ice cold and he tried to suck in as much of the liquid as he could but got only half a swallow. A few more kicks in the ribs were followed by the ever present admonition. "Sign!"

He refused. The two guards stood him up as the largest of the three punched Jacob in the solar plexus with such force as to make it seem that his diaphragm exploded. Jacob collapsed and fainted once more.

He woke up in a dark, dingy and smelly room with enough light filtering through to see that he was alone, in an isolation cell. The room stunk of urine and excrement. He started banging on the door and shouting.

After a while a voice answered, "Ah, so you woke up. We thought you were dead. We didn't hear anything for days."

Jacob asked to be allowed to go to the toilet, but was told, "Use the *parasha*." (in the Soviet prisons this is the name of a latrine bucket.) Soviet prisons, have no toilets in the prisoner's cells, only a bucket. In the semidarkness Jacob located the bucket; it was full of the previous resident's excrement. Later that day he heard noise outside the cell. A slide in the door opened and a plate with a piece of bread was shoved in. "You will get water later," said the voice on the other side.

To the best of his recollection Jacob figured he had been in Lubyanka for close to thirty days, or more, before being thrown into solitary, but could not account for those last days. How long had he been unconscious? Did Olga and Yesip make it to Bondary?

His mind was swimming with incoherent thoughts.

Olga made it to her village, but had to hide since people who might have recognized her were required to report it to the police. The new rules demanded that everyone had to report an escaped *kulak*. If one did not, and someone else knew that you didn't, you would be thrown in prison for disobeying the Soviet and made to fulfill the escaped person's sentence. Therefore, everyone was reporting.

Yesip and Olga's family decided that the best place for her to stay was in the forest. It was July and the weather was warm. They found a large oak tree with a hollowed out trunk where she could hide in case of rain or from the occasional person who came to gather berries or mushrooms. Olga loved the forest and spent her days walking and talking to the myriad of birds and animals, constantly praying for Jacob's return. In the evenings she would go to one of her relative's huts, get a meal and sometimes some sleep. As weeks passed and Jacob did not come, nor did she hear from him, she really began to fear for his life. She knew that since Jacob had no legal papers, it would take him much longer to get to Bondary. He had to walk and hop trains.

Stephan, Olga's father would often come into the forest and keep her company. Her sisters came on the ruse of going for mushrooms and berries. She could not set her foot in the village for fear of being seen and reported. On days when she could not go to the relatives' homes, food was left in another old oak tree. During those long lonely days she thought about the children, shedding many a tear, and wondering why and how did all this happened in her life. But her faith was strong and she knew that God had not forsaken them. Jacob would show up some day, but how long could she survive under these conditions. Soon winter would be coming, and if she continued in this manner she would go out of her mind.

Meanwhile, Jacob was still in isolation. When the door finally opened, he recognized the guard as the one who initially took him to interrogation and administered the punishment.

As Jacob stepped out of the cell, he collapsed. His legs buckled under him, his head spun and there was a strange feeling in his chest. The guard kicked him to get him up but Jacob could not stand on his own and had to hang on to the wall. Instead of the interrogation chamber, he was returned to the general cell and tossed inside. His cell mates were surprised to see him alive. One said that he heard Jacob had a heart atack. Even in Lubyanka, prisoners had a communication system all their own, and information filtered through. One of the urki wanted to take his boots, but another said: "Look at him, he is just about dead, wait a couple of days, he'll be dead by then, and we will get not only his boots but his jacket also."

Jacob crumbled to the floor and didn't care what happened to him. All he wanted was to stretch, hoping that the pain in his chest would subside.

He remembered reading about a heart attack in one of the anatomy books Uncle Stephan brought him and deduced that he had suffered a heart attack, when the guard punched him in the chest, and before being put into solitary. The pain was not subsiding. On the following day he was again taken to the inquisition chamber. The same interrogator sat at the desk and asked, "Well, have you had time to think? Or would you like some more of the same medicine?"

Jacob knew that he could not survive another stint of beatings and asked the man behind the desk to read him the charges against him and the confession. It did not change from what he heard the last time, only additional accusations were added. No matter what, he would be put in prison or most likely sent into Siberian exile. There was no way he could get out of the KGB prison, but if he was transferred to some other place, there may be chance for an escape. In Lubyanka, death was certain. He wanted to live and see Olga again. He signed. Seeing the signature, the interrogator intoned, "You have been found guilty of crimes against the State and as an escapee from previous exile you are hereby sentenced to a permanent re-education facility above the Arctic Circle where you will learn the way of the *Proletariat*."

It was required in the KGB prison system that prisoners who were being transferred from one penal system to another be released in "good condition." Therefore, before being sent into exile, Jacob received a cursory examination by a doctor who asked him: "How many heart attacks have you had?" This confirmed to Jacob that the pain in his chest was a heart attack. The following morning a column of about one hundred "citizens," including Jacob, was formed in the Lubyanka yard and marched through the same iron gates they had come through initially. Under heavy guard, they were taken to the rail station where a train of Stolypin cars awaited them.

Chapter 7

Permanent Exile

Eliminating the "enemies of the people" was Stalin's primary objective during the purges of 1930's and required special transport for the *kulaks* and those affected by his edicts. The Stolypin car became the state's favorite conveyance for the millions being sent to the GULAGs of Siberia. The railroad car was named after Pyotr Arkadievich Stolypin who, under Czar Nicholas II, served as the Minister of Iterior after 1906, and was known for his agrarian reforms in resettlement of poor peasants to Siberia. The car and its accommodations are best described by Alexander Solzenitsyn in his "GULAG Archipelago" treatise:

> "The *zak car*-what a foul abbreviation it is! It means that this was a railroad car for prisoners-for *zaklyuchennye*. But nowhere except in prison documents, has this term caught on and stuck. It became the universal and exclusive means for transporting prisoners in the 1930's. Therefore it would be more correct to call it a *Stalin* car rather than *Stolypin* car. The Stolypin car is an ordinary passenger car divided into compartments, except that five of the nine cars are allotted to prisoners, while the remaining are occupied by the guards. The compartments are separated from the corridor not by a solid barrier but by a grating which leaves them open for inspection. The grating consists of intersecting diagonal bars, like the ones one sees in station parks. It rises the full height of the car, and because of it, the baggage racks project from the compartment over the corridor. There are no windows in the prisoner' compartments only tiny, barred blinds on the level of the second sleeping shelves. That's why the car has no exterior windows and looks like a baggage car. The door into each compartment is a sliding door, an iron frame with bars. From the corridor all

this is reminiscent of a menagerie. Pitiful creatures resembling human beings are huddled there in cages, the floors and bunks surrounded on all sides by metal grilles, looking out at you anxiously begging for something to eat or drink. Except that in menageries they never crowd the wild animals so tightly."

According to calculations of non-prisoner engineers, six people can sit on the bottom bunks of a Stolypin compartment, and another three can lie on the middle racks in ones and twos; more can lie on the baggage shelves above. Now if, in addition to these, eleven more are pushed into the compartment (the last of whom are shoved out of the way of the door by jailers' boots as they shut it), then this will constitute a normal compartment for a Stolypin prisoners' compartment. Two huddle, half sitting, on each of the upper baggage shelves; another five lie on the joined middle level (and they are the lucky ones for these places are won in battle, and if there are any prisoners present from the underworld companionship of thieves, *blatnye, urki*-then it is they who are lying there) and this leaves thirteen down below; five sit on each of the bunks and three are in the aisle between their legs. Somewhere mixed up with the people, on the people and under people, are their belongings. And that is how they sit, their crossed legs beneath them, day after day after day.

When you were jammed into a Stolypin compartment, you expected that you would encounter only colleagues of misfortune. All your oppressors remained on the other side of the bars, and you certainly did not expect to find them on your side.

And suddenly you lift your eyes to the square recess of the middle bunk, to that one and only heaven above you, and up there one would see three or four—oh, no, not faces! They aren't monkeys' muzzles either, because monkeys' muzzles are much more decent and more thoughtful. No, and they aren't simply hideous countenances, since there must be something human even in them. You see cruel, loathsome snouts up there, wearing expressions of greed and mockery. Each one of them looks at you like a spider

60

gloating over a fly. Their web is the grating which imprisons you, and you have been had. They squint up their lips as if they intend to bite you from one side. They hiss when they speak, enjoying that hissing more than the vowel and consonant sounds of speech, and the only thing about their speech that resembles the Russian language is the endings of verbs and nouns. It is gibberish. Those strange gorilloids were usually dressed in sleeveless undershirts. After all, it is stuffy in the Stolypin car. Their sinewy purple necks, their swelling shoulder muscles, their swarthy tattooed chests have never suffered prison.

Those were the conditions under which Jacob was transported to his permanent exile. Would he be able to fend off these human wolves and survive? He was determined to do so, no matter what it took. After seven days, they arrived at their permanent destination, Aranets, a town about seven hundred long kilometers northeast of Kotlas, where Jacob and his family were initially exiled, and where he hoped his parents Zachary, Yelena and brother Sergei were still alive. Looking at the surroundings, Jacob decided to escape at the first possible opportunity and began examining the layout and situation of the camp. The guards were just shoving prisoners into the barracks paying little attention. The barrack Jacob was thrown into was empty and the door at the other end was open. Why wait, run before they get organized and are watching more closely. He ran into the *taiga* and kept going until he tripped, hitting his head on a stump, losing consciousness. How long had he been out, he didn't know but after shaking his head, which brought him out of the daze, he remembered escaping through the back door of the barracks.

He was in an ancient forest. There could be wild animals about. The object he tripped over felt large but soft. Could it have been a sleeping bear or a tiger? He had heard tigers were in the area. His brother-in-law had been snatched by a Siberian tiger as his platoon marched through such a forest during the Russo-Japanese war, and was never seen again. Jacob's survival instinct kicked in, and he scrambled up the nearest tree.

There was no sound from below, maybe it was a dead

bear? Daylight was fading rapidly and visibility was almost nil. While there was still enough light to discern the branches of the tree he decided that this would have to be his lodging for the night. In the morning he would examine the area more thoroughly and maybe find some mushrooms or berries but for now, he must put the gnawing hunger in his belly out of his mind. He located a spot where three branches joined together forming a pocket that looked comfortable. Wedging into the space, he removed the belt from his trousers and wrapped it around his leg tying it onto one of the sturdier branches; if during the night he were to roll, it would keep him from falling. He was exhausted. As he wedged himself in, the clamor of birds settling down for the night and the fatigue from the run overcame him. He fell into a deep exhausted sleep.

The first piercing rays of the morning sun penetrating the dense canopy woke him up. Night passed by so quickly, he felt like he barely slept at all. Initially he could not orient himself but the drip, drip, drip of dew from the leaves brought him back to reality. He was up a tree. The belt held through the night and he didn't fall. Slowly, the events of the previous day floated back into his mind.

He escaped from the camp without being fired upon; as he ran, he stumbled on something soft; as he fell, his chest struck a hard object, the pain in his ribs was still there. The sun was not yet completely up and it was difficult to distinguish details on the ground below. Hunger pangs in his stomach were turning to pain, but he felt that he must wait to make sure it was safe to come down from the tree. His present goal was to orient himself. Where was he? When he ran from the camp, which direction did he take? When he awoke, the sun was in his face; therefore that must be east. Boris, his brother, wrote that he was in the Urals. They were east from the camp, therefore that would have to be his general direction of travel, but how far had he run?

Finally, it was light enough to see the ground below. Slowly, he slid down the trunk of the tree making the least possible noise. Maybe the bear/tiger was still asleep and he did not want to wake it. As he stepped on the ground, he could see where the grass was bent and the branches of the bushes broken; this must be where he fell. A thick stump was sticking out of the ground; it was responsible for the pain in his side and, hallelujah! Right next to the stump was a clump of mushrooms; *borovik*i, the best kind of mushrooms. He would not starve, but he still could not see the object over which he tripped. Picking several mushrooms, he ravenously gulped them down. Then, slowly he proceeded to follow the bent grass to the place where he tripped.

The object he tripped over was not a bear but a man. The man was dead, but couldn't have been dead long, there was no odor of decomposition and Jacob knew the odor of the dead. Could he be one of the exiles from the camp who escaped like Jacob? The man was tall, approximately Jacob's height, dressed in sturdy pants and a leather *caftan* (jacket.) Who was he? The only way to find out was to go through his pockets. Jacob felt like a thief, but decided that he must search the body. The right pants pocket had some money, the left pocket a knife and some coins. The shirt pocket had a pencil. Patting the body down Jacob could not feel anything else. This man could not be one of the exiles, they didn't have money or a knife. Going through the pockets of the man's jacket he found some string, rawhide laces and a box of matches including a pouch of tobacco and some newspaper, cut in strips.

The inside pocket of the jacket contained some papers. Carefully he removed them and began to examine the find. There was a letter, still in an envelope, a stub of a used railroad ticket, and a tightly folded document. When he unfolded the paper, it turned out to be a permission slip from the police allowing the bearer to travel from Aranets to Kirov, and a work permit stating that the bearer was a carpenter who worked in the region of Ukhta. The man's name was Ivan Buryak. There was no other information about him in the document except for the date of birth, December, 1905, two years younger than Jacob. He removed the man's jacket and the belt from his trousers. The boots on the corpse were worn and looked too small. Jacob felt uneasy undressing the dead man and taking his possessions, but the man was dead and Jacob was still alive. Now he had papers and his desire to survive soared!

It did not matter why the man was in the taiga. Maybe he was running like Jacob or who knows what, but the important part was that Jacob had a document which he could produce if stopped and questioned by the authorities. It would allow him to travel more freely, and the money would buy some food. First things first, he had to get to civilization. How long would it take him to get out of the taiga he didn't know, but he knew that in the South is where people lived. Picking some more mushrooms and putting on the dead man's caftan he headed south.

How far was it to Berezniki where Boris lived? From what he remembered, the Aranets camp was about three hundred kilometers west of the Urals. He started walking. It was a difficult trek. There was no sign of human habitation. The forest consisted primarily of undergrowth with a few small pine trees and struggling gnarled oaks. He trudged south getting his bearings from the sun. Along the way he picked and ate berries. Thanks to his father, Jacob knew which mushrooms and berries were edible. Several small streams barred his way, but he was able to jump over them or find a fallen tree that provided a bridge. After two more days in the taiga he came to a river. It flowed north, so he followed it upstream. Mushrooms and berries filled his stomach but did not provide much nourishment and one of them caused diarrhea.

He walked along the river for another day and did not encounter any people. Occasional logs which looked like they were cut by men, not just broken limbs, floated by. Pressing on, along the banks of the river at the end of the third day there were still only trees and the river. The berries were really doing a number on his stomach so he decided to rest, but the reflection of the setting sun on the water provided additional visibility, therefore he could make another few kilometers. As night was falling, through tree branches he spotted a light in the distance. Could it be a village? It gave him a spurt of energy and he started hurrying toward what looked like a glow flickering through the leaves of overhanging branches by the river banks. He walked some more and finally could distinguish a light in the distance. Not much of a light, but it looked like it was coming from a dwelling. Pushing on, he finally came to what looked like a log road, the type he and the exiles built in the forest, during his initial exile in Kotlas. Not wanting to fall and injure his side even more, he gingerly stepped on the logs and reached the source of the light.

It was a small cabin with a candle in the window. Who lived there? It looked like a hunter's or a woodsman's place. As he came closer, he smelled food; his hunger intensified. He knocked on the door. After a while he heard stirring inside and then some shuffling steps. The door opened, and an ancient woman peered through the crack. Jacob said, "Babushka, I am hungry, do you have anything to eat?"

She began crossing herself and in a surprised voice asked, "How did you get here?"

"I walked on the log road," said Jacob.

The babushka once more, even more furiously, began to cross herself but, she opened the door to let him in. He smelled the food, and she again asked him, "How did you get here?"

"I walked on the log road," he insisted.

"Detka (my child) you could not have walked, there is no road, I live on an island in the middle of the river! But you look worn out, wash your hands and I will give you some soup, then we will talk."

She put half a loaf of aromatic dark bread on the table and poured him a large bowl of fish stew, called *ukha*. Jacob had not eaten *ukha* or such delicious bread since Bolshaya Sliva. They didn't talk while he ate, or rather inhaled the food. Finishing the meal, he tried to stay awake, but the full stomach and exhaustion would not let him. Babushka walked him over to a wide bench with a straw mattress and a pillow on it. He collapsed on the bench not knowing or caring where he was. All he knew was that he must be with an angel, and an angel would not let any harm come to him. He fell peacefully asleep.

He was awakened by the crow of a rooster and smell of frying bacon drifting from the stove. Babushka was cooking, and humming one of his favorite church hymns; "Let God arise, and let His enemies be scattered" an Orthodox Church hymn sung on *Pascha*, Resurrection Sunday.

She heard him stir and said, "Ah, *detka* you are awake! It is way past morning, but I knew you needed the rest so I did not wake you." Jacob rubbed the sleep from his eyes and ran to the door followed by babushka. "You see, I told you, I live on an island".

On both sides of the hut ran the river. A small rowboat was tied to a stake next to the shore. She said, "Let me feed you, and then I can row you to whichever side you want to be on." He felt relieved and trapped at the same time. The only way out, in case he had to run, was to swim. But once again he felt safe and went inside to enjoy the meal babushka prepared. He was calm in her presence and for the first time in months fear left him. During the meal they talked of life. She said she knew he was one of the exiled people. Many had come this way and she helped them in the only way she could, with food, directions and most importantly prayers. Jacob told her that he was trying to find his brother in Berezniki. "Ah," she said, "You are only a couple of days walk from the town. Just walk along the river for a day and you will come to a railroad track, follow it to Berezniki."

Jacob was still dumbfounded. How could he have walked to babushka's cabin since it was surrounded by water. Then she gave him a clue. The river she lived on flowed into a larger river downstream. Jacob had apparently missed the juncture because it was dark when he ran by trying to locate the light. She said there was a camp of exiles further up her river where they cut trees and floated them down to the town of Seryj. Sometimes, in the early spring, the logs would jam up so tightly that one could walk across. But this was the month of July and it was a swiftly flowing river and this morning, there wasn't a log in sight.

He stayed with babushka several days, eating, sleeping and resting. He did clean up the outside of her yard and chopped a pile of firewood. It felt good to do something productive of his own accord.

On the third day he decided it was time to leave. It felt like he had been with his own family. Babushka prepared him a food sack of smoked and dried fish and included a whole loaf of the dark wonderful bread. He hugged her, and they both cried. Jacob felt the hem of his jacket and pulled out one of the three remaining gold coins offering it to babushka. "My *detka*," she said, "I have no need for gold here. My gold is in the sunrise and sunset, as the sun's rays reflect off the river. You hold on to it, you have a long journey ahead of you, and who knows what lies ahead, you may need it."

They hugged once more and Jacob stepped into the tiny row-boat. At first it rocked so violently that he thought it would capsize under their weight, but then quickly like a cork it bobbed up and babushka rowed to the east side of the shore. As the bow of the boat hit the bank, Jacob stepped off without getting his feet wet. Grabbing his sack and turning around he wanted to say good-bye, but babushka and her little boat were already in the middle of the river. How did she do it so fast?

He yelled, *"Dosvidanye!"* Good-bye, till we meet again. She didn't seem to hear him and kept rowing to her cabin on the island.

Following the river downstream, as babushka directed him, he thought about the days just passed. The three days on the island rejuvenated him and gave him strength. It was a miracle that he was able to cross the river on foot. There was no log road. He had no answer, except, that God had provided another escape. He said a prayer for babushka and pressed on.

As babushka had told him, by the end of the first day he came to a railroad track and decided to spend the night. Just up the tracks he saw a lean-to where gravel and rocks were piled to shore up the rails. It was still light and he decided to write a short note to Olga hoping that somewhere along the way he would be able to mail it. He didn't know how long it would take him to get to Slutsk. Using the pencil and a sheet of paper, from the letter in Ivan Buryak's pocket, he told Olga he was alive and was on his way. He hoped to mail the letter at the next rail station. He ate a piece of bread and one small fish, drank some water from the stream and leaning against the wall of the lean-to fell asleep, facing east.

The sun woke him up and he continued down the tracks toward Berezniki. At first, it was difficult to walk on the railroad ties, but soon he was able to measure his steps, walking with ease; it even seemed that he was covering more distance in this manner. At midday, he came upon a juncture in the rails; another track joined from the south, and the switch was set to head east, toward Berezniki. He sat down to rest and eat breakfast. The smoked fish and babushka's bread were delicious.

After the meal, he lay down on the grass-covered slope adjoining the tracks; then he heard the rumble of a distant train followed by a whistle. Startled, he jumped into the nearby bushes bordering the tracks and waited. Soon smoke from the locomotive, and another whistle told him that the train was slowing down. It was a freight train carrying lumber and ore. The Urals were full of mineral mines worked by the exiles. Making sure that he would not be seen, Jacob ran along the side of the train and at the appropriate moment jumped on. He was becoming an expert at this. Settling down between cars, he watched as the train rumbled toward what he hoped was Berezniki.

On the right were the peaks of the Urals covered with snow sloping gently to a plain covered with trees and flowering meadows. How beautiful it looked. Then he recalled the stories of the exiles who spent time in the mines under horrendous conditions while mining iron ore, copper, gold and even precious stones. This land was full of riches but why did man have to exploit his fellow man to get at them? Lost in thought he just watched the countryside roll by. Towards the end of the day, homes were beginning to appear; they must be getting near Berezniki.

The train slowed down as if getting ready to stop or edge into a siding. Jacob prepared to jump off. He didn't want to be seen by any railroad men and would jump at the earliest opportunity. Then came another whistle as the train passed a semaphore. It was nearing a town. Babushka had told him that there were no major towns between the river and Berezniki, this must be it. He jumped off.

Jacob had memorized Boris' address because he was afraid to carry it in his pocket in fear of compromising his brother in case he was stopped. Now he would have to try and find it. To make matters worse night was falling and visibility was minimal. Not being familiar with the town and not wanting to raise suspicion by asking for directions he started walking. Boris had written that he lived in communal housing and Jacob began examining the building he passed, looking for anything that resembled barracks. People were coming home from work; after a while he decided to chance it and asked someone how to get to the address. All of the people looked tired and most likely would be less prone to ask questions or take time to point him out to a policeman. They just wanted to get home and rest. He asked several, but they just shrugged their shoulders or gave a wave of the hand indicating that they did not know or didn't care. Finally a man gave him directions. The dormitory was on the other side of town but the man said that one could not miss it when one saw it.

Walking through town he became part of the home bound gray mass of workers; no one stopped him or even gave him a look. Soon, from the description the man provided, he recognized the shape of a dormitory, the Communal Quarters. The place looked gray, without any trees, just a place to bed down and sleep. He entered, and was confronted by a watchman, who looked bored. Jacob asked him if Boris K. was in. The watchman told him to wait as he went to check. It was an open building without any privacy, just rows of bunks separated by thin walls. Soon the watchman returned, followed by Boris. Jacob hardly recognized his brother, he had changed so much. He was gaunt and thin, but still had that special walk Jacob remembered. Boris also didn't recognize Jacob. He had grown a beard.

When Jacob spoke, Boris' eyes widened and filled with tears as he threw his arms around his brother's neck. He told the watchman that Jacob was a friend from home. They walked back to his bunk with arms around each other and hugged some more. Both were afraid to say anything in the presence of the other occupants since neither knew what the other's masquerade represented.

It was dinner time. Boris put on his boots and they left the barracks arm in arm for the cafeteria; it was for residents only, but Boris explained to the attendant that his friend had just come into town, and asked if he could pay for his meal. The woman examined Jacob with a piercing gaze but allowed Boris to pay the fifty kopecks for the meal.

After dinner, Jacob and Boris went for a walk so that they could talk more freely; it had been months since they saw each other. Jacob told him about the loss of his children and the terrors of Lubyanka prison, his miraculous escape from the camp in Aranets, the body in the *taiga* and the "angel" Babushka. Boris listened intently, often crying bitterly, for he knew how much Jacob loved his children, they were his life. Then Boris told him that he had received a letter from their brother Sergei. Zachary and Yelena died a month before from starvation. Several weeks before, Boris sent them a package of *sukhari* (dried bread) and some bacon, but it got there too late. Sergei was still in the Toymushka camp and felt he could survive if only the *urki* would leave him alone. They still had not forgiven him for reporting them to the guards when they stole the bag of food. By this time Sergei had learned to defend himself and could handle their threats and onslaughts. Yesip, Olga's brother, wrote that Olga was at home, waiting for Jacob. Alexei, their youngest brother, was living with Uncle Stephan but felt he may have to run, people were asking too many questions about his *kulak* parents.

The brothers sat under the starry skies for a long time and talked about their past and the uncertain future. Boris felt he was safe where he was, since nobody knew he was the son of a *kulak*. He had also heard that a *Kolhoz* was being established in the area and he had "volunteered" to be a husbandman for the livestock. It would be great to work with animals again and leave this back-breaking loading job. But now it was most important to get Jacob home, to Olga.

Through his contacts at the railroad Boris was able to buy a ticket for Jacob and gave him some food and money for the trip. The bigger concern was the lack of travel papers. Jacob showed Boris the papers he found on the dead man in the *taiga* and felt he could risk it, as long as he bypassed Moscow. It was a trip of over twenty-five-hundred kilometers from Berezniki to Minsk, a long way to hide. If stopped, he could use Ivan Buryak's papers, but Boris also gave Jacob his own work documents, just in case. In a couple of months Boris would report them lost and request a new set to be issued. Jacob stayed two days with Boris. On the third day they said good-bye and walked to the train station to board the train home. This time Jacob had papers and money in his pocket and didn't have to jump a train.

The train was full of peasants and workmen. Jacob's ticket was general class. Since class distinction was eliminated under communism this generally meant that all the tickets were standing room. It was only fair that every proletariat in the USSR should travel in the same class since they were all equal, weren't they? Jacob immersed himself into this quagmire of the bodies becoming part of the nondistinctive mass of humanity.

Unbelievably, throughout the trip, no one came to check the papers. The cars were so packed and smelly that the conductor hardly wanted to immerse himself into this mass. One can only imagine the aroma of the sardine-packed unwashed bodies, many carrying chickens and pigs. Jacob tried not to leave the train at stops and stayed in the car. Four days out, he was able to trade some food for a seat with a man who was getting off at the next stop. It was uncanny to give food away for a seat since he had only recently been starving, but he had enough to eat and it was several days more to Beloruss. For the last six hundred kilometers to Minsk he rode in a seat. The train arrived in Minsk on Market Day. He got a ride to the market from a farmer on a hay wagon. The market place was his best opportunity to possibly find someone who could give him a ride to Slutsk. Then, it was only twenty kilometers to Bondary, where he hoped Olga was waiting.

This would be the most dangerous part of the journey. Even with a beard someone could possibly recognize him. The market was crowded with people, animals and the wares they came to sell or trade, as Jacob went looking for someone from the village. After wandering for a while, he saw one of his boyhood friends, Volodya. During their youth, Jacob and Volodya hunted rabbits together and climbed many a tree to destroy crows nests. He watched Volodya and when there was no one around he gave a special whistle which in their youth was an arranged signal. Volodya looked around, surprised to hear it. Jacob grabbed him and pulled him behind the wagon. Volodya turned as if to fight but before throwing a punch he recognized Jacob's voice. Volodya knew of Jacob's exile and was frightened to see him, especially the way he looked after his journey from the Urals.

Quickly Volodya told him to burrow himself into the hay on the wagon and he would wake him when he was ready to leave for Bondary. Jacob did as he was told and soon fell asleep; the fresh hay was like perfume and he dreamed of holding Olga in his arms. It seemed that he slept only a minute when Volodya was back and ready to leave. Jacob burrowed himself in the hay to get to the front of the wagon, but Volodya told him to just move the hay out of the way so they could talk, but not to show his head. During the trip Jacob learned about the happenings in Bolshaya Sliva while he was away. Many more were "identified" as *kulaks* and were now sharing Zachary's fate in the North. However, because of such a tremendous death rate of children in exile, the Soviets had relented and allowed children of the exiles to remain with their "less prosperous" relatives while the parents were "rehabilitated". Volodya also told him that one of those who had informed on Zachary and Jacob was in exile himself because he had appropriated a lot of the *kulak's* property, including Anastasia's bed. God was repaying!

The mill was under control of the *Kolhoz* but kept breaking down since they did not have anyone qualified to run or maintain the steam engine. Time flew as the old friends recalled the past and soon they were just outside the village. Jacob dropped off the wagon since he didn't want Volodya to be compromised in case anyone saw them together. He also didn't want Volodya to know where Olga was hiding. He didn't know where Olga was but felt that the first place to look would be her father's house.

At the same time Olga, was making her way from the forest to the house for supper. Each time she came, one of her sister's children would be sent out to watch the road for strangers. That evening her niece Liuba was watching the road. It was a boring chore for the child. On previous occasions no one came so she began to amuse herself with flowers growing along the fence. When she looked up, she saw a bearded man coming toward the house. The girl panicked, and with a yelp ran toward the *khata* (hut) just as Olga was sitting down to eat. "Stranger! A stranger is coming!" yelled Liuba. Olga jumped off the bench and made a dive for the open window at the back of the hut. When she landed there was a scream. She had forgotten about the black raspberry bush growing under that window and now her body was being torn by thorns but she didn't dare move!

Jacob came to the door and knocked. Everyone in the hut was holding their breath. Stephan, with his trusted hatchet in hand went to answer the door, ready to deliver a blow, should it be necessary. Even with the beard, he recognized Jacob, and exclaimed: "Yasha!" Tossing the hatchet aside, Stephan embraced Jacob as a huge sigh arose from the room. Irina, Olga's sister ran to the window whispering, "It is Yasha!" Olga was still enveloped by the thorns of the black raspberry bush but when she heard the name, she sprang up as the thorns ripped at her flesh. Her pain did not matter. She crawled back into the hut and, for the first time since Kotlas, hugged and kissed her beloved.

That evening as her sisters tended to Olga's wounds they listened to Jacob's story while she clung to her husband. She knew she didn't like his beard and at the first opportunity she would ask him to shave. That night the family let them have the separate room, while Stephan slept in the barn.

They were reunited but could not stay in the village. There were too many informers and someone would certainly see them and tell the authorities. They must hide somewhere else, but where?

While in Kotlas, Jacob wrote to his cousin Mary in America, describing their situation, asking for her help; begging if she could bring them to America. But based on the current situation in the Soviet Union, it seemed that there was no way it could be done legally or quickly. One possibility was for them to get to Finland and from there, maybe, if they were lucky and weren't caught, it could be possible. Jacob rejected that approach, since he knew that the border between the Soviet Union and Finland was very heavily guarded, and any attempts to cross would result in immediate execution. They must find a way to disappear, in Russia itself.

When Jacob was running alone, there was anxiety every day, but now there were two of them. Stress caused by the anxiety manifested itself in heart pains. Initially he did not want Olga to know but as they became more frequent and severe, he knew that he had to see a doctor who could give him a diagnosis. Did he have a heart attack in the Lubyanka prison while under the interrogation by the KGB?

There was only one physician they could trust Dr. Meyer Zelagin in Slutsk, an old Jewish friend of the family. Yesip, Olga's brother loaded a wagon with hay and told Jacob and Olga to burrow into the stack as he drove them to Slutsk. Olga would not leave her husband's side and was very concerned about the pain in his chest. Jacob was only thirty and having a heart condition at that age was unbelievable. But considering what they endured, it was possible.

Dr. Meyer was at home when they arrived and asked them to stay overnight so that he could run some tests. He knew the family had been exiled but did not know the details of their life there. At supper, and long into the night Jacob told them of the family's ordeals, loss of children, and now they had to be on the run again.

The next morning, after evaluating the test results, Dr. Meyer spoke to Jacob and Olga, "My dear friend, you have suffered a myocardial infarction, a heart attack. It was not a very bad one, but you must watch yourself from now on. I urge you to stop smoking, reduce your stress, and do not exert yourself physically. Don't work too hard, and don't drink in excess. If you follow these rules you may lead a fairly normal life and live to an old age.

"Now, these would be my instructions to someone in a situation other than yours. However, I know that it may be impossible to adhere to most of my recommendations. Smoking and drinking you must control, the rest will be in God's hands. Here is a bottle of medication called *Valeryanka;* it is a sedative to calm the heart.

Keep it with you at all times, and at the earliest sign of chest pain, take five drops in a tablespoon of water. Sit or lie down for five minutes; if the pain continues, repeat the dose again, but no more than three times. The first dose should usually relieve the pain."

Jacob and Olga were stunned by the doctor's diagnosis and Jacob asked, "Doctor, are you telling me that I am an invalid at thirty?"

Dr. Meyer replied, "Well, almost."

Shocked by Dr. Meyer's answer, Olga wept. How could they go on if Jacob could not work? What would they do?

Dr. Meyer began to calm them down. "I have given you the most frightening picture in order for you know that this is serious, but you are still young and most likely everything that I mentioned will not happen."

After these reassuring words, Olga calmed down and hugged her husband. A few more words of encouragement from Dr. Meyer, and they felt their prospects were not so grim. However the immediate situation was certainly very stressful and they had to go someplace where no one knew them. Dr. Meyer once more came to their rescue, saying, "Go to the Ukraine, to a town called Mariupol. I have a cousin there named David Dwoskin. He will help you to start a new life. I will write a letter of introduction on my stationary and tell him you are on your way."

Jacob and Olga could not find sufficient words to thank this good doctor and tried to give him one of the last ten ruble gold pieces, but he refused. Placing his hands on their shoulders, he kissed them on both cheeks saying, "Shalom. God go with you. And give my cousin David a kiss when you see him."

They left Dr. Meyer's house sobbing and hoping that perhaps someday they would be able to repay this wonderful man's kindness.

Chapter 8

Mariupol in the Ukraine

Jacob felt Mariupol was far enough out of the way that the probability of them being recognized was remote. In the village, they lived like scared rabbits, scurrying for cover from any suspicious glance or noise. What choice did they have? Stay, and most likely be identified, arrested and returned to Siberia, or run and hope for the best. They chose to run.

Their trek from Beloruss to Mariupol involved every possible mode of transportation. Mostly they walked, hopped trains, and worked at anything that would provide food or money, continually heading south toward the Ukraine. Dr. Meyer gave them his cousin's address, but they did not know whether he actually wrote the letter, and if he did, did his cousin David receive it? They pressed on, with hope and prayers in their hearts.

Several times, during the journey, they stopped to rest in places where it seemed safe. At each stop they established a signal to be used if either thought that the other was spotted or being followed. At each location they selected a spot where they could meet without arousing suspicion, making it look like a meeting of two lovers.

In one village, while staying in communal quarters, several women cautioned Olga that she had better keep an eye on her good looking husband; otherwise some woman might steal him. Olga was not troubled by their comments because, deep in her heart, she knew that their love was forever. However, just in case Jacob did not come home some night, they fabricated a story, which would be used to throw off suspicion, if needed. They didn't have to wait long.

One evening Jacob did not come back to the room and the women's tongues started wagging. When he didn't return for the second night, the women were sure he had found someone else. That evening Olga went to their designated spot and placed a small bag of provisions for Jacob, knowing that if he had to run, he would at least have food and clean clothes. The next evening she returned to the spot, the sack was still there. Her mind was reeling with terrible thoughts. Was Jacob arrested? Was he hiding? Was he spotted? No one had come to the dormitory looking for him, she therefore decided to wait one more day before running, all the time being buffeted by the wagging tongues. This wait was more troubling than the time she spent in the forest. Here, she was alone in a strange place without any potential help from anyone. What would she do if Jacob did not show up? This thought was so disturbing, that in order to keep herself from losing control, she forced herself to dwell on the few years of peace and love they shared in the past. This also brought back the exile, loss of children and family, amplified by her continuing concern for Jacob's health. There was no one she could share her pain with, except God. She agonized alone!

The following evening, looking rather sheepish, Jacob showed up. It was time for their previously rehearsed act. Olga jumped all over him, slapping his face accusing him of infidelity. Jacob admitted that he was in the wrong and begged Olga to take him back. The dormitory womens' "chorus" was on Olga's side, calling Jacob every filthy name they could think of for the occasion. He fell on his knees before Olga and begged forgiveness. This act so touched the womens' hearts that they agreed she should give him another chance because he was so good looking. But if he transgressed again, Olga wouldn't have to do a thing, the women "would kill him."

That night, as they hugged each other, Jacob told Olga the reason for his absence. While walking through town he spotted a former prison guard from Kotlas and thought that he was recognized. He didn't dare come back to the dormitory and hid in a barn for the night. In the morning as he started back to the dormitory, he noticed that another man seemed to be following him. At the earliest opportunity Jacob dashed into an alley and into the woods where he waited till the evening to return. In the morning the dormitory group saw that apparently everything was forgiven and did not bother them, but Jacob got very suspicious glances.

Another time, while still living in the same dormitory, Olga was ironing clothes when she heard Jacob's signal, warning her to run. She calmly went to the door and continued to their prearranged spot. When she arrived, she gave a whistle and Jacob appeared out of nowhere. Looking at Olga he started to laugh. She was hurt, and didn't know why he was laughing. Then Jacob pointed out to her that instead of bringing the small suitcase with all their belongings, in her hand was the iron filled with burning charcoal which she was using when the signal came. That incident convinced them that they had better move on.

It took them almost a month to reach Mariupol. Their feet were sore but they could not take the trolley since they had no idea in which part of town the Dwoskins lived. Maps were not available and the only way to get directions was to ask someon. But they were afraid to do so because it might raise suspicion and the person could point them out to a policeman. They slept in the railroad station, and finally on the second day, found the address. They didn't know if they were expected, or how the Dwoskins would react. They had not communicated with anyone since leaving Slutsk and in a month many things could have changed. After arriving at the address, Jacob knocked on the door. The man who answered had an uncanny resemblance to Dr. Meyer. As Jacob relayed the "Shalom" greetings from the good doctor, they were welcomed with open arms. The man said, "I got a letter from Meyer."

The Dwoskins didn't have much, but shared what they had. The love they showed Olga and Jacob was so genuine that they felt at home. However, they knew, they should not overstay their welcome. After several days rest they would have to find a place of their own, but first Jacob had to find work. He did not have a legal work permit but had to take a chance. David worked as a carpenter at the construction site of a new steel mill and knew that work was available unloading coal barges. Getting any job was no simple matter and required official references from a previous work site. Jacob's last work site was a GULAG in Siberia, hardly an acceptable reference, but again God came to their rescue and he was hired based on the papers he got from his brother Boris.

The job was dirty and exhausting, but he and Olga were together, seemingly safe for the time being, and had enough money for food. They shared a corner of the room with the Dwoskins while attempting to find a room to rent.

Everything in the Soviet Union requires a document, especially finding a place to live. Since Jacob and Olga were living under a fictitious name, had no official papers and very little money, their only choice was to stay with the Dwoskins until Jacob was able to obtain a work permit from his job. Olga loved their corner because compared to the forest and a hollowed out tree, where she hid while waiting for Jacob, this was a palace!

Coal loaders at the pier were required to keep a tally of the sacks they unloaded and were paid on that basis. The foreman of Jacob's gang was a shrewd fellow and would steal a sack or two from each of the worker's tally, adding them to his own. Most of the workers were simple uneducated fellows, with strong backs and could be easily fooled. This was not the case with Jacob. The foreman quickly learned he could not steal from him. Soon he asked Jacob to prepare his daily tally reports for the yard manager. After a few weeks the manager noticed improvement in the foreman's reports and asked him who was preparing them. The foreman could not readily lie and pointed Jacob out to him. The manager in turn, took Jacob to work in his office to do coal yard accounting. Jacob was thrilled. No longer did he have to lug the heavy bags of coal, eating coal dust with every breath; he now worked in a clean office as the manager's assistant.

By 1932, the Soviet Union was totally under of Stalin's grip. The Politburo, in order to have a better control of the population, decreed issuance of new internal passports to all "qualified Soviet citizens." To assemble a task force for this monumental work, orders went out to all organizations, requesting management to select individuals who were trustworthy, had good handwriting and could be released to write new passports. At that time in the USSR, all clerical work was done by hand; typewriters were few and far between, assigned only to those at the highest level of authority.

Jacob and Olga Kurdsjuk - 1932

After their escape from Kotlas, Siberia to Mariupol. This portrait today hangs at 5 Vishnyevyj Pereulok, Mariupol in the home of Pavlik (Blocha) Yudin.

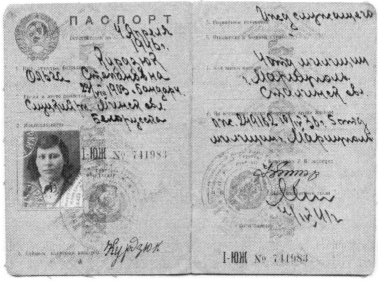

U.S.S.R Passports

No. 741983 - Issued to Olga Styepanovna Kurdsjuk
No. 741984 - Issued to Alexander Afanasyevich Kurdsjuk
These passports were written Illegally by Jacob when the
Soviet government recruited him to write
passports,becauseof his calligraphic handwriting.

82

Jacob was ambidextrous, able to write with either hand. His manager, wanting to be recognized for his responsiveness to the call of authorities, immediately submitted Jacob's name with an accompanying trustworthiness document. Hallelujah! Once more, God intervened!

Needless to say, during the issuance of passports, two additional passports were written, one for Olga Stepanovna Kurdsjuk and the other for Alexander Afanasjevich Kurdsjuk. Jacob still could not use his real first name since all documents in his possession had the first name of either his brother Boris or first cousin Alexander in Minsk. Jacob became Alexander Afanasjevich Kurdsjuk, a new Soviet citizen.

With an official passport, written with his left hand to avoid suspicions, Jacob/Alexander could now pursue opportunities previously denied him, not only at the huge Azov Steel construction project but also in education. Now he and Olga were legal citizens of the Union of Soviet Socialist Republics. His first efforts were channeled into obtaining a certificate of education. He had completed only four years of the village school, but since then read everything he could get his hands on, including many books, on all kinds of subjects, Uncle Stephan had provided.

In the USSR, to obtain a certificate of higher education one had to either attend a university, or be recommended by someone in authority to stand for a formal exam. Jacob's manager, puffed up by the work Jacob did in the issuance of passports, submitted a recommendation for the exam. The initial portion of the exam consisted of a verbal interrogation by a group of professors and practitioners in the chosen discipline. The candidate actually stood in front of this group and was grilled for several hours in subjects relevant to the chosen profession. If the candidate passed the verbal portion and was accepted by the committee, the written portion was almost always granted.

Jacob's interests lay in design, construction and finance. He chose Engineering and finance as his vocation, Civil Engineering specifically, and passed the four hour verbal exam on the first try.

His photographic memory, ability to recall the most minute facts, common sense and love for mathematics gave him the edge, so he did not have to take the written portion of the exam. His manager was thrilled and bragged to everyone what a smart man he had working for him.

Armed with a Civil Engineering certificate and the new passport, Jacob applied and got a position at the construction of the coke production facility at the new steel mill. Jacob's coal yard experience and the manager's recommendation helped him to obtain the position, thus began his new career as a construction engineer.

For the first time in his life he could apply his knowledge and efforts in a field that interested him, even though the experiences in his recent past, held him back from giving his all. How could he work at enhancing the communist system after what he suffered? But all of that was in the past, and nothing could change it. Maybe he and Olga could begin life anew.

Soon Olga was with child. A son was born, whom they named Victor. They doted over the infant, a bright and adorable child, but this happiness was not to last. At the age of seven months Victor was infected with meningitis.

Medicine in the Soviet Union was primitive to say the least, and access to healthcare was strictly government controlled. Those in upper echelons of the hierarchy received the best care first. Although Jacob was not a member of the communist party, his work in the issuance of passports and the engineering position at the steel plant placed him in the category of official staff, giving him access to the better health clinics and doctors. This however was of little help. Victor died within two weeks, and once more Olga and Jacob found themselves all alone, desperately clinging to each other, wondering how much more they could endure. Infant mortality in the '30s was high; this was the fourth child they had lost and wondered if they would ever be blessed with a child who survived?

They longed for the closeness of family and decided to ask Jacob's brother Sergei in Siberia to join them in Mariupol. By

Union of Professional Engineers-Dues Book

Issued to Alexander Affanasyevich Kurdsjuk in 1932. Upon accepting a position of Engineer at Azov Steel, Mariupol.

this time Sergei had completed his "rehabilitation" as the son of a *kulak*, but could not get work. There was plenty of work in Mariupol, especially at the steel plant where Sergei's training as a tractor operator was in demand. After exchanging several letters, Sergei agreed to come, and within a few months arrived in Mariupol. When he was released from exile, he received a passport under his real name, however, it restricted him from working in the major cities of USSR such as Moscow and Leningrad. At the age of twenty-five, the Soviet Government considered Sergei to be rehabilitated and once more he could become a "productive Soviet citizen."

Sergei, like Jacob, was a tall and handsome fellow who turned girls' heads. He was full of life and would seldom let a pretty girl pass by without a compliment. In their village of Bolshaya Sliva, he was considered to be quite a flirt and a terrific dancer. Jacob got him a job at the Azov project. While working on the site, Sergei met an attractive young office girl and started taking her for walks. Unbeknownst to him, she was dating another man in Sergei's work brigade. Once the fellow became aware of Sergei's attention for the young lady, he threatened him to keep away. If he didn't, there would be "consequences." Sergei took it as a remark of a jealous competitor and continued seeing the girl. She also showed more interest in Sergei than the "other fellow." However, the rival meant business. One day, while Sergei was under the tractor working on minor repairs, it suddenly started, lurched forward and the caterpillar's tracks ran over Sergei's entire body, killing him instantly.

In the annals of the Azov Steel Construction Project, it was reported as an industrial accident. Jacob could not pursue the issue because he would have to expose himself and identify Sergei as his brother. Whatever he did, would not bring Sergei back and would certainly negatively impact Jacob's future. He chose to let it be and go on.

Olga was expecting again and if they had to run it would be difficult. Jacob was devastated, blaming himself for Sergei's death. "If only I had not asked him to come to Mariupol, he would

86

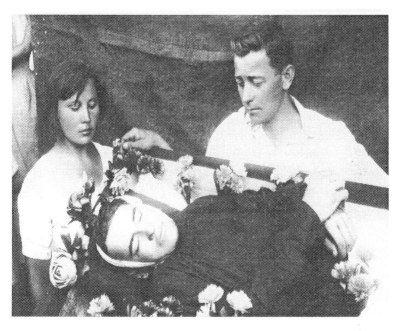

Funeral of Sergei Kurdsjuk - June 30, 1934

Killed by a jealous suitor of a girl he was dating at Azov Stal construction. Jacob could not tell anyone that Sergei was his brother since he and Olga were living under an assumed name after their escape from Siberia.

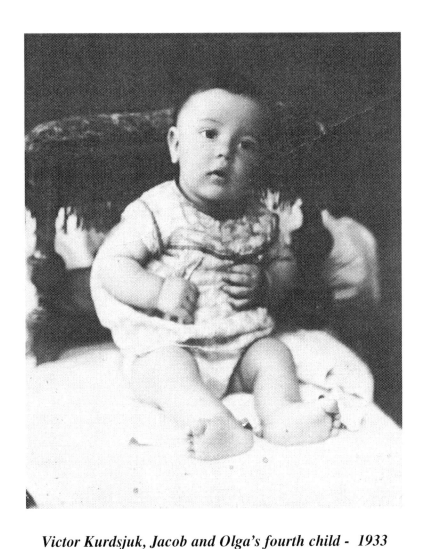

Victor Kurdsjuk, Jacob and Olga's fourth child - 1933

Victor died at the age of seven months from meningitis in Mariupol.

still be alive!" He cried and suffered so much that Olga was concerned he would have another heart attack. She tried to console him in any way she could, but nothing would relieve the pain he felt. He kept saying, "My whole family is gone, my son just died and now I am the cause of my brother's death. I don't know if I can go on. Is my life jinxed? Did someone put a curse on me? Why God? Why?!"

Under Communism, all religious ceremonies were strictly forbidden, including burials with a priest. Funerals consisted of a speech, usually given by a friend or a relative of the deceased, who spoke of the accomplishments of the departed in the advancement of communism. Then, the orchestra played a funeral dirge and concluded with boisterous Proletariat Marches.

Imagine the impact of that process on Jacob and Olga, considering what they had only recently endured because of communism. Jacob was so shaken by Sergei's death that he became very ill, and everyone wondered why a man would feel such grief for a distant cousin. Of course, no one knew Jacob burried his younger brother. Only a small wooden board marked Sergei's grave in a tiny Mariupol cemetery.

Jacob and Olga had moved out of the Dwoskin household soon after he began working in the Coal Yard Manager's office. A new five story brick apartment building was built for the Azov Steel Project workers. Jacob, being "in management," was eligible for a one bedroom apartment, sharing a bathroom. They had no furniture, but someone gave them a bed, and Dwoskin, a carpenter, made them a table and two chairs.

The construction project was in full swing and many workers from Azov Steel moved into the building and friendships began to form. Across the hall from their apartment lived a family with an infant son named Yulja. After I was born on November 2, 1934, the two mothers bonded intensely. Yulja's mother was Jewish and Mama's friendship with the Dwoskins and Dr. Meyer became a catalyst in creating the bond. Mama and Papa could not share any of their past with their new friends because they were still afraid of being found out and had to make up plausible alternatives.

Several months after I was born, Papa came home and was met at the door by a radiant Mama, while the aroma of delicious food emanated from the small cooking area. At the center of the room, the small table was set for supper with a bottle of vodka on it. Locally that size bottle was called "Three fifteen," because that was its price, and it readily fit into a worker's pocket. Papa scratched his head, pondering the occasion. It wasn't his or Mama's birthday, their anniversary was still months away so, why the celebration? Could Mama be expecting again? He was dumbfounded.

Walking over to the crib where I was sleeping he looked down and noticed something shiny under my shirt. It was a tiny cross on a blue string. He turned pale, frightened lest any one else on the floor had possibly seen it. Communism considered religion to be "The Opiate of the People," filling their minds with nonsense. It was strictly forbidden, as evidenced by the destruction of thousands of churches and the exile and execution of clergy. At the time of the revolution, Mariupol had more than 20 churches; now only a small cemetery chapel remained.

Papa's primary concern was one of the neighbors on the floor, a staunch communist who was known to inform on anyone whom he suspected of any antigovernment activities or thoughts. Mama hastened to allay Papa's fears, saying that he, Mama and the priest were the only ones aware of the baptism. That day, before Papa came home, I was baptized into Orthodoxy by one of the "janitors" in the apartment building who was actually a priest. He had seen Mama cross herself on several occasions, deducing that she was a true believer, which convinced him that her request for baptism was genuine, not an entrapment. Many priests at that time were arrested, exiled and shot when someone informed on them. After a few *"Na Zdorovyas"* and prayers, in that order, Papa calmed down, still hoping in his heart that no one had seen the cross.

Mariupol is located in the southern part of the Ukraine, on the northeastern shore of a body of water called the Azov Sea which connects to the Black Sea. The town was established in the 15th century as a trading port, with a large Greek, Jewish and multinational merchant population involved in the shipping, fishing, trad-

Anatole Kurdsjuk and Yulja Kalivanov
Boyhood friends - Mariupol June, 1936.

Auntie Maya - Mariupol Nov. 26, 1937
*She entertained Anatole and Yulja with stories
and fairy tales.*

ing and related industries. In the late nineteenth century, when coal and iron ore were discovered in the Donbas Region, it became a steel manufacturing and coal mining city, and the seaport grew.

Mariupol's climate is similar to that of Virginia or North Carolina in spring and summer, but the winters are considerably colder, more snowy and severe, with constant winds either from the sea in the south or the steppes in the north. Residents tell of one such winter, in the early 1920s, when the Sea of Azov froze to the depth of two to three feet. In the spring, an early thaw produced a quick melt while unexpected high tides caused the ice to break up very quickly. Southerly winds created high waves pushing the ice floes on shore, devastating everything in their path. Ice floes, the size of small football fields were pushed one on top of each other creating teetering ice towers; the awesome screeching was heard for miles. When the "ice towers" could no longer balance, they toppled obliterating three blocks of homes around the beach. It was as if the ice age had returned. Many were killed and the area had to be totally rebuilt.

The Sea of Azov also contains a species of fish not found anywhere else, called *chabak*. It resembles a huge tropical gurami (kissing fish) weighing eight to twenty pounds and its flesh is said to be tastier than any other. The *chabak* was harvested primarily for export, as most of the quality products at that time were in the Soviet Union, but once in a while the *proletariat* was able to find some "in the market." Smoked, salted or dried *chabak* was the ultimate *zakuska*, an antipasto, for the Azov workers whenever a bottle of vodka was put on the table.

Russians are legendary for their capacity of vodka. It serves as a release for the humdrum, colorless and apathetic life of the *proletariat*, a life with very few pleasures and only one day a week for relaxation, called *vykchodnoy* (the day off). In 1929, the new law eliminated Sunday as the day of rest and holidays were decreed by the Politburo. Therefore, most gatherings occurred on the *vykhodnoy* and lasted as long as the vodka.

Russian character is outgoing, hospitable, boisterously happy and, after a few drinks, sad at the same time. Sadness produces melancholy which at these gatherings usually turned into group songs. The song usually began with a person starting the main theme or melody of a song, which was then followed by a chorus, either repeating what the soloist just sang or adding a refrain. It has a unique Russian sound and quality. Papa had a beautiful baritone voice and at such gatherings was prodded to start many a song. The songs ranged from Ukrainian to Russian to Georgian and some even developed language of their own, after a few "*Na Zdorovyas.*"

Such gatherings provided a brief relief for Papa and his friends. Papa however, had to be constantly on guard not to let his tongue slip and say something that was out of context from the life they were living, or what they had told the neighbors of their past.

How does one live such a life? What stress must one endure that plays havoc with the mind, body and spirit? He must have continually felt like a thief, watching every word, step or move. They lived with a manufactured past, a lie; and a liar must remember what lie was told to whom and when. It was not an easy task, but they persevered.

We continued to live in the Azov Steel apartment building because it was a good location, near the trolley line affording Mama opportunities to take me to the park or the sea shore, usually accompanied by my friend Yulja and his mother. Whenever Mama needed to go to the market or on some errand, our favorite baby sitter was Auntie Maya. She was a nurse who lived on the floor above us, worked the second shift at the hospital and loved children. Maya was a marvelous story teller and kept us engrossed with many of her fairy tales. I had only a few toys. A rubber fish, a doll and an old abacus which served as a truck, a train or any other transportation our fertile imagination evoked. Yulja had some blocks and a humming top which we often spun and followed on the floor. It was a great time with Maya and we cried real tears whenever our mothers returned and she had to leave. But Mama and Yulja's mother always brought us something that took our attention from the departing Auntie Maya, until the next time.

When I was approximately three years old an opportunity came, allowing Papa to build a house on the outskirts of town. In the Soviet Union private ownership of land was forbidden, all land was the property of the government, but occasionally, local commissars allowed workers who were recognized as achievers by their management, to build a home on government property. Mostly, it was allocated to special industries which helped in the growth and expansion of International Communism. The people called it *pokazukha*, just for show, an attempt by the government to placate the *proletariat* with its compassion. Azov Steel was allocated several such parcels on the outskirts of Mariupol known as *Novosyelovka,* New Settlement.

Certain requirements were imposed on the recipient of this largesse. The builder had to utilize his own labor during "free time," and construction could not interfere with one's regular job or duties. Friends could help, as long as they were not paid for the work performed. This was the land of the Proletariat and any form of capitalism was strictly prohibited. Hiring someone to perform the work put one in the class of a capitalist, a *kulak*, nemesis of the Soviet Government and its "Free Citizens."

Mama and Papa saw this opportunity to be a gift from God and put all their efforts into getting started as quickly as possible. Finally, they would have a place where they could be truly alone, in a place of their own. The building plot was at the end of town, a mile past the last stop on the trolley line. Streets in the rural areas were unpaved, plain packed dirt, dusty when dry, full of ruts and almost impassable after rain. The mud bogged down both man and beast. Soil in that region of Russia/Ukraine is a rich black loam extending to the depth of three to six feet, a remnant of the ice age, after the glaciers melted. Most of the Ukraine was like that, flat as a table top with only a few hills and valleys created by the meltdown of the ancient ice. It was so rich that no fertilizer was needed to grow abundant crops. Just scratch the top of the soil, drop in the seed, add some water, then step back. This is why it has been called "The Breadbasket of Europe," and why so many nations fought wars for this land. Our parcel was on one of the highest hillocks providing an excellent view of the surrounding area. Several mud brick *khaty* (bungalows) stood on our street called

Vishnyevyj Pereulok (Cherry lane.) Our house Number was 7.

Each day after work, Papa would rush to the building site. Mama would prepare a meal, and taking the trolley, be there when he arrived. I remember one of these trips very well. It was during the time when Papa was fitting windows to the frames. Each window had to be placed into the opening just so, and to make any adjustments the frames had to be planed by hand. That scene and its aromas are part of a lasting memory.

When we arrived, the scent of fresh pine and the curly shavings falling to the ground looked like autumn leaves, as Papa rhythmically stroked the plane over the boards. It was enthralling! Papa looked like he was up to his knees in a beautiful fluffy cloud, ardent at his work. Mama had prepared a vegetable stew which was still hot, even after the half hour trip by trolley and a twenty-minute walk to the site. Papa set up a makeshift table on the window frames; the smell of wood and the aroma of the stew made us feel like we were in the middle of a forest on a marvelous picnic. It is imprinted in my mind forever.

Most of the adjacent homes were built from handmade mud and straw bricks. In the Ukraine these huts were called *Samankas*, self-built. The raw material was readily available and cost almost nothing. All one needed was some straw, water and labor. Papa however, decided to build a sturdier home, using frame and lath construction. It was a more expensive and time consuming process but he felt that this was going to be our home for many years to come. One inch furring strips were nailed on each side of the stud walls and the space between the strips was packed with a mixture of mud and straw. When the mixture dried, it strengthened the walls while at the same time providing excellent insulation. Mixing the straw and clay was a neighborhood affair with everyone joining in. The major problem was the availability of water. There was no running water in the area and the nearest well was a half mile away. Carrying water from the well was a back-breaking and exhausting task which fell on Mama and her women friends, but even in this there was joy. The women sang as they trudged up the hill with yokes on their shoulders while pails of water swung on each end.

A pit was dug near the house, chopped straw was mixed with the clay, water was added as everyone jumped in, feet first. It looked like a disorganized comical dance in which everyone held on to their neighbor in an attempt not to fall into the mud and was reminiscent of how the Jews must have made bricks in the ancient times of the pharaohs. A similar mixture with more finely chopped straw was used as stucco on the outside of the house. After the clay dried, it was whitewashed with a mixture of chalk and lye.

The shell of our home was completed before winter and we moved from the apartment in September. Papa got permission to use one of the steel mill trucks together with a driver and moving our few meager possessions took only one trip.

The New Settlement stood between two small military airports used as training ground for new pilots. Private aviation did not exist in the USSR. Everything was controlled by the Party. The children on our street were constantly entertained by parachute jumps out of the old bi-wing wood and cloth "Jennies" providing us with a great deal of excitement, especially when it seemed that one of the parachutists would land on our street. None ever did, but it was still thrilling each time we saw one heading our way.

One day, while I was having lunch, the excited cries of my friends made me rush to the street. A parachute was landing! In the summer we never wore shoes, running around *bosenky* (barefoot.) Mama did not allow me to run around barefoot, especially on the street. This time however she was not around to stop me as I dashed to freedom. I ran across the street, when all of a sudden I felt tremendous pain in my right foot. Looking down I saw blood gushing out. I had stepped on a broken bottle.

A new house was being built just across the street and there was a large pan of water right in front of it. Screaming with pain, I ran toward the pan and plunged my foot into the water in an attempt to clean the wound. Alas, I did not know that the pan contained lye in preparation for white washing the walls. My screams doubled in intensity and I felt my underwear filling up. Mama heard my screams and rushed toward me. As she picked me up, blood from my foot ran all over her dress and a warm brown liquid flowed down my leg, all over Mama. I had laid my foot open, the blood was gushing out, and my bowels let lose. Mama poured iodine on the cut, which made me scream even louder, as she attempted to bandage it. To this day I have a problem with calluses created by the scar tissue. I never again ran out into the street *bosenky*.

One mile from our house flowed the river Kalka, famous in Russian history as the site where Russian knights were massacred by Tatar hordes in the 14th century. It was only a few miles from our new house. After defeating the Russian nobles, the Tatars gathered the enemy wounded and built a platform over their bodies, then proceeded to have a great victory feast.

Mama had a "green thumb" and everything she planted grew. One of the items we moved to our new home was a tall rubber plant, called ficus, with large broad and shiny leaves; it looked tropical. As the truck passed under the trolley lines, the top of the plant got tangled up and broke off. Mama and I were riding in the back of the truck and she grabbed the broken stem as it floated down. It was planted as soon as we got to our new home, later it grew into a second rubber tree plant, and became a decoration in our sitting room. I recall that incident very vividly, but Mama insisted that this was not possible because I was only three years old at the time.

Summers in Mariupol were very hot and humid. Cooking meals indoors was a difficult task as we had no fan and air conditioning was as yet unknown in the USSR. Many built a brick oven and stove combination outdoors, Papa built one for Mama. It was her pride and joy and gave her the opportunity to watch me at play as she prepared the meals. I usually invited my friends into the yard since after my accident with the foot I was not allowed to go beyond the fence, Mama enticed them with wonderful goodies she prepared.

Although Papa's salary was better than most workers, it was still not enough to live on. Mama helped by selling vegetables and sauerkraut she made from the cabbage grown in our garden. When available, the staple of each Russian meal is bread. During the summer, Mama baked our own bread in the outdoor oven. Once the bread was baked it was set to cool on a board next to the oven. She usually baked six to seven loaves at a time, if there was enough flour. However often it was less, since money was in short supply. After we moved to the house, we were living on a week-to-week basis as far as food and money were concerned. Money was needed for materials to finish the four room bungalow. While we lived in one room Papa worked on the remaining space.

One incident of the bread baking process is part of my memory and another reminder of how God works in his mysterious ways. The bread was cooling on the board while Mama was attending to something in the house. I was playing with our dog Bobik when I heard the barking of dogs beyond the fence, they were chasing an elderly beggar woman. She was waving a stick behind her back in attempts to fend them off her heels. There were many beggars in Mariupol at that time and when- ever Mama saw one she would always give them something; either a few coins, a glass of water, some fruit or vegetables from her garden. She always said, "We are giving to *Bozenka* (God) whenever we give something to those less fortunate than ourselves." As a child., I was taught that God was all powerful, did many good things for people who believed in Him. Therefore, it was good to be on His good side and never anger Him.

When the woman came to our gate, I ran to see what she wanted. She was very old, her face was full of wrinkles but her eyes were the brightest blue. She cleared her throat and with a very raspy weak voice asked, "My child can you spare a crust of bread?" A crust?! Mama had just baked five loaves of it and they were still hot. I ran to the cooling board, took one of the loaves and brought it to the babushka. Her face lit up like the sun, she crossed herself several times, blessed me many times as a tear ran down her cheek. She put the loaf into her bag and walked away slowly humming under her breath. I thought nothing of it and continued playing. Some time later when Mama came out of the house and went to check the bread cooling by the outdoor stove, I heard a piercing scream and a gasp. One of the loaves was missing. She proceeded to look all around checking to see if it had fallen to the ground. Finding nothing she ran to me asking if Bobik or some other dog had come into the yard and stolen the bread. I told her about the beggar babushka. She ran out of the yard, down the street, trying to catch her, but she was nowhere to be seen. When Mama came back, she was crying. She grabbed me by the arm and proceeded to administer her hand to my backside while at the same time telling me that we would not have enough bread for the week. How would we survive?! Needless to say, that week I could not sit very well and was confined to the yard without my friends who thought the punishment was too harsh.

It was difficult for me to understand. What was so terrible about giving babushka the bread and why was I being punished? Mama and Papa always gave. Later Papa told me we were really short of money that week - but we didn't starve. Subsequently we were shown that God had orchestrated this incident.

Whenever I misbehaved, Papa seemed to know about it when he got home. We had no telephone but he always knew, even before he spoke to Mama; he knew about the bread incident. Finally, some days later, I got up enough courage to ask him. Initially he said that it was a special gift God gives to all parents. I knew that God knew everything, but did Papa really talk to Him? I could not figure it out how God did it. Papa kept me in suspense for several days. During that time I was a perfect angel and behaved totally. Finally by the end of the week when he saw that I was really troubled, he sat me on his knee as we faced in the direction of the steel mill and told me that he had another way of helping God. He said, "See that very tall smoke stack? Well, every day I climb the stack and using binoculars look into our yard. You know I am watching if a red light is blinking."

We lived between two airports and a light was always blinking. At the age of five I believed my father, and from that day on my behavior became exemplary, until I forgot about the blinking light.

I had five friends on Vishnievyj Pereulok, three boys and two girls. My best friend was Anatoly Kaluzin. He was my age and lived two houses away; we shared our most intimate five year old secrets and were always together. On the other side of our house lived Pavlik, he was older than I but was very small for his age and, as usual, children coined nicknames for their friends who were "different." Pavlik's street name was *Blokcha*, the flea. Across the street lived Henka, the oldest and biggest boy on the street. He was somewhat retarded and preferred to play with the younger children where he was teased the least and could bully us with his size. Whenever we played games which required strength, we always wanted Henka on our side, especially when we played war. The game consisted of attackers and defenders. Those defending the turf would hide behind any obstruction while the attackers using dried mud as grenades, charged. The black dried mud exploded when it hit a wall or fence creating a cloud of dust, just like real grenades. War was one of our favorite pastimes.

Another favorite game was called tsurki, usually played by older boys since it required more dexterity. It is very similar to baseball, but is played with sticks. A six to eight-inch *tsurka* was made from a chunk of wood and its ends were sharpened to a point so that it would stick in the ground. A hunk of dried earth served as a launching ramp. The objective of the game was to strike the elevated *tsurka* with a bat stick causing it to fly up, then, while it was in the air, to hit it with the thicker stick, hopefully further than home. While the *tsurka* was flying, those in the field tried to catch it with their bare hands. Usually at least three players were needed on each team; those "in the field" tried to catch the flying tsurka and throw it to the player who covered home, who then would attempt to tag the runner before he crossed the line. When two players were tagged, the team in the field came to hit and the hitters went into the field. We usually agreed on the maximum score before the start of the game, but the game often ended when the players had to go home. Mothers usually called us long before we wanted to stop, and it was always during the most critical part of the game. Mama and Papa considered tsurki to be too dangerous for me, and continually told me about the boy who lost an eye when the tsurka hit him, but usually I sneaked out when Mama was not watching and played until I was caught and called home. As mentioned earlier, the game is somewhat similar to baseball, and probably is the basis for an ongoing argument as to its origin. I am told there is a similar game in the USA, called pegs, played with sticks and slightly different rules and field layout. However, it is best to leave this discussion for another time.

Mama was busy all the time. She planted a garden, hatched chickens and Papa bought a piglet from a villager who worked at the steel mill. Our home was beginning to become lived in. Inside walls were plastered and painted. Trim was installed around the doors and windows and I was given a room of my own, next to Mama and Papa's bedroom. At first it was very strange for me to be alone in a room, so Mama and Papa left their door open, and I felt safer. Papa built a picket fence around the front of our house and the garden was protected with wire mesh. Chickens were in a pen together with "Masha" our pig. I loved Masha and would scratch her back as she was fed. She became so spoiled that she would refuse to eat unless someone scratched her back. My other pet was our dog Bobik, but he was more of a watchdog than a pet. He did play with me in the yard running back and forth on a chain attached to his collar. This gave him complete access to our yard and we had no concerns of intruders.

One day, as Mama was returning from market, I met her on the street, because I knew she was bringing me something special. It turned out to be a straw hat with a blue ribbon around the brim. It was the best hat I ever had and I ran to show it off to my friends. Everyone wanted to try it on and I was glad to share it, proud that I was the only one who had one. We were playing in the street for quite a while, when all of a sudden I had an urgent "nature's call." We did not have an indoor toilet, it was a privy in the back of the house and to reach it the quickest way, I had to run through the middle of the yard where Bobik stood guard. I yelled to Mama "I've got to go!" She called back *behi*, meaning go ahead. I do not know how Bobik interpreted her command, but it must have sounded to him like, "Go get him!" In nothing flat he was all over me snarling and biting. Mama heard my screams and ran yelling toward me. Bobik recognized her voice and immediately stopped his attack,

Azov Stal Engineering Crew - Mariupol October, 1934

*Jacob in back row, black jacket, on his left is Ivan
Kalivanov, Yulja's father.*

but not before he took a chunk of flesh out of my arm and bit my stomach. As soon as he recognized my voice, he began to whine and cry, trying to lick my wounds. This happened just before Papa came home. Poor Bobik, he knew that he had done something very wrong. Crawling on his belly he whined even more sadly when Papa came in. Papa seeing the blood all over me went wild and began beating Bobik with a club; if Mama had not stopped him, I am certain Papa would have surely killed him. Bobik was beaten for protecting the yard from a "stranger" in a straw hat with a blue ribbon.

It was fortunate that on that day Papa got a ride home from one of the drivers who lived in the area. When the truck driver heard my screams and saw the commotion he stayed around, and was able to drive us to the clinic about two miles away. The doctors stitched and bandaged my arm, and then told Mama that the dog must be tested for rabies. The test required several days and to prevent any infection from this dreaded disease I would have undergo a series of twelve antirabies shots. Bobik was taken to a vet, and I had to begin the shots right away. The antirabies shots are extremely painful and have to be administered in the most sensitive part of the human body, the abdomen. The serum itself burns when it is injected, saying nothing of the needle. Mama and Papa had to physically hold me down for these shots while my screams echoed throughout the clinic. The shots had to be administered every other day. After the first time, when I knew it was shot time, I did everything in my power to run and hide. Mama and Papa begged, cajoled and promised me anything if I would only go, but to no avail, I had to be taken kicking and screaming. Thanks be to God that I had to endure only four shots, until the results of Bobik's test were found to be negative. Papa bought me the biggest ice cream cone I ever had. Mama cooked a celebration meal and Bobik for the first time was petted by Papa while he in turn, licked his hand. All was forgiven. One more of life's crises was over, but Mama and Papa became more vigilant as far as I was concerned. I was their only surviving child of the five , and the only one who had lived past the age of five.

Vera and Pavlik, who lived next door, were very fortunate they had a *Dedushka*, a grandfather. He did not play with his grandchildren but sat in the front yard under a mulberry tree. He resembled the writer Leo Tolstoy; a tall man with a flowing white beard down to his belt line. He wore a long white shirt bloused over his trousers belted with a white rope. I never saw him smile but it was known on the street that he possessed a great deal of wisdom. In Russia elders are respected and revered. One summer when it was very hot, Pavlik and I were playing in the shade of the mulberry tree while our friends went down to the Kalka River to swim. Pavlik and I were not allowed to go, because we could not swim and might drown. As we played, Dedushka called saying: "Give me your hand." I was startled since it was the first time he had ever spoken to me.

I obeyed, and he proceeded to lead me into the house. We lived next door to Pavlik but I had never been inside. In Russia one does not go in unless invited. That day the sun was very bright and as we entered, it took some time for my eyes to adjust. In the left corner of the room I saw the glow of a *lampadka*, a vigil light. Behind it hung a picture of a person with long hair and a beard, just like Dedushka's, except the hair was dark and the face had a piercing gaze. The light from the *lampadka* cast a golden glow on the picture and Dedushka's face. Still holding me by the hand he led me toward the corner, bent down and reaching under a small table brought out the largest book I had ever seen.

Sitting down on a creaking chair he placed me on his left knee and opened the book. Immediately a strange aroma floated up and filled my nostrils. Its pages were aged, yellowish and the words were written in an ornate and strange script, unlike any I had ever seen, each page also had an ornate border. Crossing himself and muttering something under his breath, Dedushka took my right hand placing my index finger on the open page. As he did, I felt a slight tingle, like a static shock racing up my arm. It did not hurt but felt rather pleasant. Holding me even tighter with his left arm, he said, "Son, you are touching the word of God! Study, obey and live by it!"

Madona and Christ

Representation of the B.M. Kozelshansky Icon.
By the permission the St. Petersburg Ecclesiastical Seminary
Committee. St. Petersburg, 8th of Janurary 1902, under
Archbishop Antonin.
Printed by Chromolithography, of E.L. Fesenko, Odessa.

When I came home I told Mama of this strange experience of my young life to Mama. She told me that the book was called a "Yevangeliye," The Holy Bible, and that the picture by the vigil light was an icon of Christ The Savior. By the way, Dedushka's last name was Svjatodukhow. Translated into English, it means "Of the Holy Spirit."

I was so drawn to this tall, dignified and ancient man that every time there was an opportunity to be with him, I took it. He told me many stories from the great book and taught me how to talk to God. Pray! Sometime later *Dedushka* Svjatodukhow left Pavlik's house to return to his village and I never saw him again. However, before leaving he blessed me with an icon of St. Nicholas the Wonderworker and our family with an icon of Virgin Mary and Christ Child.

To this day we have a reminder of him and his goodness, as we look upon an icon of The Virgin Mary and Christ Child. The wood is riddled with worm holes but the print is as beautiful as ever. It occupies a place of honor in our present home, behind a *lampadka* in our Bright Corner.

Life began to settle down once the house was completed. Mama had more time to contemplate the expansion of her garden and domestic stock. The chicken pen was enlarged for additional birds and its inhabitants were supplying enough eggs so that Mama could even sell some at the market, and we could have chicken soup whenever we wanted. She also decided to plant an orchard of apple, plum and apricot trees. The fruit not only gave us dessert in season but, after being dried, provided the ingredients for compote during winter. Papa bartered two dozen trees from one of his "acquaintances". At this time, he was managing supplies and materials used in construction of the the steel mill. The plant managers usually promised their superiors more than they could deliver and often Papa would "help them out" by allocating additional materials when they were running short. They in turn provided Papa with what he needed, and he often invited them to our house for a *"Na Zdorovye."*

Mama was a great cook and could make a meal out of anything. Spring and summer were the favorite times for "visitors." The magnet was Mama's *okroshka* (cold cucumber soup). It became so well known at Azov Steel that all of a sudden Papa had many "friends" and started getting rides home instead of having to walk. Someone always brought a "Three Fifteen," or a larger bottle of vodka. Together with Mama's bread, okroshka and garden vegetables, it became a feast.

We were getting settled at Vishnevyj Pereulok No.7, and Papa began collecting galvanized pipe in anticipation of drilling a well for our home. This would save Mama having to haul water from the open well and would also be a boon for the whole neighborhood. Well-water was used for cooking, but for everything else we used rain water collected in barrels and cisterns. However the summers often were dry, so often the only choice was the well. Laundry was done by hand on a wash board, larger items Mama took down to the Kalka River. She washed, while I had a fishing expedition. I loved fishing, but until I was older I was not allowed to go alone.

In 1939 Mama's sister, Irina, and her son Stepan came for a visit from Beloruss. Their visit coincided with a reward vacation Papa received from Azov Stal Commisar for his accomplishments in completing the chemical extraction facility ahead of schedule. It included a trip to a resort in Sochi, on the Black Sea, where mineral cures were said to heal the heart, just what Papa needed. It was the first of several such trips Papa was to take and I believe it helped his heart. Stepan was three years older than I and attended third grade, and I was so proud to have "an older brother." In Russia your first cousin is considered to be your second brother, having Stepan with us was great.

I finally had someone close to my age in the family. Most of my friends on the street had brothers and sisters, I was the only one who had none. Many a time, I would come home crying because I could not understand how brothers and sisters could fight. All I wanted was to have someone to share my thoughts with and to love. Aunt Irina stayed for three months and during that time Stepan taught me many things including how to draw with ink pen on glass.

Jacob and Azov Professional Workers - 1940
Jacob in center of front row wearing a gray suit.
In Kislovodsk on the Black Sea. A reward for completing the
Chemical plant at Azov Stal ahead of schedule.

Jacob and Azov Stal Engineers - Sochi, June 1935
Jacob seated on right.
Black Sea - Sanatorium for heart patients where they
were sent for the Narzan mineral waters cure.

It was a great summer. Since I was supposed to start first grade that fall, he also told me what school was all about, bu t he had to return home to begin fourth grade in September.

Not long after Stepan and Aunt Irina left, Papa's younger brother Boris came to visit from the Urals and brought his daughter, Yelena, with him. As a gift, he brought Papa a *kazukh* (sheepskin coat) which became my favorite place to snuggle into. In later years, this coat also saved us from freezing. Yelena was about my age and we became friends as we played with Bobik and my cat, Murka. Papa had built a large bird cage in which we would shelter wild birds that we captured in the fall and released in the spring. We would put Murka in that cage, place it on the abacus and pretend to play circus. Murka was the tiger and we made believe we could train her. It was not the cat's favorite pastime and she hissed and spat at us. One time Yelena was too close to the cage and Murka swatted at her with its paw causing a gash on her face. It is still visible to this day, a memento of her visit to Mariupol. Papa's gift to Uncle Boris was a bicycle. Uncle Boris carried it on the train to the Urals and later wrote us that he was the envy of everyone in town. Uncle Boris was the only relative of my father's family that I ever met.

1939 was our year for visitors and the greatest one was from my maternal grandfather, Stephan Makarenko. Grandfather Stephan was a plain village man who had spent his entire life within walking distance of Bondary, where he was born, just outside of Slutsk in Beloruss. Making the trip to Mariupol was certainly an undertaking for a man who, at the age of seventy, had never been on a train or more than fifty miles from home. Grandfather Stephan stayed with us for two weeks during which time Mama and Papa expanded his horizons. He was interested in everything. Each time he saw something new, he would shake his head in disbelief and Papa would have to go into a detailed explanation of how "it" worked.

One beautiful *vykhodnoy* we took him to the beach by the Sea of Azov. Grandfather had never seen such a large body of water; lakes in his region were his only comparison. As we stood on a bluff overlooking the beach, we watched a ship sailing away

Uncle Boris - Jacob's Younger Brother
*In the Urals wearing the Kazhuh which protected us from
cold and rain on the 500 km forced march by the SS.*

Irina With The Children - 1941

and it appeared to get smaller and smaller. Grandfather watched it very intently as it moved toward the horizon. Finally he turned to Papa and asked, "Sonny, tell me, are those people shrinking in the boat? How are they made big again?" Grandfather had no concept of horizon.

Grandfather had a full beard and a mustache which he twirled up on both ends. Most of the time a small curved pipe was clenched in his teeth, even when it was not lit. Tobacco had permeated his beard with an aroma unfamiliar to me. Papa smoked cigarettes, only when he could afford them. They were half paper filter and half tobacco; the smell of cigarettes was quite different from grandfather's pipe. Most men smoked *makhorka*. It is, I believe, another pure Russian smoker's invention. It is made from finely chopped stem of the tobacco plant, most workers could not afford as real tobaco leaf. The chopped stem is then rolled in strips of newsprint to fashion a cigarette. Cigarette paper was not available, instead, newspaper was cut or torn into strips, folded in half, the *makhorka* sprinkled into the fold, then rolled between fingers, and sealed with saliva. As a matter of fact any kind of paper was scarce in the USSR.

I remember that during my rabies process, the doctor wrote my medical record on the reverse side of wall paper with a purple design. Can you imagine the chemical composition of the burning mixture which contained not only tobacco and printer's ink but also chemicals used in the paper manufacturing process? But, this did not matter to the addicted who craved tobacco more than food or even vodka.

Grandfather and I spent a lot of time together taking walks and picking fruit. But best of all, we went fishing. He made me a fishing pole from a very straight branch of a locust tree, tied a strong linen thread to the thin end of the pole and fashioned a bobber from a cork and chicken feathers. Papa brought us several hooks from the steel mill. The river was very good to us and I caught the biggest fish ever. Grandfather had to help me land it.

When it came time for Dedushka Stephan to leave, Mama prepared not only food for the six days of travel it took to get to

Slutsk, but also a valise full of items and goodies not available in Bondary. We walked him to the trolley stop and in the tearful and long good-byes did not realize that the trolley was pulling away, there was no way to stop it! Grandfather flipped his duffel bag over his shoulder, grabbed the valise in his left hand and ran after the departing trolley. My last glimpse of him was seeing him grab the handrail with his free hand, jump up on the trolley step waving good-bye. One wave and he was gone. Not bad for a man of seventy plus. I was glad that I also had a *dedushka* and Pavlik was not the only one. Grandfather Stephan lived until he was eighty nine and died in Bondary in full possession of his faculties.

Later, we learned the details of his death from a letter written to us by one of Mama's sisters. Grandfather gathered all of his family together, most of them lived in or near Bondary, and told them that he was getting very tired and needed a long rest. He blessed his children, grandchildren, and great-great-grandchildren gathered around his bed. Then after crossing himself, folded his arms on the chest, took a deep breath and fell peacefully asleep.

In 1940, at the age of six, I fell in love. The object of my affection was Liuba. She was the daughter of Mama's middle sister Antonina, the girl who watched the road when Papa returned from Siberia. Papa was able to get Liuba enrolled at the university in Rostov on the Don, about a hundred miles from Mariupol. Liuba was the most beautiful woman I had ever seen, even prettier than Mama. She was tall, with gorgeous brown eyes and a short auburn flippant hairdo. When she arrived at our house she carried a small suitcase which contained all of her possessions and, slung over her shoulder, was a guitar. Liuba also brought me the most marvelous toy. It was an airplane which "flew" as it rolled on a string with a balancing weight suspended underneath. I was the envy of everyone on the street and we "flew" the plane from sunup to sun set.

It was the month of May, flowers were in bloom and the *fialka,* (a night blooming violette) was in its prime. In the evening, I would sit at Liuba's feet and listen to the most beautiful contralto voice accompanied on a guitar as she sang *"Suliko,"* one of the very haunting and popular songs of that time. It recounted the longing of separated lovers in the Caucasus. I was enthralled by her songs and the wonderful aroma of the night blooming *fialka*. I spent so much time with Liuba that I almost forgot my friends. They began calling me a love-sick calf.

Rumors of war were getting stronger and Papa wanted to make sure that Liuba could get home to Minsk before anything started. He bought her a train ticket and Mama once again prepared a basket of food for the journey. My favorite bantam rooster "Korolek" sacrificed his life for Liuba's dinner but, I was in love and forgave her. We rode on the trolley to the railroad station and waited hours for the train. To me the time flew, since I could not take my eyes off Liuba. Before she got on the train she kissed me on the cheek, I hugged her and cried. We were never to see each other again, but we did receive a letter from her a week before the war with Germany began on June 22, 1941. She had arrived home safely.

Chapter 9

World War II - Invaded by "The Reich"

Even before the war between the Soviet Union and Germany was declared, preparations for its eventuality were taking place in the Ukraine. Since we lived between two military airports, air attacks by the invaders were a certainty.

To provide shelter against such attacks, Papa and the neighbors began to construct a bomb shelter. A trench was dug in the form of the letter "Z." The shape was said to diminish the impact of air pressure in the event a bomb exploded nearby. It became a community project with each neighbor contributing digging time whenever possible. The trench was seven-feet deep and five-feet wide. Benches were carved out of the earth at the back of the shelter. Papa obtained some steel beams for the ceiling, metal sheeting for the roof and heavy wooden beams were placed under the steel sheeting as supports. A direct hit would not save the occupants, but we would be safe from any bombs falling in the area. Interior walls were lined with boards to keep the soil from cascading down the sides. A six-inch diameter pipe protruding through the roof, was installed at the rear of the shelter and would provide air to the occupants in case they we were buried by a nearby blast. Once the sheeting was placed on the roof, and the breathing pipe installed, heavy branches were placed over the metal sheeting and the excavated soil piled on top.

Although no one said it, but from the outside it looked like an ancient burial tomb; it was too gruesome to contemplate such thoughts. Entry steps were carved out of the soil and topped with thick boards to keep them firm. Shelves were built around the perimeter of the interior and would be used to store water, food, blankets and other essentials the neighbors would contribute. The shelter comfortably held twenty people and with a tight fit, thirty could be accommodated. Children found the whole process exciting and could not wait for the day when we could use the shelter for our "War Games." However, our parents told us that the shelter was off limits for games and the first infraction of the rule would result in very sore bottoms.

In December of 1940, Papa received his army induction notice. It read:

"YOU ARE DIRECTED TO REPORT TO THE COMMANDANT FOR DEFENSE OF THE CITY ON _____ TO FULFILL YOUR OBLIGATION TO THE MOTHERLAND.

YOU ARE REQUIRED TO BRING A METAL CUP, AND A METAL SPOON, AND A CHANGE OF UNDERWEAR. EVERYTHING ELSE WILL BE SUPPLIED.

DISREGARD OF THIS NOTICE WILL RESULT IN ARREST AND IMPRISONMENT!

SIGNED - MILITARY COMMISSAR OF MARIUPOL."

Needless to say Mama went into a panic. She and Papa knew that, should he be sent to the front, he would not return. Papa took the notice to the Commissar of the Azov Steel Works, whom he knew very well, they had split many a "Three fifteens" together. Papa explained to him that his work at the steel plant would contribute much more to the war effort than being on the front lines. The commissar agreed and issued papa a "permanent deferment" for the duration of the war. Only a major catastrophe would require Papa to be called to defend the Motherland. He continued to work at the steel mill and was placed in charge of the coal yard. Demand for steel was increasing with every day and the mill worked around the clock.

Immediately after the start of the war, the town council of commissars began to make plans for the defense of the city. Mariupol's steel production and manufacturing had to be protected at all costs. Bombing by the German Luftwaffe began almost immediately and our shelter was occupied daily. Air raid sirens were installed in the city, but the warnings came just before the bombs started to fall, giving us little time to reach the shelter. A more reli-

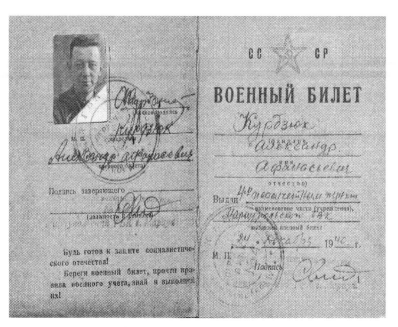

Selective Military Certificate

*Issued on to Alexander Affanasyevich Kurdsjuk requesting
him to defend the Motherland.*

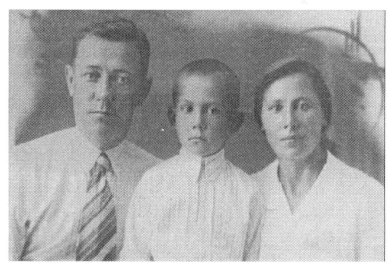

June 1941, Before Papa's Call -Up Into The Army

able air raid notice was provided by our dog Bobik. The Luftwaffe used the *Stuka* dive bomber as its primary aircraft. The sound of its engine was so distinctive that when it dove, it sounded like the scream of a banshee, frightening everyone. Bobik heard the sound of the bombers long before the air raid sirens sounded, and we found that we could trust his warning, rushing into the shelter as soon as he began to howl. He saved our lives many a time.

During one particular air raid, small antipersonnel bombs rained down from the sky. They exploded, sending shrapnel in a circle at a twenty-five degree angle cutting down everything in their path. After the raid was over, we crawled out of the shelter and viewed the devastation. Several of our fruit trees were cut down at the root. The chicken fence was in splinters as was our outhouse. One of the bombs shattered the chicken coop and there were dead chickens on the ground, some still flapping their wings, others were scattered all over the yard. Our first priority was to get the live chickens back behind the fence since they were our primary source of meat. Those that were killed were collected in a bag for later examination to see if they were edible.

Our home did not look damaged, at least we thought it was not. The house had no basement but Papa had dug a root cellar below the entry corridor, where vegetables and meats were kept during winter. Cabbage, beets, potatoes, carrots, sausages, hams, including a barrel of salted pork from the last pig we slaughtered were stored there. This was our food for the year and any loss presented a serious problem. Mama walked into the porch and said she smelled bacon frying. She knew she didn't leave anything on the kitchen stove before running to the shelter, so where was the odor coming from? Sniffing the air, she discovered that the smell was coming from the root cellar. Raising the lid she looked in, there were splinters on the cellar floor; looking up, she noticed a hole in the roof. Papa was still at work and she was afraid to go down alone. I offered to do it, but she wouldn't let me.

She ran over to get help from our neighbor Mr. K, who came over right away. Just before he started down the steps, we heard the sound of a truck engine. It was Papa. He got a ride from a truck driver who lived in our area. Seeing that Mama and I were safe, Papa motioned for the driver to go on and check on his own family.

Once Papa calmed down, Mama told him about the "frying bacon" in the root cellar and the hole in the roof. The cellar had no electricity so Papa lit the kerosene lamp to take with him as he climbed down the ladder, while Mama continually admonished him to "be careful!,"as she prayed out loud. Raising the lamp for better visibility, Papa gingerly stepped on the cellar floor. The damage was obvious. A bomb had penetrated the roof and the floor imbedding itself in the pork barrel. Apparently sufficient heat had been generated by friction to fry the bacon.

What was to be done now? Reporting the unexploded bomb to authorities would certainly cause the bacon to be confiscated and we would never see it again, leaving us without meat for the year. The fins of the bomb were visible above the brine and everyone began to offer suggestions as to how to remove it. Could the bomb be a dud? We heard that some of the bombs could have delay fuses and would explode several hours or even days later. Several did not explode in our yard and the neighborhood, including one that splintered our chicken coop. That night we slept at Mr. K's house while Bobik guarded the house. A Russian proverb says: "The morning is wiser than the evening" and we chose to heed its warning. That evening a myriad of options of how to "save the bacon" were offered and discarded, none seemed safe enough. Mama and Papa came to the conclusion, that to die over a barrel of pork was foolish; they had lost so much in their life, and knew that God would provide. Had He ever left or forsaken them? No!

The police were called and soon showed up with an army bomb disposal unit; apparently ours was not the only unexploded bomb from the raid. Dutifully the police wrote us a receipt for the barrel of pork, promising to return it when the bomb was diffused. Of course, we never saw it again.

The chicken coop was so badly damaged that repairing it was futile. Therefore, we would have to rebuild it in another spot. Since the bomb which shattered it did not explode, Papa very carefully dismantled the remaining boards, making sure none of the wood or soil fell into the hole. Once the wood was removed, he planted a small cherry tree over the crater. The ball of the roots was just the right size to cover the hole. He then stepped back and threw several spades of dirt over the roots, said a prayer and walked away. Several days later he fenced in the tree making sure no one stepped on the surrounding soil. To the best of my knowledge, that bomb is still in the ground.

Mariupol stands on a peninsula several kilometers wide on a strip of land connecting it to the mainland. The defenders of the city decided to dig an antitank trench across the isthmus to prevent the advancing German forces from entering the town. Men, women and youths were organized into "defense battalions against the Nazis" as continuous propaganda blared over the loud speaker radios,

"Comrades and citizens of Mariupol unite!
Keep the Fascists out of your streets!
Defend the Motherland!
Repel The Aggressor!"

Radioes in the USSR were very primitive. Actually, they were only speakers without the ability to tune in any other station; there were no other sations. The speakers were connected by telephone wire to a central broadcasting location and the Soviet citizens coined a special acronym for these radios, "LCHD." In Russian Cyrillic letters the phrase says "Lopaj Chto Dayut," translated, it means: "Eat What You are Fed," a perfect instrument for propaganda.

The defense trenches were still being dug when the first German tanks and motorized personnel carriers of the Wehrmacht and "SS" descended on Mariupol on July 30, 1941. This happened a little over a month after the official declaration of war. In German the onslaught was called Blitzkrieg, a Lightning War. It certainly was that. The antitank trenches did not stop them. The Azov Steel Works were in full operation as the Nazi invaders occupied the town. The town "Defense Committee" was still discussing how to repel them and no one anticipated such speed and fury.

120

Mariupol's population at the time was approximately one quarter of a million people, mostly Ukranians, Russians, Jews, Greeks and a few other Soviet ethnic groups. It was almost unbelievable that on the day of occupation there were only two casualties. One was a policewoman, who was run over by a tank as she ran yelling: "We are under attack!" The other, was a German soldier on a motorcycle, who in his zeal to occupy the town, drove into a police station demanding surrender. He was shot by a policeman.

In the Ukraine, as well as other parts of the Soviet Union, most people were sick and tired of communism and looking for an alternative. Many of the citizens welcomed the Germans with cheers and flowers; little did they know what was to follow.

Under Communism, any citizen under suspicion would be arrested and would seldom be seen by the rest of the population. The individual was whisked away in a *Chernyj Voron*, a "black crow" car, operated by the NKVD or GPU. The German tactics were more brutal and in full view of the population. Initially this instilled fear but later turned to such hatred of the occupiers that it was said to have been one of the major factors in defeat of the German forces in Russia.

Takeover by the Germans was swift and complete. The steel mill continued operation and never stopped production and in a few months it became normal to go to work.

After occupation, the first action by the "Waffen SS" was to identify, arrest and execute Jews and members of the communist party. A card carrying member of the Communist Party lived next door to us. One afternoon the SS descended, dragged him out of the house and executed him in front of his wife and family. This was my first exposure to such brutality. To see someone die so suddenly had a horrendous impact on me. Later, death became a daily companion. The man's daughter, Liuda, was my playmate. Thirty days after the occupation there were no Jews or communists to be found in Mariupol.

When Papa first learned of the executions, he tried to get to the Dwoskins in an attempt to hide them. He went by night to their house but when he got there, the house was all dark. He knocked on the door and peered through windows, but no one answered. Thinking they were hiding, he slipped a note under the door, asking David to meet him the next night in a place familiar to both of them. From there, Papa was planning to take them to safety in a village outside of Mariupol. He made the attempt four days in a row but no one showed up; it meant that David did not get the message. On the last attempt, Papa was arrested and only the pass to Azov Steel issued by the SS which allowed him to walk after curfew, prevented his execution.

Many weeks later we learned that the Dwoskins were one of the first Jewish families to be taken. Only their son, Vowa, survived; he was at the front in the Soviet army.

The antitank trenches, so dutifully dug by the residents of Mariupol, became graves for the mass executions. Those to be executed were taken to the site by truck, stripped naked, lined up next to the trenches and machine-gunned. No attempt was made to cover the bodies, the next group to be executed became their cover.

People who lived close to the trenches recall the screams and moans of the wounded. The execution site was off limits, and anyone approaching it was shot. There were stories of some victims who crawled out of the pit at night seeking refuge among the nearby residents. Some were given shelter while others were turned over to the patrolling SS. Those who are familiar with the history of Russia and the Ukraine know that there was no love lost between the citizens and the Jews. Pogroms were frequent and brutal, especially during the times of the czars.

The winter of 1941-42 was severe. Food supplies soon disappeared and residents of Mariupol had to survive on what they were able to squirrel away in root cellars, or able to barter for in nearby villages. Anything edible was consumed on the spot. Every source of potential nourishment was exploited. A new source of food came from the sunflower mill, where seeds were pressed into oil. What remained, after the press, still had considerable nourishment. It was called *makuha*.

In the Ukraine sunflower seeds are the main source of oil, and thousands of acres were devoted to its planting. Because of the rich soil, plants grew to a height of seven or even eight feet and cones holding the seeds were the size of garbage can lids. Those grown on individual plots of land were a boon to the children at harvest time. We used the stalks to make teepees and the empty cones became the outside covering as their rough surface held them in place. It was fun to build a hiding place of our own. The structure gave us many hours of fun and when the stalks dried they were used as fuel in the winter.

Removing the seeds from cones was a party. Blankets or tarpaulin was spread on the ground, cones were dumped nearby and it was the children's job, using sticks, to pound the cones to dislodge the seeds. The seeds were then thrown up in the air as the wind blew the chaff away. Somehow, we managed to have seed fights during the process. As long as the seeds did not fly off the blankets, it was OK.

Next, the seeds were taken to the oil press. Some were first dry roasted and shelled before being pressed; others were pressed with the shell on. The shelled seeds produced the most prized *makuha*. Oil flowed into cisterns and later decanted into bottles. The unshelled *makuha* was used as cattle and swine feed while the shelled *makuha* was for human consumption. The oil was rich in nutrients, better than animal fat and the crumpled-up makuha was added to many foods. It was also made into our favorite sunflower candy. *Makuha* mixed with honey or condensed sugar beet molasses, produced *a halvah like,* Middle-Eastern delicacy made from sesame seeds mixed with honey and nuts and sold in specialty stores.

Food was crucial for survival but, to the Russian male, vodka was just as important, sometimes even more so. After the occupation vodka disappeared and any liquid containing alcohol became its substitute. Aftershave lotion, perfume and some fruit extracts disappeared from the face of the earth. Men were desperate for a drink. Most conversations were held at arm's length, because the aroma from the speakers breath was indescribable.

Since potatoes and grain were the staples of life, few ingredients were left for making vodka. Papa's job at the steel mill gave him the opportunity to obtain materials for a still, but what would they use to make sour mash? Discussion of this predicament became the highest topic of conversation among the neighborhood men, and I believe formed the first joint venture in our area. Those who wanted to participate in the rewards of the project would somehow get the necessary ingredients; thus began a serious search for potato, beet, carrot and any other vegetable peels which in any remote way contained starch or sugar. Soon mounds of this "material" began to show up at our front door, some of it in "ripe" form. Mama was furious and told Papa that she was not going to allow a garbage dump or brewery in her home. If Papa wanted *samohonka* (home brewed vodka), he would have to do it away from the house. Ever so slowly, enough ingredients were collected and placed into a steel drum Papa brought from the mill. It was winter, therefore the odors wre tollerable otherwise, I am sure there would have been a divorce in our family.

Have you ever smelled sour mash as it was fermenting? If you have, the "aroma" leaves an unforgettable lasting memory. It stinks! But the desire for a drink was overwhelming, and the odors were tolerated for the promise of the first sip. The brew was bubbling in the barrel as Papa complained to Mama that it was taking longer than anticipated for the mash to "mature" because it was in the cold chicken coop. Mama would not relent. During this process, I think we had the happiest chickens in the neighborhood and I didn't dare ask Mama how it affected the egg production. Almost daily someone would stop by to inquire if the brew was ready. Finally, the long awaited moment arrived. Papa said the still would be fired up the next day. Men's faces shone with anticipation and all agreed to assemble at sunup to begin the process.

It was a cold winter. Every man came dressed in his warmest clothing. Some wore double and triple layers, while the more fortunate wore their *Kazukh* and all wore the traditional Russian *shapkas* (hats) with ear flaps tied under the chin. It was a Kodak Moment, as the men gathered in a tight circle around the still — anticipation on every face. Papa presided over the process like a "Major Domo."

I am sure I heard prayers uttered under breath for success of the venture. Fire was started under the mash barrel as Papa placed a large glass under the condensing coil and the long wait began. When the first drop of liquid hit the glass, there was a loud sigh around the circle as men simultaneously licked their lips. From that moment their eyes never left the glass as drops of clear liquid began their musical drip, drip into the container. Someone asked "How much longer?" And was immediately accosted with verbal abuse. How these men kept their patience I will never know, but the Russians are known for their patience. Just remember how much they suffered over the years.

No one made a move until the glass was about three quarters full. At that moment, Papa leaned over and gingerly, as if lifting the most precious chalice of liquid in the world, removed the glass from under the condenser, and without missing a drop placed a new glass under the drip spout. Standing up, he lifted the glass showing the contents to the assemblage and in accordance with Russian tradition proposed a toast, *"Daj Boze zavtra toze"* meaning, "May God grant us the same tomorrow!"

He crossed himself, brought the glass to his lips, took a healthy swig of the contents and his breathy response of "Ahhh!" was proof that the process had worked. Then the glass was quickly passed around the circle. Each man, after taking a swig, repeated Papa's "Ahhh!" For the rest of the day it was a joyous celebration and the stagger line from our house by the participants to their own homes, was something to behold.

Mama would not let Papa sleep in their bed that night, neither did she speak to him for several days. But he was a hero on our street! How long did the *samohonka* last I don't remember but Papa was "happy" for quite a few days.

Not much later food was running out. Our root cellar was almost empty, even the *kapusta (sour kraut)* barrel was showing bottom. The most important staple of Russian life, bread, totally disappeared. Flour could not be found anywhere and very few villagers showed up on market days; those who did, were selling rotting cabbage. The only way to survive was to make a trek to the nearest village in hopes of bartering anything for food. The nearest village for us was ten miles away, but rumors were circulating that they had sold out everything and were chasing everyone away. The next source was another village more than thirty miles to the north. Nevertheless, it was the only choice!

The previous year, for my birthday, Papa had one of the workers at the steel mill make me a sled with wide metal runners. It could seat four but required a good bit of effort to pull it back up the hill. I never had any problems getting volunteers to pull the sled, since most of the children did not have one of their own and wanted a ride on mine. Papa decided he would use my sled in his search for food. He hugged both of us as we got down on our knees and prayed. Mama arduously praying for Papa's safe return. She prayed so hard that tears ran down her face. Papa left and said he would be back in three or four days, no more than a week.

On the day after Papa left a strong blizzard came out of nowhere. The temperature dropped to ten degrees below zero and over three feet of snow fell. With the blowing wind our door to the outside was covered almost to the roof line. Mama and I shoveled the snow to make a path to Bobik's dog house. He was curled up safe inside but we decided to bring him into the house. Bobik was a watch dog and never allowed into the house and we had a difficult time getting him to come in. Once inside he curled up by the stove and fell asleep. We were safe and warm inside but how was Papa surviving? Did he make it to the village or safety before the storm hit? We didn't know and prayed even harder.

After four days Mama began to worry. She knew that the roads were completely covered and only military vehicles could traverse the snow. On the fifth day we heard from our neighbors that the trucks were bringing in frozen bodies found on the roads, lining them up in rows in the marketplace for people to come and identify their loved ones. Papa was still somewhere out there but we believed that God would protect him and bring him home safely. Mama spent most of the day on her knees praying before the icon of the Virgin and Jesus but there was still no message from Papa.

On the sixth day she decided to go to the market place.

When we arrived, a shocking scene presented itself. Frozen bodies lay everywhere, in various contorted positions. Some looked like they just sat down by the road and then toppled over, others looked like a curled up ball. Some were waving their arms in the wind as if trying to hail someone. Other bodies were missing limbs, most likely broken off during the collection process. The occupying German army used the Russian Prisoners-of-War to collect the corpses. A number of women were crouched over bodies bobbing back and forth, raising their arms to the heavens and crying; I guess they found one of their loved ones.

After walking through the rows of bodies and peering at the contorted faces for several hours, we did not see Papa and began to tremble from the cold. It was sub zero, windy and with the wind chill we did not know how cold it really was. Mama was concerned that I might get frostbite. We returned home on the trolley, walking the last kilometer in snow up to our knees. When we arrived home we hoped that Papa would be there or at least there would be a message. He wasn't and there was no message. That night I slept with Mama in her bed, cuddling so close that I almost pushed her on the floor. She hugged me very tightly and through the night her body shook with deep sobs.

The next morning we got up early and Mama cooked me some of the remaining oatmeal saying that it would give me strength and keep me warm. I didn't see her eat any herself. When I asked, she said, "I had some when I was cooking yours." I didn't believe her.

As we were getting bundled up to repeat the trek to the marketplace, Bobik who was sleeping next to the warm stove, gave an almost inaudible bark, I thought he was dreaming but then he jumped up and ran to the door tail wagging. We didn't hear anyone at the door and Mama opened it to see if anyone was at the fence. There was no one there. Then she looked toward the back yard and gave a cry. Grabbing her coat she ran across the snow toward a figure hunched over and pulling a sled. It was Papa!

When they stumbled into the house, Papa looked like one of

127

the frozen men in the marketplace. The only difference was the steam coming from his mouth and nostrils. Mama sat him down on a chair by the stove and began to scrape the snow and ice from his face and coat as Bobik danced around Papa's feet whining and wagging his tail. It was only then that Mama realized she had no shoes on.

As the layers of ice melted away, we could see the exhaustion on Papa's face and knew that had not God directed him home, the next day he most likely would have been one of the frozen corpses in the marketplace.

We pulled the sled inside the porch and waited for the snow to melt, but it was taking too long and we were anxious to see what Papa brought. As he lay down on the couch next to the stove, we pulled the sled into the kitchen and began to unpack it. There was flour, honey, sausages and two frozen chickens. I think they were alive when he traded for them in the village but the trek home in subzero temperature froze them to death. No matter, Mama thawed them out, just like Papa near the stove and we had some delicious chicken soup that night.

We survived the winter and were very glad to see the birds return in the spring and the fruit trees bursting into bloom. I took the bird cage out into the yard, opened the door and watched my winter visitors take wing with a chirp. Several minutes later one of them returned to the cage gave several chirps as if saying "thank you" and flew off into the sunny day. Mama and Papa made a solemn oath, that if at all possible, they would store as much food as they could for the next winter so that Papa would not have to endure another trek to the villages. The next time he may not survive and where would that leave us?

Liberated from communism people began to seek the church. Some of the churches during the Soviet Regime were converted into warehouses, museums or were simply blown up. With the German occupation, churches were allowed to reopen to celebrate Liturgy of the Orthodox Faith. One such church opened not far from Novoselovka. At the first opportunity Mama took me to church. I had never been in a church and did not know what to expect or do, what was it all about? Mama, however, had taught me how to make the sign of the cross in the Orthodox way. Placing the thumb, index and middle fingers together and starting from the forehead to the chest, then moving to the right shoulder and from there to the left, making a slight bow during the process toward the icon or altar.

As we entered the church the perfume of incense hit my nostrils. It was pleasant and reminded me of the scent when *dedushka* Swyatodukhov first opened the *Yevangelye* and introduced me to the Word of God. The choir was chanting a beautiful melody as the priest intoned prayers. It was the holiday of St. Nicholas, with whose icon I was blessed by *dedushka* Swyatodukhov. The church was small and packed with people continually crossing themselves in the manner Mama taught me, bowing toward the altar. When the priest faced the people, Mama took a deep audible breath and began to cry. Later she told me that the priest was the same "janitor" who had baptized me when I was two months old. The icons on the walls and the peace I felt made a tremendous impression on me and I told Mama that I would like to come back.

After Liturgy as we left the church and started walking home we heard several shots followed by screams just ahead of us. People with panic stricken faces were running in our direction. As we approached the spot where the shots were fired, we saw a young man sprawled on the ground, blood flowing from his head. His body was not moving and he looked dead. A woman leaning over him was pulling her hair and screaming, *"Boze Moy! Boze Moy!"* - "Oh My God! Oh My God!" While the people surrounding her were pointing and shouting, Mama quickly took me aside from this scene and asked the nearest person, what had happened. A man explained that the young man and his mother were walking in the direction of the church as two SS officers were walking with a dog on a leash in the opposite direction. As they passed each other, the dog lurched torward the boy tangling the leash in his legs. Trying to extricate himself the boy accidentally kicked the dog, who gave a yelp. One of the SS officers took out a pistol and without saying a word shot the young man twice and continued walking, as if he had just swatted a mosquito. The young man's mother screamed and tried to stop the SS officer. He just turned and without breaking stride whacked her on the side of the head with the pistol and she fell beside her son.

I remember our neighbor being shot by the SS because he was a communist party member but what did this boy do to deserve death?

We had just left the church, where we prayed to God for protection and safety, and here we were in a situation that God should have prevented. Why didn't He? Mama said He was our protector. I was bothered and confused. What seven year old would not be? I looked up at her and asked: "Why?" She grabbed me by the hand, squeezing it so hard that it hurt, as we hurried away from the place. She didn't say anything on the way home, she just cried. Several days later she took me in her arms and explained that God did everything in His own wisdom and some day, when we are with Him in heaven, we will know. It was not the answer I was hoping for but Mama knew and she always told the truth.

A similar incident occurred when Papa took me to work with him at the Steel Mill It was to be a special time as I had never been to the place where Papa worked. Several days before we had a large load of coal delivered to our house, but when we got to the coal yard at the Steel Mill, the huge mountains of coal overwhelmed me. There were many men with shovels working in the yard. Some were loading trucks while others were spreading the coal on the ground. Papa said they were Russian-Prisoners-of-War. Guarding the prisoners were several German soldiers with police dogs on a leash.

I busied myself around Papa's office, when I heard a loud shout from the yard and saw one of the guards take two men aside, telling them to dig two holes. When the holes were dug, he placed the men next to them and shot each in the head. I saw their heads explode as blood and brains flew in all directions. The German then told several other prisoners to cover the bodies with coal and dirt. None of the other Russian Prisoners of War made an attempt to do anything about the brutal act they had just witnessed. Papa said it was not the first time this had happened. The SS did this almost every day to keep the other prisoners in fear. He muttered what I knew to be an obscene word and returned to his abacus. The incident definitely upset him and I saw his knuckles turn white, and blood drained from his face.

I was so shaken that I asked Papa to take me home, but of course he could not. I had to stay the balance of the day looking at the two graves which were soon obliterated by the next load of coal dumped in the yard. I had nightmares for several days, so much so that I slept with Mama and Papa in their bed.

The occupation continued and many similar incidents became a daily occurrence as the population boiled with anger, all of us began to grudgingly adapt to our conquerors. Men spoke of revenge at the gatherings in our house. Papa was looked upon as leader by the neighbors who often came to him for advice and counsel. The Germans considered the occupied population to be beneath them and referred to us as *untermensh* (subhuman), as they brutalized people at every opportunity. The worst were the Waffen SS. Rapes of local women was a daily occurrence. Vera's mother was attacked by one of these men. It sent terror throughout the neighborhood as women began to fear even going to the well for water. The SS did anything they pleased, taking anything they fancied, from women to food to household items. Worst were the troops who were garrisoned in peoples' homes. Nothing and nobody was safe; we all lived in terror.

Chapter 10

"Nach West"- The Forced 500 Kilometer March

As the occupation continued, conditions in Mariupol were getting worse and worse. In January of 1943 conscription of young people for work in Germany began. A family, who lived at the end of our street, had two of their daughters taken. It was the beginning of enslavement labor from our area. Everyone was told that it would be only for a short time since Hitler and the Third Reich soon would be victorious, and in the end, those who worked for the Reich would be rewarded. No one believed it, but what choice did we have?

Rumors were circulating that a strong front was being established by the Soviet army around Stalingrad and that the Germans were taking heavy losses. In Stalingrad, fighting was said to be hand-to-hand for every street and building. To support their forces, the Germans brought in the Rumanian army under General Antonescu to hold down areas they already occupied. We in Mariupol were among the first to be "blessed" by the new Rumanian occupation force.

One day we saw a cloud of dust approaching our area. At first, we thought it was another group of tanks heading for the front. To our surprise it was the Rumanian Army on horseback, with only a few motorized vehicles. Because our house stood on a hill and provided a good view of the area, the Rumanian general decided that it would be a perfect place for his headquarters. For us, it could not have happened at a worse time. Papa and his friends had just the day before slaughtered a pig and we had no idea of how or where to hide it. If we didn't, it would certainly find itself in the Rumanian military soup kitchen. The carcass was wrapped in blankets and placed in the bomb shelter because it was cool. The entrance was covered with branches and weeds, hoping that it would not be discovered.

The field kitchen was set up in our yard as cooks began to prepare the evening meal. Our stash of potatoes was confiscated.

Mama's garden was stripped of everything edible and what was not taken, was trampled by the soldiers and horses. Mama was hysterical because so much of her hard labor and produce was destroyed. Brandishing a ladle, she charged the Romanian general. Papa thought she would be shot for sure but the general listened to her harangue and let her go. The next morning the troops formed and continued east. But before leaving, a soldier brought Mama two sacks of potatoes, some onions and cabbage, saying that this was from the general. Mama could not believe her eyes. She was so touched that she gave the soldier a jar of cherry preserves to give to the general. Where they got the potatoes and cabbage from we did not know; most likely from some other local resident's garden. But we were glad to have them. Once more God showed His mercy and provided for our family. We would not starve.

As soon as the last of the troops disappeared into the valley, our first job was to get the butchered pig. Thanks be to God that they did not stay any longer. The cool temperature and dampness of the shelter kept the meat from spoiling. Mama and her friends immediately began the arduous task of cleaning the entrails which would be used as casing in preparing a variety of sausages. Every portion of the animal was utilized. The bladder was cleaned and became a container for the head cheese consisting of diced internal organs with a substantial amount of sliced bacon. The mixture was liberally salted and a variety of spices added including saltpeter which served as a preservative and enhanced the color of the meat. Today this preparation does not sound appetizing but at that time it was delicious.

Several months later we saw the same Romanian soldiers drifting through our area. They were totally disorganized after their defeat in one of the first skirmishes and decided that home was better than the Russian front. It was a ramshackle group and many of them wanted to trade their *pushka* (rifle) for some *mamalyga* (corn bread). Their retreat was a foreshadowing of things to come.

We saw more and more German convoys heading west, while at the same time attacks by Russian planes increased with very few German fighters challenging them. Could the rumors be really true?

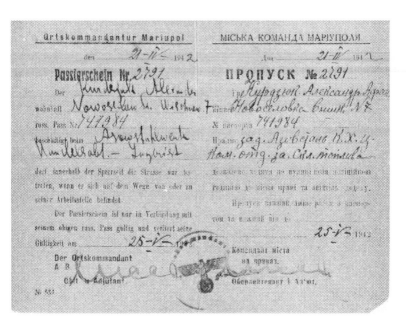

Entry Pass to Azov Stal
Issued by the German occupying forces to Alexander
Affanasyevich Kurdsjuk on May 24, 1942 as Manager
for Fuel Distribution.

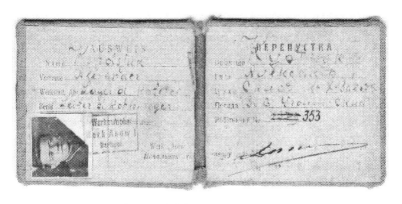

Special After Hours Pass

Issued to Alexander Kurdsjuk
Allowing him to walk the streets after curfew.
This document saved our lives many times..

Did this mighty Wehrmacht suffer a defeat against the poorly equipped Soviet forces? Apparently there was something to it and everyone began to anticipate the days to come with hope and trepidation. What would the Soviets do to us when they returned? We most likely would be branded as collaborators, because we were in the occupied zone, and most likely shot. If not, then certainly we would be sent to dig trenches at the front. Papa was very troubled because he knew that since he worked at Azov Steel he would be considered a collaborator. His past life under communism told him his days would be numbered once the Soviets returned, and he began to prepare for an alternate way to survive.

He continued to work at Azov Steel all the while looking for some way to protect his family and himself. The Germans were also preparing for this eventuality and began issuing documents for evacuation to workers at the steel mill. Papa received a pass. The evacuation was initially to proceed to Nikopol, a city approximately 500 kilometers west northwest of Mariupol.

It was the end of summer and we were gathering what was left of the garden after the Romanian destruction. This was the first year the fruit trees, which Mama and Papa planted, began to bear fruit. Mama made jellies and stuffed apricots into large mouth bottles. She was so happy with the fruit harvest and lamented the loss of her garden. The butchered pig was saved and would provide us with meat for the winter; all we had to do was to survive the remaining time of the German occupation.

Rumors were rampant of the imminent return of the Soviets. Bombings by Soviet aircraft were getting more frequent and people spoke of guerrilla activity in the area. Not much later an evacuation order, with a specific schedule, was issued by the military Gubermeister of Mariupol. Our area was to be evacuated on the seventh of September, only four days away.

Men living on our street came to our house asking Papa what he was going to do. He didn't give them the answer they were looking for, saying only, "Let's think about the alternatives available to us and prepare for any eventuality. Go home, discuss it with your families. I will do the same and we will talk tomorrow."

That evening as he was returning to the house, he stumbled on the front steps clutching his chest. His face turned ashen as cold sweat covered his brow. Mama gasped as Papa shouted "Get the V*alerianka!*" Only once before did I see Mama give him valerianka. It was just before the war and he had to be sent to the hospital. Valerianka, a greenish liquid, was an extract from a plant which grew in our area. Mama kept it in a safe place in their bedroom. Later I learned it was the source of valium, a sedative. Mama put several drops into a spoon, added some water, gave it to Papa and immediately made him lie down in bed. He had a heart spasm. We were very frightened. Where or to whom could we turn for help? The town of Mariupol had just received its orders for evacuation; rumors were flying that Soviet partisans (guerrillas) were in the area and everyone on our street was in turmoil. That night we went to bed praying that Papa would be better in the morning. He was not, and Mama asked me to fetch my friend "Flea's" father. I stayed with Papa until Pavel Yudin came. Mama explained the situation to him and he went in to see Papa. They spoke for a few minutes then Pavel came out and told Mama that he was going to get a message to his father in the neighboring village to come and fetch us. That evening Grandpa Yudin arrived. We immediately wanted to leave for Seredinovka but Grandpa told us that the roads were filled with troops; he was concerned that we might be taken for guerrillas and shot. We decided to wait until morning.

Papa began a diary at the beginning of September 1943. I will use his words to continue our story. Amplification and my comments appear in italics.

September 2, 1943

An order was issued to the workers of Azov 1 for voluntary evacuation to the town of Nikopol. There are very few volunteers. I am continuing to report to work but requests for coal by the Wehrmacht are few. Orders received are not being picked up by the drivers. Russian prisoners of war, who are working in the yard, seem agitated anticipating something. There are fewer German guards and those present seem to have lost interest in maintaining order in the work force. I am dispensing coal to whoever says they need it.

September 3, 1943

Today is a repeat of yesterday except that those who cooperated with the Germans seem panicky. There are only a few troops visible in town. Toward the evening we see a huge red glow from Taganrog, a town east of Mariupol, what is burning?

September 4, 1943

The steel plant remains open and people are attempting to work but without energy, it seems that most are awaiting the return of the Soviets. There are many rumors that speak of the many changes in the Soviet regime since the start of war, some say that the collective farms (*Kolhoz*) have been disbanded. Today was the last day I went to work. Glory to God! It looks like the occupation forces will soon leave, as evidenced by their retreat from Taganrog. Yesterday we saw a huge fire in the East, and learned that the former Cosak village of Nikolajevka and its neighboring village Budjenovka were burned. For the past two days we have seen very few refugees from Taganrog and the surrounding areas. It looks like a partisan front has been established. The people in Mariupol are in a panic in anticipation of the coming events. What is awaiting us?

September 5, 1943

The Military Governor of Mariupol issued an evacuation directive to all residents. All must evacuate, those refusing will be shot. The following schedule was published:

9/6/43   The Port and surrounding area

9/7/43   Novoselovka, our area,

9/8/43   Remainder of Mariupol,

9/9/43   the Left shore, and the Ilyich factory

The population is in a panic. Where can we run to and hide? I am feeling pains in my chest and hope it is not another heart attack. What will the Germans do to those who refuse, or cannot evacuate? Based on their treatment of the population, that question has its own answer, it will be certain death! What are we to do? Can we hide anywhere? Many are planning to hide in the sewers or run off pipes including wells. Others have built false walls in their homes just for this contingency while quite a few are running into the steppe and plan to hide in the tall grass.

It is a catastrophic situation!

Toward the evening the pain in my chest is getting worse, a heart attack is definitely coming. Several large buildings on the outskirts of town are burning and we hear explosions from the Azov factory.

People are milling around not knowing where to go. Our yard is filled with neighbors asking me about my plans? Some say they have heard that the partisans and Ukrainian police in the area are preventing people from leaving, some residents have been captured. By the evening I have no energy at all and am in bed. What are we going to do?!?

In any case I am trying to find out from the visitors if anyone knows how far the partisans are. Apparently a group of strong young men was organized to reconnoiter, but they came back without any new information. Where could the partisans hide in the open steppe?

September 6, 1943

The night is filled with constant explosions. Buildings, factories and homes are being destroyed. My coke production factory at Azov Stal is all in flames; eleven years of my effort have been wiped away. The Benzene storage tanks are dynamited. Rectification factory No. 4 and everything the Soviets wanted to destroy before the German occupation, have now been obliterated by the Germans. I am in bed and feeling worse by the hour; but the neighbors are keeping me informed. They tell me that in the port side of town everyone is being herded like cattle. Some have escaped the

139

city. Tomorrow the neighborhood men are planning to leave, and hope that the retreating SS army will not harm the women and children. My neighbor "K" stops by quite often and does not want to leave without me. I can't get up. Tomorrow our region is scheduled for evacuation.

Oh Lord, don't leave me! Help Me!

September 7, 1943

All men on our street have left, I am the only male remaining. My neighbor "K" stopped by to say good-bye. I am still in bed, can't move and feel in a hopeless situation, my family is overwrought not knowing what to do. Asked my neighbor to get a message to our friends in the village of Seredinovka, possibly grandfather Yudin can come and fetch us. I do not know if he will be able to come but, we are preparing to leave our home and hide. I asked our elderly neighbors the Pasynkovs, who are in their seventies, to move in and occupy our house during our absence, praying that the SS will not harm them.

In the evening grandpa Yudin arrived and I immediately wanted to leave for Seredinovka but he told us that the roads are filled with retreating Germans and traveling at night would be dangerous, we could be mistaken for partisans and shot. Most likely we are spending the last night in our home.

September 8, 1943

Throughout the night more and more of Mariupol is burning. Explosions are shaking the earth, everything is being blown up; the Germans are leaving nothing standing, only the scorched earth remains. We arose at 4:30 a.m. in hopes of escaping to Seredinovka. I can just about stand. The pain in my chest is constant. We left the yard about 5:00 a.m. Bobik whined and cried like never before, possibly sensing that we will not see him again. I released him from the chain allowing him the complete run of the yard, looking at him I also cried.

Later, while in the DP camps in Germany, we learned of Bobik's heroism. He defended his yard to the death. When the SS came into the yard to check if anyone was in the house,

Bobik charged the first man and ripped out his throat, the second machine gunned him to death.

Once again everything we own is being left behind. How many times in our life have we had to leave everything and run? Belaruss, Siberia the Urals and now Mariupol. How much more can one endure? We are taking only the absolute necessities and sufficient food for about two weeks. We leave Vishnyevyj Pereulok heading toward the airport road, but are stopped by the SS who force us and everyone else into a column, pointing it towards the city. I attempted to show them my evacuation papers issued by the Burgemeister of Mariupol, all I got was kick in the groin and the butt of a rifle on my neck, followed by the now familiar to us German expression, "Untermensch! Schweinhund!" I am so weak that I collapsed to my knees. I guess our plans to hide have been seriously disrupted, if not completely eliminated.

The road we are marching on and the connecting side streets are filled with people, everyone has been driven from their homes, mostly women and children, all are being treated like cattle, even very pregnant women with small children get no concern. They are marching us down Shevchenko street. As we go, soldiers enter every home along the way and in many instances we hear gunfire from inside. Most likely they are shooting those who attempted to hide under their beds or wherever possible. Grandpa Yudin wants to dash away and hide. As we pass a tiny house with a very old woman in the yard he makes a run for it; the guards did not see him as he stood next to her, they look like they belong together. Most likely we will not see him again, I shout a farewell blessing, and he is gone.

He left us his 18 year old swayback horse named Zorka (Dawn) and a two wheeled *bedarka (cart)* as he dashed into the Franko Street yard. The candy factory on Franko is burning; also many other buildings are in flames. Nothing is seen on the streets except us, who are being forcibly evacuated. At the cross roads police are blocking the side streets, any attempt to move outside the column is threatened with execution. We are herded into the area of the 238th division barracks and parade grounds, the same

141

place from which Jews were taken for execution. This point is not missed by many and some began saying their farewells to families and friends in anticipation of what was to come. The place is filling up, by 11:00 a.m. the yard is full. We are being treated worse than cattle many a neck has felt the butt of a rifle or worse. Oh Lord, is our fate the same as the Jews?!?

At around 12:00 o'clock the gendarmes opened the gates as a hush fell over the place. Is this it? We are being pushed out of the yard in the direction of Kalchik. As we look back at Mariupol, all we see are flames and smoke. At the airport even the smallest buildings are being set on fire, some are billowing acrid black smoke; most likely these were fuel storage locations. By now the column of the people has extended over three kilometers. Most carry only a small pack or a bundle in their hands, there was no time to pack. Every type of cart is being used, some have horses and wagons; cows are harnessed to other carts. It is amusing and sad at the same time to see these unfortunates. It is a column of elderly, children and infants, only a few men are visible here and there. The situation is absolutely horrible. Women with children are falling behind. As we approach the antitank trenches, the column is stopped, and screams are heard. Oh Lord, is this the end? Are we only minutes from death?

These same trenches were used to execute the Jews and Communists when the Germans occupied Mariupol in July of 1941. According to statistics, thirty-five to forty- thousand Jews lived in Mariupol during the Soviet regime, after thirty days of occupation, Jews became nonexistent and Communist party members were either executed or in hiding.

One day, at the start of the occupation, as Papa and I were walking in Downtown Mariupol, a man came running toward us with a very frightened expression on his face, grabbed Papa's arm and pulled us into an alley. He then breathlessly continued: "Alexander Affanasjevich you should not be walking around like this, they are executing all the communists!" This man had worked in Papa's department at Azov Steel and assumed that Papa was a member of the Communist Party because of the position he held. Papa was never a party member.

As previously noted, Papa could not use Jacob as his first name after his second escape from Siberia, and used his cousin's name, Alexander. Therefore his Patronymic became Alexander Affanasyevich rather than Jacob Zacharyevich.

After what seemed like an inordinate amount of time the column began moving past the tank trenches. Many women crossed themselves, audibly giving thanks to God for sparing us, for the time being. Along the march we began to meet men who had left several days before, many were meeting up with their families. Cries are heard everywhere, grief is seen on many faces, but the faces of the reunited are radiant with joy, even under these circumstances. Other men are searching for their families, but the SS and gendarmes are not allowing them to walk against the forward motion of the column. Where are we going? We hear explosions at the Maxim Gorky Kolhoz and by 8:00 P.M. are herded into a police yard at Volodarsk. It is an open area, there is no roof and people are settling down on the ground where they stand. There is no food; we must survive on what we brought with us. There is a water cistern in the yard but getting to it is impossible. We are thirsty but Zorka is really suffering. The worst situation is the lack of sanitary facilities, there are none, and people are forced to use the nearest bush or siding. Mothers with children are suffering the most.

September 9, 1943

There is no moon as we spend the night under the open sky. Fires are forbidden and the stars provide little light. We have been separated from our friends and finding them in this environment is impossible. We are more than twenty kilometers from Mariupol, and the glow of the burning city is ominous.

In the morning we are rousted out of the yard and the column is pointed towards the village of Boyevoye. Volodarsk is full of troops. On the road it is impossible to see or breathe due to the dust raised by the retreating military vehicles, while the heat is adding to this torture. Most of the roads in this region, as in most of the Ukraine are unpaved, just packed soil, and it has not rained for weeks. The retreating troops are confiscating better looking horses and wagons in the column. Pleading and begging does not help.

Our Zorka is old with a sway back and so far has not been taken, also the wheels of our cart are held together only with bailing wire some of which is wearing thin and most likely will break soon. Have to find some wire for repairs.

By mid-morning a Soviet aircraft appeared out of nowhere strafing the column. A woman in front of us was killed. A horse had half of its head shot off and is running around dragging a small cart as the blood from its head sprayed everyone in its proximity, finally a soldier ended its misery by shooting it. Panic is everywhere and the SS are not allowing anyone to stray from the column, a move to the left or right results in death. Today we have seen several people killed. It seems that from now on death will be our daily companion.

My health is still bad, I considered riding on the cart but am afraid that the wheels would break, which would be a disaster for Anatole and my wife, therefore all of us are holding on to the cart and walking. By 5:30 p.m. we arrive at the village of Boyevoye and meet up with our neighbor "K". He, his son and wife have been pulling a cart for three days and are exhausted. The night is spent in the open; we are surrounded by police and the SS.

At 9:30 a.m. once again we are rousted up, formed into a column and are forced to march toward Zakharovka. Today it is more difficult since the terrain is hilly creating stress and strain on the exhausted people and animals. Often we have to assist Zorka with the load by pushing the cart. In my condition I am not much help. Once we get to a flat part of the road, we attach our neighbor's cart to our wagon, giving them some respite. The column is closely guarded and those falling behind are continually prodded by rifle butts. The smallest infraction results in execution on the spot, and the body is thrown to the side of the road. Lord, how many have been killed? We saw at least three shot today. By 4:30 p.m. we are halted for the night, still under the open sky. Thank God the weather is warm and it is not raining.

September 11, 1943

At 6:30 a.m. the police and SS are up and agitated. Throughout the night we hear continuous artillery fire from the direction of Rozovka; the fighting is getting closer. We are told that the column is heading toward Pology, but someone said that the town has already been occupied by the Soviets. Suddenly the column is split into two groups; some are being directed toward Belocerkovka and part of the guard is going with them. What is happening? Why are people being separated?

Along the route we are traveling, German soldiers are digging in. To the right we hear cannon fire and see the smoke of explosions. The further we go the fewer guards are visible and the SS have not been seen for a while. As the saying goes: "They must have smelled the gunpowder and ran!"

There seems to be some elation in the column. We are halted, and hope to stay the night in Belotserkovka, but all of a sudden the SS appear and are forcing us to continue to Belmanka. Everyone is hoping that by tomorrow there will be no one left to push us.

September 12, 1943

Last night it started to rain and we attempted to find shelter in the homes or barns of the villagers; they are reluctant to let us in and seem to be afraid of us, we did find a roof for the women and children, I spent the night under the cart. This morning we do not see any guards and feel better. There has been no shelling from "the front" and all are hopeful that today or tomorrow we will be able to turn around and go home. It is Sunday, even away from home it seems like a holiday. The rain continues, foreshadowing cooler nights. If we can't return, will we be able to find shelter?

September 13, 1943

In the morning there was an onslaught of the military, and once again we are forced to continue West, in the direction of Polovky. Every day along the route of the march we see burning windmills, storage barns and any building which could possibly provide shelter is set on fire. As we enter the village of Vershina, the windmill is burning and our hopes of returning home are fading. Fires are seen all over the landscape. Quite often a dust trail is seen in the distance as a motorcycle is dispatched and within a few minutes there is a column of smoke, nothing is being left standing.

Ukraine is very flat, similar to Kansas, and one can see for miles. On several occasions we saw a village in the distance and thought that we could reach it by nightfall, but it took almost a day's travel to get there.

September 14, 1943

We spent the night in the village of Popovka, only a few guards were visible at night, by morning all have disappeared. Do we dare to turn around and head for home? There has been no information about Mariupol. Who is occupying it today, Soviets or Germans? As we were musing about our chance to return, a troop of German regulars appeared and are forcing us to continue west. During the seven days we have been on the move we have not seen anyone going anywhere but west. By the evening the troops disappeared and we are spending the night in the yard of a villager in Chernigovka.

September 15, 1943

This morning the armed forces made sure we left Chernigovka immediately and the local residents are being forced to go with us. For the seventh day we are moving into *neizvestnost* (uncertainty); by my best computation, so far we have traveled about one-hundred and thirty kilometers from Mariupol. I can't believe that there is no end to this. By 7:00 p.m. we arrived at the German Volksdeutch village of Krasnyj.

Germans migrated to the Ukraine during the 1900's after Czar Nikolai II married the German princess Alexandra of Hesse and started to build villages of their own design, after occupation, they began building the New Deutches Reich.

September 16, 1943

Yesterday only sixteen families arrived at the village of Krasnyj, others from our column were routed in different directions. Where are we all going? Only God knows. It looks like this colony was evacuated more than a week ago. In the morning, we discovered a great deal of goods and animals, but have not met any residents. The provisions we brought with us have run out and we are going from house to house hoping to find something edible; our search was quickly rewarded. It seems that the former residents left in quite a hurry as we found flour, eggs and chickens for the taking. The trees in the orchards are laden with ripening fruit, plums, pears, apples and many other varieties. We spent the day replenishing our supplies, undisturbed by anyone. This place seems like paradise, if one can call it that in our situation. An evening rain forced us into the homes for shelter. It was strange and frightening to occupy someone else's house. Every room is filled with straw and hay, why? It is very strange to contemplate what is ahead of us. It may possibly be the end to our wanderings.

September 17, 1943

We are still in the Krasnyj Colony, here war does not seem to exist, everything is quiet. Toward the end of the day, two homes at the end of the village caught on fire. We have no idea how it happened. Did the partisans start the fire or was it the result of spontaneous combustion? Aside from that, the whole day was quiet; women cooked chickens and made jam from the delicious plums. We hope and pray that we will not see the Germans again and plan to wait here for the front to pass.

September 18, 1943

In the morning our hopes to return home once again were dashed when at 6:30 a.m., without any warning, a troop of fire setters on motorcycles roared in and began setting the homes on fire; when they found us we were sure that we would be executed. This time, however, my documents for evacuation issued in Mariupol saved us as we once again were arranged in a column and pointed west. My neighbor "K" was unable to snatch one of his bundles from the house before it burst into flames, and it burned with the house. Because the homes were filled with straw, setting them on fire was a very simple task.

A tracer bullet fired into the house made it flare up like gun powder.

September 19, 1943

Our hopes to return home collapsed once more. For a whole day we passed through similar German colonies, all in flames. Both sides of the road are littered with dead cattle and horses. Anatole had to continuously brush sparks from his head and cart; it was an inferno and we could hardly breathe. Our poor old horse was panting so hard that we thought it would collapse at any moment. The cattle must have been shot quite a while ago as their bodies are distended from the heat. Some already exploded from decomposition, scattering their entrails all over the place. There are also human bodies on the side of the road but no one is doing anything about burying them. Who knows, we may be joining them soon.

That evening we reached the village of Raskoshnoye (Plentiful). The residents are primarily Ukrainians and it looks like they occupied the Volksdeutche homes after they left. Six Soviet fighters passed overhead firing at a collection of German troops and civilians around them. We don't know if there were any casualties and will be spending the night in the yard of a resident. The village is filled with troops, equipment and herded civilians.

The SS searched our cart and took away the jam and jelly Olga made just a few days ago. They also wanted to take our Zorka but her pathetic appearance and sway back saved us again. At 5:30 a.m. the troops rousted us making sure we leave Roskoshnoye immediately. Homes around us are set on fire, the situation seems critical and hopeless. We are moving in the direction of Melitopol. The six wagons from Mariupol are sticking together. We are now traveling on a macadam road. Those who disobey orders are executed immediately as we continue moving through German colonies. The homes which had not burned are incinerated before our eyes; these beautiful buildings are collapsing one after another. At the next village named Orlow, which seems more prosperous that the others, it is impossible to get any water. The heat is intense amplified by the burning buildings on both sides of the street; breathing is difficult and the smoke is scorching our eyes and lungs. Anatole can't raise his head and keeps brushing cinders from his head and body. Today has been our hardest day since being captured; we have traveled over 35 kilometers.

Toward the evening we cross the Mlkiy River and enter into Terpennyj. As we walk, mines are being laid on both sides of the road and the SS are digging in on the banks of the river, they are preparing a defense line. Trenches are being dug by men, women and even children; we are "invited" to participate in this effort and were released to the village by 9:30 that evening.

September 20, 1943

It has been 12 days since we were captured and banished from our home in Mariupol. At six this morning we are told that we will be heading toward the village of Veselaya (Joyful) with very few troops to push us ahead. The fields around us are full of wheat and corn still standing, and our horse is enjoying every mouthful whenever we stop. By 2:30 p.m. we are halted at Pervomajsk and told that it will be our overnight location.

September 21, 1943

This morning, here in Pervomajsk, my neighbor "K" traded a pair of boots for a horse. We fashioned a harness from several towels and by 8:30 a.m. left the village. We have not seen many troops along the way, they are probably massing at the Molochnaya River. Civilians like us are overflowing every assembly point. We are running out of food and hunger is an ever present companion. There has been no food distribution from the army, just the opposite, they steal and take from us. Once more we are under the open sky; thank God for the pleasant weather and the absence of the SS.

September 22, 1943

Left Pervomajsk at 7:30 a.m., the weather is magnificent and we hear no firing behind us, it almost seems that there is no war, except when we look upon our surroundings. We are continuing west, and once in a while encounter military vehicles not only going west but in various directions. The civilians are pointed only West. By 3:00 p.m. we stopped at a village called Hawrilovka, since there was still quite a bit of daylight, the women decided to bake some bread, but could not, as none of the villagers would let them use their ovens, so we hope that tomorrow we can bake. The food we brought from home and what we added in Krasnoye is running out. Where will we get some more? God will have to provide.

September 23, 1943

This morning the women baked some bread, enough for several days. Four of the wagons from Mariupol left hurriedly before us, promising that we would meet up on the road. Only my neighbor and I remain with our families. We departed Hawrilowka at 10:40 a.m. but could not find any of the Mariupol people, not only in the steppes but also villages where we stopped on the following days. At 4:00 p.m. a storm appeared in the distance, it looks dark and fierce, we must find some shelter. The nearest village is about 4-5 kilometers away, can we make it? Suddenly it became very cold, but thank God it has not started to rain. Just as we entered the village of Anatoleyevka, the skies opened up, but we were able to get under the roof of a barn. Seeing us soaked, disheveled and miserable the owner did not chase us out. We were out of the wind, in a dry place and the cold was not so bad.

In several places where we stopped for the night, the residents invited us to spend it in their homes. We accepted one invitation, and were sorry for it. The homes were filled with fleas, bed bugs and other vermin due to the infrequent bathing of the occupants, earthen floors and straw mattresses. From then on, we preferred to stay in the barns or under the open sky, if it wasn't raining.

September 24, 1943

In the morning the Burgemeister of the village, because of the large number of hungry refugees distributed 5 kilograms of wheat to each family. This was the first time, since leaving Mariupol, we received any food. Many who still had some provisions of their own left early in the morning, we stayed for the food distribution. The temperature this morning is very cold but started warming up when the sun rose. We are heading toward Nikolayevka and arrived there at 4:00 pm; our numbers are getting smaller by the day, where are the people disappearing to?

September 25, 1943

This morning, in the conglomeration of refugees, we encountered some of our friends from Mariupol, many pulling small wagons or pushing wheelbarrows and decided to stick together. We were herded out by 8:30 a.m. and pointed in the direction of the Dnieper River, towards Bolshaya Lepetikha. During the day as we passed through the village of Yekaterinovka where we were stopped and forced to bring in the harvest of corn and wheat which was still in the fields. In a way it was a help, since we kept a sack of corn for ourselves, and Zorka.

Since we are so close to the Dnieper River, I decided that we should attempt to reach Karpovna, in the region of Kirovgrad and possibly meet up with my friend Sizorov from Mariupol who was born in this region. Possibly, if allowed, we could spend the winter with him. As we head toward Dnieper we are continually troubled by rumors that all crossings are overwhelmed by refugees, and that the possibility of obtaining a crossing permit is remote. It is said that the line waiting to cross extends for five kilometers, and the town of Bolshaya Lepetiha is full of people. If one does not obtain a crossing permit from the *Ostkomendature* (The Eastern Military Command), they are forced to go into the fields and harvest what is still standing. We pulled off the road and decided to follow the dictates of a Russian Proverb: "The morning is wiser than the evening," and see what will happen tomorrow. As usual we are spending the night under the heavens, not far from Bolshaya Lepetiha, on the other side of the village of Yekaterinovka. The weather has improved, maybe we won't freeze; people are saying that yesterday a Soviet aircraft bombed the ferry, two horses were killed and several people drowned.

We remained in the Dnieper Delta for several days wait-ing to obtain a crossing permit. The delta was full of animal and bird life, but mosquitoes are a real pain, although they seemed to bite only in the morning and evening. We kept dry and saved from pneumonia by placing the perina (a feather quilt) on the ground; Papa and Mama would lie down on ei-ther side while I crawled in the middle. We covered ourselves with the kazukh Uncle Boris gave Papa, and thus stayed dry from the morning dew and even light rain.

One morning, when I awoke and turned my head, I felt something scratch my face. I tried to brush it aside, thinking it was a bug, but it was something very different, a snake skin. I jumped up and screamed, scaring Mama and Papa. Mama was deathly afraid of snakes and began crossing herself reciting fervent prayers as Papa went looking for it. Of course it was nowhere to be found. After the skin was examined by Papa and those around us it was determined to be one of the nonpoi-sonous variety found in this region and there was nothing to fear. Mama would not accept the explanation and insisted that we leave the delta as soon as possible.

This morning, for the first time since leaving Mariupol I de-cided to give some attention to my person and try to become a human being again. Found my razor and shaved, it may help me to obtain a crossing permit. The women baked some flat bread and somewhere got additional food. God bless them, they almost al-ways find a way to feed their family.

Even though it was Sunday, I decided to go to the *Ostcomendature* office. When I arrived the Commandant was at his desk and I presented my evacuation papers from Azov Stal. He examined them carefully and said that I only had four days left to get to Nikopol. Taking a sheet of blue paper he issued us a pass to cross the Dnieper. I reminded him that I had my friend "K" who was traveling with us and asked for a pass for him. He gave me a stern glance and shouted: "Raus! Get out!"

Pass in hand I went over to the SS control officer and asked if we could move up the line. After looking at both of my documents he said "Schnell," hurry up. I did not need any more encouragement and ran all the way to our wagon. Quickly we threw everything in and almost at a gallop drove to the crossing. When we finally stopped, our Zorka was panting so hard that I was afraid she would collapse. I had my neighbor in tow and the SS officer passed us through. It was another matter at the ferry. The operator insisted that the pass was only for one wagon, we had two, and would not let us load. What could we do? I did not want to leave my friend behind, and persuaded the operator to let him board; the price of persuasion was my wrist watch, the only thing of value I had. Once on the ferry, I was not sure that we would make it across. It was a rickety affair and we were afraid that it would flip over and drown us. Everyone was praying. It seemed like it took forever to cross since we had to pull on the towropes ourselves. It was dark and we didn't see where we were heading, but kept pulling, when suddenly we felt the bump of the opposite shore. We made it! Once on shore we drove about a kilometer and stopped in the Dniepropetrovsk Delta region for the night. Thank you Lord for saving us! No matter how difficult life is we continue to fight for survival.

September 27, 1943

We spent another day in the delta region among the willows, reeds and mosquitoes. How good it was to rest, but what will happen in the coming days? Since we crossed the Dnieper, there is no one to push us west. However, the prospects for tomorrow are uncertain. Fall is upon us, and winter is not far behind. What to do? Where do we stop? We have no food to sustain us for the winter. Our only hope is God's mercy. We remained in the delta on the 27th and 28th of September as countless herds of sheep and swine were driven West past our campsite. We bought a sheep from one of the shepherds; slaughtered it immediately and feel at least for a while we will not starve. Toward the evening a paramilitary looking person arrived in the area and began issuing commands to all that we must go into the fields and bring in the harvest. Anyone refusing to participate will be shot. I grabbed my evacuation documents and the crossing pass, with the Ostcomendant's signature, and informed him that I must reach Nikopol within several days. He, wanting to show his authority, cursed me out and said: "What are you waiting for, get going!" Within minutes we harnessed Zorka, threw the perina and kazukh in and galloped towards Novyj Gai.

We are moving on a wide road with columns of people like us. As we stared talking to them, we found out that they were coming from Nikopol. We pulled over, stopped, and began to review our situation. Where do we go from here, towards Nikopol? People are saying that the Germans are driving people out of the town. We crossed over the wide road and decided to head *Kuda glaza vedut*, where ever our eyes will lead us. By the evening we came to a community named Chervonoye and decided to stop for the night. The residents are not friendly and do not believe us when we tell them what we have been through during the past three weeks. They say: "How could you be forcibly expelled from your homes?" No matter what happens, we decided to overnight in the middle of the village.

September 29, 1943

In spite of not being welcome, we stayed more than half a day, still trying to determine what to do and, which way to go? We feel fortunate that since crossing the Dnieper River we have not been pursued or bothered by the SS or the police and decide to ask permission from the local military authorities if we could spend the winter. We asked at Chervonoye and Novokamenka, but were refused and settled down for the night on a large government farm, a *Kolhoz*. It is filled with people like us. There are some from Nikopol, Cherkask and both sides of the Dnieper River. Again, where do we go? We must save ourselves somewhere!

September 30, 1943

We will spend the next several days in Novokamenka and rest the horses and our cow. The rest and good food which we found in Krasnoye and from the standing fields, should revive them and us, then we will move on, but to where?

October 2, 1943

Every place we pass through, I attempt to get permission from the local military command to stay. We are heading toward Kherson-Nikolayew, towards Snegirovka but then changed our mind and decided to take the route to Kirovgrad in hopes of finding my friend from Mariupol but, were denied a pass and now will head towards Novyj Bug, near Kirovgrad. We are without water. The villages along the way have no wells and people are drinking rainwater collected in cisterns or barrels. It has not rained in weeks so every bucket is precious and people are unwilling to share.

October 3, 1943

Left Novopavlowka at 11:30 a.m. and arrived at Novomirovka by 3:00 p.m. We are trying to conserve the animals, without water, they and we will perish. In this village I found several Belorussian families of former *kulaks* who settled here after being exiled in the 1930's. During the German occupation none wanted to return home to Beloruss, saying there was nothing to return to since their families perished in Siberia during the exile, just like ours. One of the men invited us to stay in his yard and shared their supper with us. This new friend says there may be a possibility to remain in the village and he will vouch to the authorities that we are his relatives. Tomorrow once more we will attempt to get added to the village rolls. There is water about three kilometers away, but is said to be quite salty.

October 4, 1943

A day of rest, with these good people. We went to the local Authorities, with our Belorussian friend and once more tried to get permission to stay the winter, but were refused. Tomorrow we will start looking again.

October 5, 1943

In the morning we said our tearful good-byes to our *zemlyak* (fellow countryman) and are traveling toward Novyj Bug. Some residents told us that in a village, about two days travel from here, the local military is allowing people to be added to the rolls. Every day the weather is getting colder, especially at night. The children are at the point of exhaustion; somehow the women are keeping up their strength. How much longer can we survive under these conditions? At 4:00 p.m. we stop at Vladimirka; this place also has no water, but one of the residents shared a bucket with us.

October 6, 1943

At 7:30 a.m. we started moving towards New Yuryevka. On both sides of the road the weeds have grown so tall that a man on horseback is not visible. It is frightening, like traveling through a tunnel, we can not see what is on either side of us; there could be partisans. If they could exist anywhere, this would be the place. After traveling for almost thirty days through table top flat land where one could see forever, this is terrifying; we arrived in New Yuryevka by 4:30 p.m. As before, we are sleeping under the open sky. No-one here is even offering us a barn with a roof. But by this time we are used to the fresh air and the stars. By tomorrow we should reach Novyj Bug and maybe find a roof.

October 7, 1943

When we arose in the morning it was freezing. We moved out by 6:30 a.m. in order to get to Novyj Bug before the end of the day and, moving faster kept us warm. It feels like there may be frost tonight. That afternoon we attempted to see the military governor and get assigned to the village, but the place is full of people from the East and the rumor is that very few are being accepted for the list. What are the criteria? Most likely it is bribery that gets one in. We have nothing of value to offer. Water here is also scarce, someone said that water is available from a huge cistern erected by the Germans, but that is ten kilometers away and we have no container large enough to bring the water in.

October 8, 1943

Considering the conditions in this place, we started toward Kirovgrad by 8:30 a.m. This morning it is warmer than yesterday. Again we are moving through the weeds forest, heading north. Pushed our Zorka all day long, arriving at the village of Ingulski just before dark. I do not know if we could have survived in the weed fields, it would have felt like spending a night in a cemetery. It is really cold and we are looking for a stack of straw or hay to spend the night in.

October 9, 1943

We moved out toward Kirovgrad by 7:30 a.m. hoping to get into town before dark. This morning it is still warm almost warmer than yesterday, but towards the evening a tremendous storm arose with pelting rain and hurricane force winds. Women are given shelter by one of the villagers; Anatole was so happy.

As we were searching for someone to give us shelter, I began to shiver so badly that Mama and I huddled against each other and a tree to keep from freezing and being blown off our feet. We were soaked through to our skin. It was getting dark and we still did not find a roof. While standing by the tree, I noticed a light in a window towards the end of the village, and said to Mama: "If these people will not let us in we will have to sit by the roadside and freeze to death!" We approached the little hut and knocked on the door. Soon we heard footsteps as a gray haired wrinkle-faced babushka opened the door and invited us in.

She had the bluest eyes, and I felt in my heart that I knew her. Then it came to me! She was the one I gave a loaf of bread to in Mariupol when I was five years old. No one will ever convince me that it was not she. We told her that Papa and Zorka were still out there, she told me to go and fetch him right away. I left Mama with the babushka and ran as fast as I could to where Papa was waiting huddled under the wagon, and could not wait to tell him of who took us in. The name of the village where the babushka lived was Shelkovoy (Silky). But, I did not dare ask her if she was ever in Mariupol and specifically on Vishnyevyj Pereulok, when I was five.

I knew she remembered me.

October 10, 1943

The next morning the babushka gave us breakfast and we left

157

Shelkovoy stopping at a bazaar in Bobrinetz. Everything here was so inexpensive; we have not seen prices that low since before the beginning of World War II but what did we need? Some sugar and butter, was the only thing we bought. Meat did not look good and we still had some of the mutton. At Ostrovoye, when we spoke to the residents, one of them told us that we were moving in the wrong direction to reach Kirovgrad. Tomorrow we have to correct our route.

October 11, 1943

We left at 7:30 a.m.

At this point Papa's journal ends and I will continue based on my recollections and our subsequent talks.

It was about thirty kilometers to Kirovgrad and I feel we could reach it in two days. We pushed Zorka hard and on the first day made twenty kilometers. Almost had to spend the night in the middle of the steppe, but saw a small village slightly to our right and made it there before sunset. One of the residents gave us permission to stay in the barn; our first night under a roof in many days. God must have directed us to this spot since they had a well with drinkable water; all of us drank our fill, including the animals.

On the following day the owner was also going to Kirovgrad and would show us a short cut. He was familiar with the city and gave Papa directions to the address Nikolai Sizorov gave Papa in Mariupol. We rose early and continued to Kirovgrad. When we arrived at the address we found Sizorov's brother who was aware that we might be coming, his brother wrote him from Mariupol. He didn't know where his brother was but told us that we were welcome to stay. There was no military activity nor did we hear any artillery shelling. We stayed three days. We also learned that Mariupol was occupied by the Soviets. Papa went to the local *commendatura* to find out if any others from the Azov Stal had showed up. A number had and in three days a caravan of trucks was assembling to take us to a designated location. Upon return,

Papa discussed it with the others in the group as to whether to join the caravan or stay behind and let the front catch up with us. We were no longer being driven by the SS. The choice was ours, how and where to go from here.

That evening a friend of the person with whom we were staying stopped by and brought disturbing news. He had been overrun by the Soviet front, and having been a *kulak* like Papa, hid for a while. What he saw and told us made up Papa's mind to continue west. He said that men who stayed behind were immediately put into work battalions and sent to the front to dig trenches, but many were executed on the spot. Any hint of collaboration with the Germans, no matter how remote, placed you on the execution line as an "enemy of the people"; for people like him and Papa, it was certain death. He escaped by crawling through fields and finally bypassing the front headed for home somewhere near Kirovgrad.

Will the time ever come when we will be accepted as normal human beings and not as sub-humans or enemies of the people?

We gathered whatever belongings we had and stuffed them into the large valise that Papa made when he and Mama ran from the Urals. Papa sold the cow and left Zorka and the wagon as a thank you to Sizorov's brother for putting us up. I knew that it would be my last day with Zorka and begged Papa to let me ride her bareback to the river for a drink and a bath. He boosted me up on her back and I began to trot to the river. Initially it felt great but by the time we reached the river I was beginning to have a sore backside. She was all skin and bones and her backbone lodged squarely between my cheeks, bone to backbone. I walked her back and could not sit for quite a while. Our parting was sore and sorrow all the way.

Next day we drove to the collection point for the Azov group. I cried as I kissed Zorka good-bye. She had saved us and we would never forget her. We were loaded on trucks and driven to the railroad station where a train was waiting. Papa's pass got us on board. The train consisted of third class coaches and freight cars, we were put in a coach. I had never been on a train and the wooden seats looked neat, even though my backside was sore.

We stayed at the station until evening at which time the train started west. By the middle of the next day, we arrived at Pzemysl in Poland.

Here we were unloaded and once more the demeanor of the German guards changed, once again we became *untermensh*. As we got off the train we were herded into groups and began a long march to a camp. Questions as to where we were going were answered with kicks and rifle butts. The one day holiday was over.

We were brought into a large building and told that before we go any further, we had to go through a disinfecting process. All had to strip and go into the next room where the disinfectant was to be applied. Someone in the group screamed, "We are going to be gassed just like the Jews!"

I didn't know what he was talking about, but Papa was apparently aware of what was happening. He clutched me to his naked body and said, "Forgive me my son, I did not mean to bring you to this death."

Just as he said it, an acrid mist descended from the shower heads in the ceiling. All held their breath, but soon the doors at the other end opened and a now joyous "Raus!" was heard. I don't think many minded that command. We were not gassed but only disinfected and still alive!

Somehow we located our clothes, which had been sprayed with DDT, and began to look for Mama. Papa saw her leaning against a wall crying and clutching our valise. Once more we were together, and that was all that mattered. We returned to the hall where a soup line was forming. Soup was being poured into cups made from tin cans and a slice of bread was given to each of us. We had not eaten for 24 hours and devoured the bread and soup. When we finished a Gestapo officer got up on a platform and told us that we were going to board a train for our next destination. The loading was to begin immediately. Clutching each other's hand, Mama, Papa and I headed for the platform.

Alas, the passenger cars we had come in were gone and replaced with a row of freight cars with their doors slid open. As soon as we got close to the platform we were shoved to the nearest box car and told to climb in. Many refused to enter, and were helped along with the point of a bayonet. Papa put me in the car first then helped Mama up with the valise, just before a bayonet was about to meet his back, he jumped in. The floor of the car was filled with straw and several shelves were built against the wall, this was to be our home until the next stop. Where would that be? The situation was a familiar one to Mama and Papa, the cattle cars were just like the ones used to transport them to GULAGs of Siberia. Papa grabbed the top shelf next to the window and boosted me and Mama up. As we were settling in more people were being packed into the car; I don't know how many of us there were but sardines had more room. The door was shut and the train began moving. The jolt of the cars caused many to lose footing as we began to examine our new surroundings.

The cattle/boxcar was just that, four sides with a sliding door, which was now shut and locked. We found this out when several men attempted to open the door. We were in a sardine can prison. When would the door be opened again? How would we be able to relieve nature's calls? And food, would we get any? All these thoughts raced around in our minds while packed bodies began to exude their individual odors making each breath an experience in taste and smell. The only ventilation consisted of the four small windows at the top of the car, these were flung open as the movement of the train began to draft out some of the aromas. Not long into the trip, we found out that our toilet was a barrel in the corner of the car; it didn't have a cover. Embarrassment was forgotten and those in need began to use the "facility." Those standing, sitting or lying next to the barrel made an attempt to turn their heads, but it was futile. Soon the already present odors were refreshed with the smell of human urine and excrement. The lye and disinfectant powder next to the barrel provided little relief, it rather caused more fumes to be released from the decomposition of the contents. We were on the top shelf next to a window and able to breathe some of the fresh air mixed with the escaping odors and the smoke from the steam locomotive. Huddling next to each other we attempted to keep warm. It was the beginning of winter. Where are we being taken?

The clickety clack of the wheels on the rails and exhaustion soon lulled many to sleep. Those who had room to lie down did, others leaned against the sides of the car or slept standing up, leaning against a neighbor. The train sped on with no stops, only curves slowed it down. The barrel was getting full and was close to spilling over. All contributed whatever luggage they had to brace it against the wall. This not only stabilized it but also created a barrier to view. Our valise, since it was quite large, was one of the foundations for this project and we were praying that there would be no spill; all we had to our name was in it. All night we had been passing through country with only a few lights visible through the windows. As darkness turned to the gray of the morning we felt the train slow down and pull into a small siding. Sounds of doors being slid open created excitement and concern at the same time. What's next? As the door in our car opened, we were confronted by four wehrmacht soldiers with machine guns at the ready. We did not hear the familiar Rauss! and waited for any commands of what we were to do. It became apparent that this was a barrel emptying stop. Carefully several men edged the almost full to the brim container to the door; thanks be to God nothing spilled. The soldiers directed them to jump down and carry the barrel out of our sight. Soon they returned with the empty barrel and a can of disinfectant, and a lid. After about fifteen minutes, there was the noise of a truck pulling alongside of the car. We had heard it stop and go earlier. Since our car was in the middle of the train we had to wait and see. It was a food truck with barrels of barley soup, our only meal of the day. The next six days were a repetition of the first, and soon we were passing through towns and cities with unfamiliar architecture. We were in Germany. The trip took its toll on all of us, one elderly woman died in our car, and was removed with the next day's barrel brigade, her elderly husband did not even protest, he was in a catatonic state.

These are the names of the towns and villages we passed through during the 500 km march:

Note: 1 mile = 1.497 kilometers

Seredinovka, Volodarskoye, Boyevoye, Zacharovka, Rozova, Belotserkovka, Belmanka, Polovky, Vershina No.2, Chernigovka, Krasnyj, Roskoshnoye, Terpenyj, Veselaya, Pervomajsk, Horilovka, Anatoleyevka, Nikolayevka, Bolshaya Lepetiha, Karpovna, Yekaterinovka, Dnepropetrovsk Delta, Novyj Gai, Chervonoye, Bolshaya Aleksandrovka, Novokamenka, Novomirovka, Vladimirka, Yurjevka, Ingulskyj, Sukhaovoy, Bobrinez, Ostrovennoye, Kirovgrad.

Chapter 11

"Arbeit Macht Frei"
At Slave Labor Camp No. 4939
The Alfred E. Nobel Dynamitfabrik

We arrived at the camp in November, 1943 after a grueling one week journey from Pzemysl, Poland. During normal times the trip took one day, on this journey we were shunted to the sidings so many times, in order to allow military trains to pass, that it took almost six days. Arriving at Wurgendorf, we were once more moved to a siding. This time, however, we heard the locomotive unhitch from the cars as we waited for the doors of the cattle cars to be unlocked and opened. As the doors slid open, we were confronted by a series of barracks surrounded by barbed wire with watch towers at the corners and in the center, all topped by machine guns and search lights.

Unloading began what to us by now was the typical German fashion, *"Raus! Raus! Schnell!"*

We were told to get out and wait by the freight cars. Soon guards with rifles and Billy clubs showed up and marched us into the compound. We were assigned to barracks No. 4 in the middle of the camp, not far from the watch tower. Mama said it was almost like the camp in Kotlas and began to weep recalling all of the suffering. Those who stopped to look around were kicked into the barracks and told to find a place.

The barracks' interior consisted of rows of triple decked bunk beds on both sides of the aisle with a potbellied stove in the middle. The stove was cold and it was freezing. We were one the first families to be processed and Papa immediately went to the center to occupy the bunk nearest the stove. Our trip in the cattle cars and their previous experiences in exile made us want to find the warmest spot possible. Each bunk had a straw-filled mattress on top of wooden slats and a very thin blanket, there was no pillow. Mama and Papa immediately put our belongings on the bunks to show that we occupied the space. Several others wanted the bunks nearest the stove but moved on when Papa put up a protest. As we began to settle in, we heard the now infamous cry: *"Schnell, Raus! Raus!"* and were told to line up in front of the watch tower. Because of the cold, mothers huddled children against their bodies and we didn't know what was coming next. It was the middle of afternoon, the sun was shining but did not provide any warmth. It felt like zero degrees. We stood there shivering for about twenty minutes, when we heard the roar of an automobile engine. A huge black convertible car pulled up next to the center tower. A Gestapo officer in an immaculate black uniform with a red and white swastika arm band on his sleeve stepped out holding a leather riding crop. He mounted the platform by the tower, as the loudspeakers blared, *"Achtung!"* He spoke, first in Russian, then Polish and finally some other language I did not understand. His speech was short and to the point, "You are here to work for the Reich, and are expected to fulfill your quotas under specified rules. Any infraction of these rules will be dealt with. You will be fed the best food available. Now, go to the dining hall and receive your evening rations. There will be no talking on the way. That is all."

How does one expect a group of over three hundred people, especially women and children, to keep quiet under those circumstances? However, it was undoubtedly planned to show us that they meant business. Out of nowhere additional guards appeared with clubs in their hands. Anyone who talked received a swift crack on the head, back or neck. Women tried to shield their children and received brunt of the blows. Many heads were bleeding. Welcome to the Third Reich!

We were brought into a long building with rows of tables and benches, at the end of which we could see what looked like a serving line. We were handed a bowl of soup, a piece of bread and a cup of brown liquid which someone called coffee. In Russia no one drank coffee, tea was the main hot drink.

Examining the contents of the soup, we found that it was mainly liquid, smelled bad, and had some indistinguishable vegetables floating in it. Someone said it was kohlrabi, a kind of turnip. The bread was dark, almost black and very hard. To bite it without cracking your teeth one had to first soak it either in the "coffee" or the soup. When we bit into the bread we found that it contained particles of wood, some of us even got splinters in our gums. This we later learned was to be our mainstay called *Ersatz Brot* (False bread). The brown "coffee" liquid smelled like burned toast with an indescribable bitter taste. It was called *"Ersatz Cafe."*

The most surprising item in the cafeteria was the silverware. It was stainless steel, with "DYNAMITFABRIK" stamped on the handle of every utensil; we marveled at the luxury. As we turned in our bowls, cups and utensils, they were counted and we were searched. On the subsequent days, if one did not turn in the issued utensils, you were locked up in a dark smelly cell for the day.

As we marched back to the barracks, there was less talk, all of us remembering the beatings. Some still got whacked on the head. Mama kept her hand on my mouth. When we returned to the barracks our belongings were scattered all over the place. They had been opened, searched and items such as razors, mirrors and scissors were confiscated. It took us most of the afternoon to gather things up.

The barracks were still cold. Several men went outside in attempts to find some wood and eventually returned with wood kindling and two pails of coal. Fire was started and soon the stove was red hot; everyone crowded around it to get warm. There was indoor plumbing, a toilet with two washbowls and a trough for urinating. It was a communal bathroom. The bowls were not screened and everyone had to use them in full view of the others. There was a shower room with two spouts but only one valve, cold water only.

The guards began distributing patches by nationality. These had to be sewn onto every outside garment and were similar to the Star of David the Jews had to wear. Our patch was a blue and white "OST" about three by three inches; in German it meant east and designated Russian origin. There was "UKR" for Ukrainian, "POL" for Polish and several others.

No other clothing was issued. We had to wear what we came

in. On the following day the camp guards separated us into groups. Children were set aside for the time being while men and women were marched off to Dynamitfabrik. When they arrived all were assigned specific jobs. Papa, being tall and strong was assigned to unload rail freight cars. He had to use a jackhammer to loosen the compacted content of the car, and then shovel it out into a wagon. Mama was put on the manufacturing floor.

When we first saw the factory, we thought it was a mine. Everything was underground in stone caverns and cement tunnels, with trees camouflaging the site. The only objects that could possibly have betrayed it as a manufacturing facility were four greenhouses with tall smoke stacks. Our pictures were taken and we were issued a pass which had to be worn around the neck at all times, designating our work area. If you entered an area other than your own, you were punished, usually with a beating. Entry and exit to the factory was through a single gate. Each morning the workers were rousted at 5:00 a.m. with a rousing, *"Aufstehen! Raus!"* and after "the sumptuous breakfast" of ersatz brot and cafe we were marched one and a half kilometers up a tree lined road to the factory entrance. Then in accordance with our pass, we were redirected to our work stations.

Dynamite manufacture is a fairly simple process. The components making up the mixture are blended somewhat like bread dough in a bakery. The mixture is then fed into a rolling machine which extrudes a cylindrical piece about one and a half inches in diameter and ten inches long. The cylinder is then wrapped in wax paper and sealed at both ends, by crimping.

Apparently there were many strengths of dynamite because when the machines stopped, we had to change the wrapping paper as directed by the German foreman. Mainly, the paper was white with red stripes, others were white with green stripes and the least popular was white with yellow stripes. We never knew what the color coding meant, but were fairly certain that it indicated the explosive factor of the mixture. Dynamite is inert and very safe to handle, until a blasting cap is attached. The explosive charge in the cap causes the nitroglycerin in the mixture to explode. Finished shells

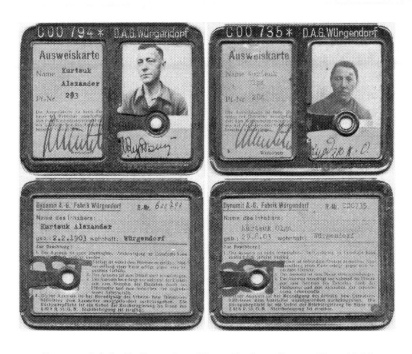

Dynamitfabrik Pass for Slave Labor Camp No. 4939

Pass No. C00794* - Alexander Kurtsuk
Pass No. C00735* - Olga Kurtsuk

The pass had to be worn around the neck at all times.

Children under fourteen years of age did not get a pass as above, but had to wear a special orange tag around our necks signifying that we could move about the manufacturing floor, since we had to clean the equipment in all areas.

were scooped up and placed in a box. Then each box was weighed. Every color code had to be of a certain weight. If it was less than specified, more shells were added; if more than the specified weight, shells were removed until the required weight was achieved. Then the boxes were moved to a conveyor belt which carried them to the next level where labels were applied. Men and women did most of the heavy work. Children over the age of ten, because their hands were small and could reach into tighter spaces, were used to clean the gears of the manufacturing equipment.

Although I was only nine but tall for my age, I. was placed on the cleaning crew. Denatured and wood alcohol was used as the solvent to remove the packed-on mixture in the gears and cranks. Fumes from the alcohol made us light-headed and we could only work no more than two hours at a time before almost passing out. Then we were given a five minute break. If we worked longer, accidents happened. Many fingers, hands and arms were lost in the process.

To achieve the required production quotas, machinery was stopped only for a short time. When the horn sounded, it was our time to work and we had only a few minutes to clean the gears and get out of the way before the equipment was restarted. We moved from one station to another and soon became experts at our tasks. Children learn quickly unless they have a distraction, such as an injured buddy.

To dissuade people from drinking the wood alcohol, printers' ink was added, making the fluid dark gray, almost black, without affecting its solvency or its punch. We were warned of the effects of wood alcohol; if it was drunk, blindness, the shakes and finally death would result. Many men did not believe the warning and began sipping the mixture. Soon, during the winter months, a morning ritual began in the barracks. One of the men was designated to look for charcoal in the stove. He would remove it from the previous day's fire and hide it. Later, it was crushed, placed in a paper filter and the ink tinted alcohol poured through it. After several passes the liquid became whitish gray. The more passes the clearer the liquid became, making it visibly more palatable to drink.

When-ever these "filters" were discovered by the guards, the possessor or the nearest person was severely beaten, some were shot. One was hanged, and his body left on the scaffold for two days, as a warning to others. Maybe hanging was better than dying or suffering from wood alcohol poisoning.

We worked 12 to 16 hours a day, with a break for food after a six hour shift. The mid-day-meal was usually a combination breakfast and supper. It would have been interesting to determine the calorie count of the food, but no one did. I believe that it was basically a survival diet, no more than 700 calories per day. The bread, which consisted of about 40-50% sawdust expanded when liquid was added filling the stomach, that reduced the hunger pangs, but addied little sustenance. During the two and a half years in the camp, this was our daily diet. We never saw an egg, milk, meat or fresh vegetables. We did try to supplement our "greens" by eating leaves of sour grass which grew by the edge of the camp fence.

In Russia the sour grass is called *shchawel* (sorrel) and is used to make either hot or cold soup. Mama made the best *shchawel* to which she added a diced hard boiled egg and sour cream, but this was back home in Mariupol, these ingredients and taste were only a memory. One day, to our complete surprise, we did see some meat floating in the soup. The rumor had it that several days before a gorilla had died at the Siegen Zoo. However, the rumor was never substantiated or denied.

Children under ten, who did not work at the factory, were assigned various cleaning jobs in the camp. It was a daily ritual, except on "holidays." I believe we had only two such holidays during our imprisonment.

The camp commander or *Hauptfuhrer*, as he preferred to be called, lived just outside the camp in a large wooden house surrounded by two barbed wire fences. Inside the fence was a garden with flowers but we were never allowed to approach it. One day as I waited to go to work, a guard came, grabbed me by the neck and took me inside the commandant's compound. I did not know why, but later learned that I was selected because I was learning to speak German and was able to communicate with the guards. A woman came out of the house and told me to sweep the sidewalks and the porch. I did as I was told, and before I was taken back to the camp, she gave me a slice of real bread and half a glass of milk. I was overjoyed and told her that I would do the job every day. But this was not to be, I was told to do it only once a week. I believe that her largesse helped to keep me from starving. Sometimes I would drink the milk while making believe that I was chewing on the bread which was safely hidden in my pocket. I wanted to share it with Mama and Papa, but they seldom took it and made me eat it. Sometimes Mama or Papa would find a piece of potato floating in their soup. They would wrap it in a piece of the wax paper, used for the dynamite shell casings, hide it in their pocket or underarm and bring it to me. After several months, I was told that I would not have to go to the factory but should remain in camp and do whatever Frau Hauptfuhrer told me to do.

Mama and Papa were concerned but since they could not affect the decision, they felt it would be better for me since there was a possibility I could get better food. Soon I was being sent to the village to pick up the Frau's groceries. I guess they felt that I would not run away since Mama and Papa were still in the camp, and where would I run to?

Please try to imagine how I felt, seeing, smelling and carrying foods which we had not seen for months. It was almost maddening, but I always hoped that the Frau would give me something. Even if I wanted to steal anything, I could not. Everything I brought back was placed by the grocer in a metal container with a locking lid, only the frau had a key. Once I was told to go to the butcher for some sausage fluid. The fluid, in which sausages were cooked; it was used by the Frau to make soup. While the butcher was pouring the liquid into the container, I noticed that he slipped a piece of sausage into the pot. He replaced the lid, locked it and told me to return the container, *"Schnell."* The walk back to the camp was about one and half kilometers, but to me it was an eternity. I could smell the broth and hear it sloshing around in the container; once in a while I heard the thud of the sausage against the side, it was awful. Saliva was forming in my mouth and I could not wait until I got to the camp. I ran most of the way, hoping to get a reward. It was not to be; I only got small cup of the liquid to drink without any bread. It was greasy, but I could smell and taste the sausage.

As spring approached, the Frau was starting to plan her garden and told me to turn over the soil. I did the best job I could, taking a small shovel full and dragging the job out as long as I could. The soil was fluffy when I finished and I got a glass of apple juice. By this time my German was becoming quite understandable and when the Frau called for me to do some more work on the garden, I told her how good Mama was in planting and growing a garden and that she could grow vegetables better than anyone on our street in Mariupol. She smiled and said that I was a very clever boy.

Next week Mama was told to report to the Frau and worked there four days a week. We were all overjoyed since Mama and I could be together at least some of the time. The garden was planted and I was sent out into the farm field next to the camp to gather cow dung for fertilizer. I was told to pick up only the dried stuff since the fresh droppings were too strong for the plants. Thank God for little favors. If you have ever been in a field where cows dropped their load, you would know what I am talking about. I had to shred the dry droppings and spread them around the plants. Frau was very happy with the way Mama cared for the garden and said she had never seen better vegetables, but daily she would come out and count all the cucumbers and tomatoes, making sure we did not steal any.

Mama and I were spending most of the time in the camp, but the barracks life did not change for us, except in one way. The straw that we slept on began to harbor fleas and bedbugs. The fleas were the least of the problem, and were probably the result of infrequent bathing, but the bedbugs were the real menace.

The bedbug is part of the tick family, and looks almost like a tick. It is dark red in color, flat with six legs and lives by sucking blood from its host. The bug does not like light and only shows itself at night. In the barracks there was only one small light at the entrance and in the bathroom; moving about at night was very difficult. The windows had no cover, giving the guards the ability to look inside. At night, the bedbugs would attack in force and we almost had to scrape them off our bodies. Killing them individually would not solve the problem, there were too many. When a bug was crushed, it gave off an awful odor, similar to that of a stink bug. DDT which was sprayed on our clothes and bodies did not kill the bugs. The only solution was fire or boiling water. The infestation was so great that workers were getting sick from the bites and could not perform to the expected standards. It was at this point the commandant decided to have a "clean day."

All mattresses were carried out, emptied of straw and the straw burned. Pots of boiling water were prepared and poured over the cracks and joints in the bunks, it was the bug's favorite hiding place during the day. All our clothing was placed into a huge fumigator and our underclothes were boiled in a cauldron and we were herded into the showers. The water was cold but the soap felt great. The incident almost turned into a holiday except when, while still almost naked, we were made to scrub the floor, walls and ceiling of the barracks using a very smelly soap-like substance. Looking back at the scrambling bodies over the structure reminded me of hell as it is depicted in Michelangelo's "Last Judgment" in the Sistine Chapel, in which naked bodies are shown slipping, sliding and falling into the abyss of hell. Women had to finish mopping up the floors, while men were put to stuffing the mattresses with fresh straw. That night we had the most blissful sleep in months, aided by the aroma of the fresh straw and no bed bugs.

Lest the process sound like a jolly time, strict camp discipline was ever present, any infraction of rules or delayed response to a command brought a truncheon on the neck or back. Bleeding had to be stopped by pressure or a piece of rag, no medical aid was available.

Summer went into fall, and our production quotas were increased, the Reich needed more dynamite. Now the average work days were closer to sixteen hours, my "vacation" with the Frau was finished and I was returned to the factory. I had been working there for two weeks when a guard came in, grabbed me by the neck and pushed me out of the production center. I tried to ask, what was the matter, what had I done? But the only response I got was a kick in the tail, a whack with the club and a *"Zei Ruich!"* (Shut up!). I knew that it was almost the end of the shift and begged him to let me see my parents; another whack on the neck. As he kicked me down the road towards the camp, I saw the commandant at the bottom of the hill standing with a group of German civilians. On the way I tried to think of any infractions I had committed but none came to mind. When we finally got there, the commandant said to the civilians: "This is the *auslender* (foreigner), who speaks some German and would suit your needs."

I still did not know where I was going to be taken, or what I was supposed to do. Just at that time the workers appeared on the road to the camp. Papa, saw me first and breaking out of the line ran toward the spot where I was being held. The commandant's grip on my hand was so tight that it was turning blue. Mama also saw me, screamed, and came running. The Commandant said that I was going to another place and would stay there for as long as it was necessary. Papa begged: "Where are you taking him?" the response was a kick in the groin, a whack with the riding crop across the face and a *"Schweinhund!"* Mama screamed once more and fainted. Several of the women workers tried to revive her, but could not.

I was led away by the civilians while Papa was kicked back into the line and marched back to the camp. Mama was being carried by the women and I didn't know if she was alive or dead. The civilians now took charge of me, and I asked them in German: *"Wohin?* Where are you taking me?" They said: "To herd cows." I screamed the answer to Papa hoping that he heard me. I think he did because he waved his hand in my direction.

I was brought to a farm near Siegen, about twenty kilometers from Wurgendorf, where I was put out in a boggy pasture to watch sixty cows and a bull. The water in the field was over my ankles and the *Holtzshuhe* (wooden sole shoes) I was wearing soaked up the water and weighed a ton. I had to stay with the herd all day or until it was time for milking, then I had to lead them into the milking barn. Milking was done by hand and I could sneak a sip almost at will, this was the only positive aspect of my new environment. I had to sleep in the barn with the cows, inhaling the wonderful aromas they produced. The food I received was of better quality, but it was never enough. I stayed on the farm for a month not knowing what was happening to Mama and Papa or whether I would ever see them again.

By this time, every night I could hear planes flying overhead their engines straining. Once in a while search lights would illuminate a plane as flak exploded around it. I saw one plane shot down and several parachutes float down as it fell, but it didn't land in our area. Some hours later I could hear the planes return but their engines were no longer straining, they had delivered their bombs.

As winter set in I was returned to the camp since the cows were being kept in the barns. It was a wonderful reunion with Mama and Papa; we cried with joy for hours. One of the guards had told Papa that I was working on a farm and being treated well.

Several weeks after my return to the camp, we were rousted at sunup and made to line up outside by the tower. We knew something serious was afoot since there were more guards and they were treating us more severely than usual. Clubs and rifle butts were flying. As we stood in the morning cold, the commandant appeared flanked by four huge Gestapos. He didn't mince any words and demanded that the perpetrators of the sabotage be handed over immediately, if they were not, an inmate would be executed every hour until the guilty party was brought forth. We did not know what the sabotage was about, and stood there for hours while the Gestapo grabbed and roughed up a number of men and women. How they selected their victims we didn't know, but we suspected informers.

At about ten o'clock we were told that a most hideous crime against the Reich had been perpetrated. Several tons of dynamite would not explode because someone had bastardized the ingredients. Of course the Gestapo did not accuse the German stewards who actually controlled the mixture and no one stepped forward to accept the blame. The Gestapo took a man and one woman and shot them in front of the assembled workers.

Some time was given to let this action sink in before the Commandant once more stepped forward and said that two workers will be shot every hour until the guilty are identified. He was true to his word; one hour later two more men were executed as women screamed and men cursed. Then there arose a commotion on one side of the assembly and we saw men dragging two women to the Commandant. The women were either Hungarian or Yugoslavian. The Gestapo immediately took them away as we awaited the outcome. Several hours later the women were brought out. It was evident that they had been beaten severely, their faces were almost unrecognizable and they could hardly stand. The Gestapo announced that the women confessed to the crime and had implicated several men. Punishment would be carried out immediately. They were taken to the ever present scaffold and hanged. One of the women cried out some unintelligible words, just before the trap was sprung but, the noose strangled her words. They died slowly, kicking their feet and swinging their arms, while the whole camp stood watching the carnage. We continued to stand for over six hours, while the guards continued searching for the remaining "criminals." Many a skull was cracked that day, but no one made a move to help or tried to run. Soon, three men were brought forth and hanged on the same scaffolds with the women; we assumed they were the ones implicated by the executed women. Then, we were kicked, beaten and punched into the barracks and the doors locked. The remainder of the day and the night was spent locked up without food or water. The bathroom faucets and toilet tanks were drained before the water was turned off. Sanitary conditions became unbearable, many of us had dysentery.

No-one had any idea what would happen next. In the morning we heard the usual, "Raus!" and were marched to the factory without breakfast. Everyone was still stunned by the happenings of the day before and work proceeded very slowly until a group of guards showed up with clubs and instilled in us the need to work faster. That evening we were served the first food in two days, bread and coffee only, no soup. We also learned that the sabotage was the result of several women carrying sand in stockings suspended between their legs which they dumped into the mixture. That day all stockings were confiscated including men's socks. When we returned from the factory, the bodies were still on the scaffolding and remained there for several days, until they began to give off horrible stench, then they were taken down, dumped into a hole and covered up. Thus ended the only resistance against the Reich at Wurgendorf.

Bombing raids increased with every passing week, often the planes came during daylight hours, flying quite low. We knew they were either American or English. One plane was shot down and two crew members parachuted into Wurgendorf only a mile or so from the camp. I did not see it but my friend who was in the camp that day told me about it.

I've often wondered how I could find out who the airmen were.

Daylight raids on supply trains to the factory also increased. We almost never saw or heard the planes, when out of nowhere, as soon as a locomotive came chugging up the rails, two or three American twin fuselage planes swept down like hornets strafing it and the cars. It seemed like they were hanging on sky hooks just waiting for the opportunity to strike. The strafed locomotives looked like beautiful steam fountains. Sometimes the fighters missed their mark and strafed the camp since it was right next to the tracks. Two children were killed. One of them was my friend who was cut in half by several .50 caliber bullets. I was in the factory at the time.

With all these happenings we knew that the allies were on their way and that we would be freed soon. The German workers however kept saying that Germany and especially the Luftwaffe had secret weapons and aircraft in the works which would blow the allied bombers out of the sky and inflict terrible damage upon allied cities. There was also considerable talk of a new super weapon that was almost ready to deploy. They said that this weapon would change the war overnight. We heard the buzz bombs as they headed for England and saw the contrails of the V-1 and V-2 rockets and thought that this was what they were talking about. It was the most likely scenario.

By early March of 1945 we noticed considerable change in the manner in which we were being treated by the guards and the German supervisors at the factory. The beatings became less frequent and our work days were reduced to less than 10 hours. To us this indicated that the Allies were close to winning the war. The mood in the camp got a shot of adrenaline. Each time we saw the planes overhead, flying at ever lower altitudes, we knew that our rescue was just around the corner.

In the middle of March 1945, the Hauptman announced that every one, without exception, had to pick up a new pass. If one did not pick it up, rations would be denied. We were told it was required by the "new rules" instituted by the Reich and that the documents would be issued on the following day. Lines were formed at each barracks and the gestapo gave every worker a green passport-like document with the German swastika eagle on the cover. It read,

"ARBEITSBUCH FUR AUSLENDER"
(Workbook for Foreigners)

Inside was a photograph of the individual, several official stamps and an issue date of March 17, 1945. Subsequently we deduced that it was a subterfuge by the Nazis, an attempt to state that the slave laborers were actually volunteers and worked of their own free will. The ruse did not work. Children did not receive the above document. We were considered under age and. in accordance with child laws were not allowed to work. Another ruse!

On March 29, 1945 we were marched to the factory as usual, but at the entrance we saw sand bags being laid out in a machine gun nest fashion. Everyone was elated and frightened at the same time. By two o'clock in the afternoon the processing equipment was shut down and we began to clean it. Then we heard the infamous "Raus!" This was certainly something new since it was still three hours untill meal time. As we emerged from the underground tunnel, we saw that three machine guns had been set up across the

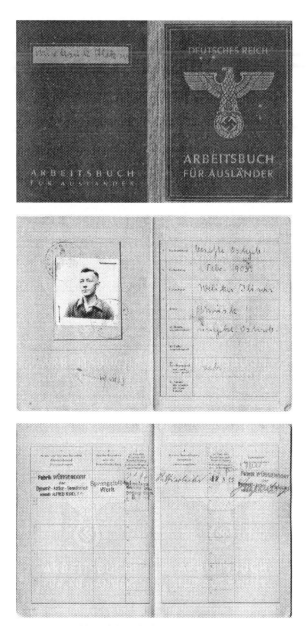

Workbook for Foreigners

Issued on March 17, 1945 by Wurgendorf Dynamitfabrik to show that the Slave Laborers were actually "Volunteer Workers." A ruse, before the end of The Reich.

roadway leading to the exit gate, and they were manned by the SS. We stopped dead in our tracks sensing that the machine guns were set up to kill us before the allies arrived. The guards started pushing us forward but no one moved until we saw that some of the guards were walking out in front of the machine guns. If they were going to shoot us, they would certainly also hit the guards. Slowly we started moving forward, clutching each other and saying good bye to the person next to us, because we still felt that we would be shot.

As we came closer and closer to the factory gate, those in front picked up the pace while those in the rear began to have hope and moved forward. As more and more workers came through the gate, all began to run, knowing that if the shooting started, we at least would have a chance to possibly get away. Our guards started running also, away from the road and into the fields. At any moment we anticipated the staccato of the machine guns, but none came. As we ran towards the camp, accustomed like Pavlov's dogs to the ringing of the bell, we heard another familiar sound, the rumbling of tanks. When we turned the corner into the camp we could see them coming down the hill. They didn't look like the German panzers and we could see a big white star on their turrets.

They were Americans!

The camp was in chaos, people were running everywhere. I ran toward the barracks in hopes of finding Mama and Papa. They were not there. What do I do? Do I stay here or do I run? Then I remembered what Papa said: "If you see the front coming, run for the ravine and stay there," I did just that. Jumping into the ravine I saw many others there already. Papa saw me first. He grabbed and hugged me, Mama was right behind him. The rumbling grew louder and louder, then we heard the cracking of wood and barbed wire as tanks ran over the fences which had been our prison for so many months. Then they turned, heading toward the factory. We heard a volley and saw the guard tower splinter into kindling. We were rescued!

After a few minutes the tanks stopped as a small open truck moved in front of them. It was our first view of a Jeep. The soldier in the front seat stood up and started making hand signals to the tanks. As if by magic they stopped and turned their turrets north. Soon troops on foot came running into the camp. They all looked alike. One could not distinguish who were the officers and who were privates. We ran out of the ravine and threw ourselves on the necks of our rescuers. The only words out of our throats were, "AMERICANS! AMERICANS! AMERICANS!"

As we were celebrating we heard the first salvo of the American tanks firing toward Siegen. The cannonade continued for about fifteen minutes. We dropped to the ground anticipating return fire but none came. When we stood up, the American soldiers came toward us and in their hands they held olive green boxes. They approached the children first and were inundated by the whole camp. I got a bar of chocolate and began to strip the paper from it; the aroma was enthralling and I could not wait until I could take a bite. Just then over the loudspeaker came a voice in a language I did not understand or recognize. The soldiers stopped handing out the packages and turned toward the place where the tower used to be. We then heard an announcement in German and Russian, informing us that we should not eat all of the chocolate or other food right away because it could give us stomach cramps and possibly kill us.

How do you stop eating something in your hands which you have not seen for years? Many didn't and got an awful belly ache. I gave some chocolate to Mama and Papa and ate the rest myself but did not get sick. I guess some of the milk and food I got while working on the farm helped my system tolerate the richness of the chocolate. Subsequently it was explained to us that since our diet for the last two years was so bland and lacking in calories, ingestion of the rich food would cause our system to go into convulsions. Therefore we had to proceed slowly and not gorge ourselves on the American goodies. Sure!

Euphoria reigned over the camp. People were jumping, dancing, hugging and singing. Several men charged the commandant's house, but found no one inside. In a way I was glad because I knew that they would tear him to pieces. I wanted my revenge also, but Mama always said that the Bible teaches us, "I will avenge, sayeth the Lord", but I knew that many of us wanted to be His instrument at that moment. Soon we understood and began to accept what had happened and were fairly certain that the Germans would not return. All the guards disappeared and I saw only three taken into custody by the Americans. One was snatched by several men who began to beat and kick him unmercifully. I am sure they would have killed him if the Americans had not stopped them.

The camp was in a joyous chaos, everyone was running around, laughing and screaming. We were free! Then an announcement over the speakers told us to return to our barracks and await further instructions. It took several hours to get the people to comply. Then we saw several huge trucks come through the compound gate and stop in the middle of the camp. The truck beds were full of barrels with soldiers in white caps and aprons; they looked like cooks. We heard over the loud speakers that food would be served, and we should proceed in an orderly fashion. Sure! As soon as we smelled the food, it became a riot. The cooks tried to distribute it in an orderly manner, but there were so many hands reaching for it that they just put the bread and a can of soup into the nearest hands. It was the most delicious green peas with ham soup I had ever eaten. As a matter of fact, I had never eaten green peas soup with ham. The bread was soft and white, like cake and had no wood chips in it, a feast!

We knew that few of us would sleep that night. Who could sleep when there was so much going on? It seemed that all the American soldiers smoked, but as soon as they took a few puffs on the cigarette they would flip it away and in a few minutes light another one. What a waste! And, what an opportunity for all the men who have not had a cigarette in months or years. Men would grab the tossed cigarette and while it was still lit take a puff and smile, as joy danced on their face when they inhaled the sweet tobacco aroma. Boys were also dashing around grabbing every flipped cigarette butt. I collected a handfull and brought them to Papa, others were stuffing them into pockets and any place that would hold them. Soon there was a flourishing trade in butts and tobacco.

As the evening approached we noticed a mound of small round silk bags and made an attempt to grab some but were sternly rebuffed by a huge American with an "MP" armband. It turned out that the bags contained gunpowder which was removed from the shell casings as the tanks fired on Siegen. Apparently, during manufacture, every shell was filled for the maximum range the projectile could travel. If the distance was less than the maximum, bags were removed and tossed aside. The mountain of gunpowder grew as tanks continued firing. We were wondering when the powder would be picked up. To our surprise one of the MP's fired a tracer bullet into the mound and it flared up like a volcano. I was sure the flame must have reached over forty meters into the air and was seen for miles.

Chapter 12

Rescued and Hiding Again

We were rescued by the army of General George Patton, the Third Armored Division. On their sleeves the soldiers had a red, yellow and blue patch showing a tank with the number "3" superimposed on it.

The morning after our rescue, at about six a.m., those of us who were sleeping were rousted out of the barracks and told to get our belongings together because we were being moved. Moved to where? As the trucks were lining up, we heard the unmistakable whistle of artillery shells which initially fell above the camp. Soon many more were exploding all around us. Panic broke out and everyone started running every which way. In the confusion I got separated from Mama and Papa.

The American soldiers were just about throwing people on the trucks, and as soon as one was full, it roared out of the camp. I yelled for Mama and Papa but with the noise of the trucks, screaming of the people and exploding shells, my voice was drowned out. I did not get on a truck and kept running around looking for them. Soon, I found myself just about alone, all the people were gone only the soldiers remained. An American officer grabbed me, threw me in a jeep and we took off. I kept screaming in German and Russian that I want my parents but it was to no avail. We drove for a while and then stopped on top of a hill. I could not see the camp but there was a lot of smoke from the general direction we had just come from.

Apparently the Germans, in a last ditch effort, decided to counter attack, and fired on the American tanks which had just rescued us. I was still in shock from being separated from my parents and tried in every way to get some American's attention. I did not see any of the trucks that took the people away from the camp, and did not know what happened to them. Finally, in an attempt to quiet me down, a soldier came up to me and

187

started speaking German. He hugged me to his chest and I felt that he was really concerned. After I stopped crying and explained to him what had happened he said that he didn't know where the people were taken but as soon as the fighting stopped he would make inquiries. The shelling did not stop until several American planes flew over and dropped bombs on the German artillery. Huge columns of smoke arose in the distance and there were no more shells.

I stayed by the soldier's side all day; finally he went over to a huge truck with antennas on the roof, it looked like the field headquarters. He told me to stay right where I was as he went inside. After a long time, he came out and told me that the people from Wurgendorf were taken to a camp in Wetzlar, about fifty kilometers away. However, this army division would not be going that way and I would have to stay here until a Red Cross truck showed up to take me there. I was afraid to leave this kind soldier but he had to leave and get back to his unit. Before he left me, he went inside the headquarters van and came out with another soldier who was dressed in a cleaner uniform and also spoke German. I was told this was the captain who was involved in the re-settlement activities of the labor camps and I had to stay with him. What choice did I have, I had to do what I was told. Almost three years in the camp taught me obedience on the spot. I stayed by the headquarters truck all day and in the evening was taken to the mess tent.

Many scents which I had long forgotten floated into my nostrils, while new unfamiliar smells tackled my nose and brain. Sausages, potatoes and something called Spam was being served. I had never tasted Spam but it looked like meat, and that couldn't be bad. Many of the soldiers were not eating their Spam; it smelled great to me. That night I fell asleep on a cot in the truck crying, and wondering if I would ever see Mama and Papa again. I was ten years old, and had to grow up before my time since the war had exposed me to so much, but still many of the childish feelings prevailed. In the morning the whole unit moved to another location. I did not have a hat and one of the soldiers gave me his cap. When I put it on I felt like one of them.

We moved around for several days but the Red Cross truck never showed up. I wondered if there really was one and began to be concerned. The soldiers treated me very kindly, all gave me candy. One of them gave me a pouch which I could sling over my shoulder and somewhere they found a pair of boots which were almost my size and I got rid of the awful *Holtzshuhe*. With the hat, shoes and a satchel slung over my shoulder, I looked almost like one of the soldiers. I even learned several American phrases like "OK", "Hi, Joe!" and "Hey You!"

Many weeks later the Red Cross truck showed up. Hallelujah! The captain said they would be going to Wetzlar that afternoon and would take me along. He was not certain if we would be able to locate my parents since everything was in chaos and apparently some of the people from the camp were taken to locations other than Wetzlar. There were no lists. God! Help me to find Mama and Papa!

The captain saw how distraught I was and got permission to go with me to Wetzlar. When we arrived I was overwhelmed by the sight. It was the biggest camp I had ever seen, it seemed like thousands and thousands of people were milling around everywhere. How would I be able even to start looking for Mama and Papa? Apparently it had been a training center for the German army and consisted of many one, two and three story buildings around a huge parade ground. We drove through the gate and pulled up to a large brick building. People were running in and out with stacks of papers in their hands. It had to be the camp headquarters. Inside the building were hundreds of people working, typing, speaking on telephones and filing things in drawers. Most looked like Germans and I began to wonder if this was another concentration camp, but there were many American soldiers among the workers, therefore, my fright abated. One soldier started looking through a stack of papers and asked me, "How do you spell your name?" What is spell?"

The captain told me to write mine and the the names of my parents on a sheet of paper. The soldier took the paper and went

Anatole Kurdsjuk

Wetzlar 1945

Wearing the Army cap, shoes and trousers given to him by soldiers of Gen. Patton's Third Army 1st Division, after he was separated from his parents in Wurgendorf.

Anatole Kurdsjuk with his Mama
April, 1945 in Wetzlar DP Camp where after six weeks of separation, he was reunited with Mama and Papa.

Wetzlar Displaced Persons Camp - 1945
The camp to which Olga and Jacob were taken by the American Armed Forces after the liberation from Wurgendorf.

back into the office complex.

We waited and waited. After about an hour he came back and told us that according to the lists, Mama and Papa were part of the group brought to Wetzlar. - but where were they in the camp? This they could not tell me since people were just dumped in the camp and settled where they found space. Inventory rolls would be taken in a few days, or once the refugee stream subsided. As we waited more and more trucks rolled in with people from other camps; at this rate it could take months!

The day was ebbing away. Toward evening I began to notice a number of small fires springing up on the parade ground, it looked like people were cooking. While the soldier went looking in different barracks, I went looking on the parade ground.

Mostly women were huddled over their individual fires which burned between two bricks or stones. On the stones stood cooking utensils of every shape and kind, ranging from tin cans to enamel pots and everything in between. I started walking. Every woman I passed, I asked if there was anyone here from Wurgendorf? Few shook their heads, "No," while others concentrated on their cooking saying nothing. Every woman I passed, I bent down and looked in her face, searching for Mama and the OST patch. I walked about for two hours; it was getting darker and darker and it was difficult to recognize faces. The only light was coming from the cooking fires, and on the huge parade ground it was becoming almost impossible to see anything clearly. I decided to return to the office, but lost my bearings and didn't know which way to go. Then I saw the two lights by the gate and decided to follow a straight line path toward it. As I was hurrying toward the light I brushed against a small woman with an OST patch still on her coat. Bending down to look at her face, my heart skipped a beat. It was Mama!

I cried out, "*Mamochka*?!"

She looked up and fainted. Her head just missed hitting the stones while her shoulder knocked the pot over. I started waving my army cap over her face, to give her more air, and praying both thanks to God for His miracle while asking Him to wake Mama up. After a while she let out a moan and as if jabbed by a needle jumped up and started hugging me. Once again I was in the arms of my wonderful Mama. I was almost as tall as she was, but she picked me up in her arms and started running toward one of the barracks kissing me all the way and crying. She ran into the corridor yelling, "Papa! Papa! God has returned Anatole to us!"

All the doors to the rooms were open, out of one of them came Papa. We all fell to the floor in a jumble of hugs, kisses and tears. Their fifth and only remaining child was back in their arms. How long we lay there I do not know, nor did I care, there was love all around me and it felt so wonderful! Mama and Papa were telling everyone that God sent them a miracle. Suddenly I remembered that I was supposed to go back to the office where the captain and the soldier were waiting. I tried to convey it to Papa but he would not listen, all he kept saying was, "*Moy synok, Moy synok!*" (My son, My son!), with tears streaming down his face. Some time later I was able to convince him that we had to go to the office.

On the way I told him of my life during our separation. When we got to the office the captain was waiting outside.

I ran to him yelling, "My Father! My father is here!" When Papa came to the captain, he fell on his knees hugging and kissing his shoes. This time I knew that Papa would not be kicked and started crying with joy myself. The Captain lifted Papa up and told him he had to return to his unit, but would come back when the fighting was over. He also asked Papa if he could adopt me and take me to America. This thought was out of the question in my father's mind, we were just reunited.

Wetzlar is the site of the Leica camera factory. The camp or *kasserne*, as it is called in German, was one of the main training areas for the Wehrmacht ground troops. The barracks were stone and brick with large rooms for enlisted men and several smaller rooms on each floor for the officers. Many rooms still had uniforms and other military paraphernalia hanging on hooks. Papa was able to secure one of these smaller rooms which became the home for ten people. To us, after the concentration camps, it was like a hotel. Most of the camp occupants were Polish with a few Russians and Ukranians. We had metal bunk beds and many of the families separated their spots by hanging blankets on ropes between the beds. This provided some visual privacy but every other noise or conversation was public knowledge, especially at night when activities of the young couple in our midst became amorous.

Our food was provided by the United States International Refugee Organization, IRO, and distributed by the American Armed Forces. Camp cooking facilities were not operating and food had to be heated or prepared by the recipient, which is why the women were cooking on the bricks. Every day a truck would pull up to the barracks and soldiers would distribute green packages and cans of food. I wormed my way to the tailgate of the truck and yelled: "Hey Joe! OK?" One of the soldiers looked down, smiled and gave me a big green can and a loaf of bread. I said: "OK Joe!" and ran to the room. I had no idea what was in the can, but it was big and heavy. I knew we had bread and that was good enough.

Everyone was examining the goodies they received, trying to figure out what the packages and cans contained. Everything was in "American." A person on our floor had an English dictionary, and became the most popular man in town. Papa's Russian/English dictionary for which he was almost executed in Wurgendorf was in the valise, somewhere in the camp; it was lost during the move from Wurgendorf, Papa was sure that it was somewhere in the pile of suitcases he saw off loaded when they arrived.

Examining the can, I was able to figure out one word, "BUTTER". I did not know what peanut meant but I knew what butter was. We had not seen any real butter for years and now I had a huge can of it. Mama was so excited that she started clapping her hands and dancing like child. All that butter! We didn't have anything to cook in it but we had the bread. Bread and butter, what a feast! Everyone in the room was also excited about the butter. One woman across the hall said to Mama that she would trade her two potatoes for a spoon of butter. Mama agreed. Papa came back with a can opener, it was one of those throwaway GI-type and it took a while for us to cut the lid open. Once the can was opened and the lid peeled back, we knew something was amiss. This butter was not yellow but brown. Was it spoiled? Or, was this some American specialty butter made for the army? It smelled sweet and aromatic, so it seemed that it should be edible. Since it was our butter, Mama was going to use it first. She peeled the two potatoes, she got from the woman, sliced them and headed out to the parade ground to fry them in a pan borrowed from one of our roommates. Almost everyone followed her.

Once the fire was going, she placed the frying pan on the bricks and scooped out a healthy spoonful of the "Peanut Butter," placing it in the center of the pan. It sizzled and sputtered, but would not melt. We waited and waited but it just burned, only a little oil trickled from the blob. What kind of butter is this? Everyone said it was spoiled and the woman wanted her potatoes back. What we thought was a boon turned out to be a bust. Gathering everything up, we returned to the barracks. The man with the dictionary looked up the word "peanut." Based on his explanation we were almost certain that this butter was not for cooking. In the morning Papa and I went to the main office in hopes of getting a better explanation on how to use this Peanut Butter. The soldiers, to whom we explained our dilemma of the previous evening, went into convulsive laughter. They explained to us that peanut butter was used to make sandwiches and showed us how to make a peanut butter and jelly sandwich. We didn't have any jelly but they had a jar of grape jelly by the coffee pot. One of the soldiers made a sandwich and gave it to us. It tasted great and we returned to the room proud of our discovery. Soon we traded some peanut butter for several spoonful of cherry preserves, Mama boiled some water for tea and we had a wonderful meal.

When the German army retreated, the camp was left full of armaments. Rifle rounds with wooden bullets used for target practice, grenades and other explosives were everywhere. We also found some rifles but their barrels were jammed with dirt, sticks and tar. The camp was populated primarily by adults and only a few children were visible, but children find other children very quickly and soon there was a soccer game on the parade ground. I don't know where we got the ball and playing between the cooking brick was tough, passing the ball was even funnier; it never went where we wanted it to go. It just bounced off the bricks. When we got tired of playing football one of the older guys said he had a real game to play, but one had to have guts to play it. What nine or ten year old would say he had no guts? We all would play.

He selected mostly the taller boys and told us to follow him. We all went to the other side of the camp and into a bunker. On its shelves were boxes and boxes of target bullets.

The game was called "Chicken," and went something like this: A fire was started using the scraps of wood from the broken crates. As the fire grew, heavier sticks were added. The instigator of the game got a box of shells and started handing out five to each of us. Then we drew numbers by lot, number one had to go first. The bullets were tossed into the fire and we had to start counting to fifty. If one ran before the count reached thirty or before the bullets went off, he would be considered "Chicken." The real hero would be the one who stayed the longest. I pulled out number 7. The fellow with No.1 stepped in front of the fire and threw his shells in, starting the count before they even reached the fire. The game's instigator yelled, "Foul!" and said that the count had to be started again. As the issue was being "'discussed" with much yelling and shouting, the first shell exploded, and the bullet went zinging over our heads. We dropped to the ground. Not many "brave souls" lifted their heads as the other four shells exploded in rapid succession. Then it was quiet. The number 2 guy said it was a stupid game and refused to play. The instigator called him "Chicken" and there was a chorus of about two other voices who repeated the call. The rest of us threw the bullets away.

All of us have had enough bullets zinging over our heads, and survived, getting killed now was really stupid, since the war was almost over or at least we thought so. Some of us did go back and played the game again, but this time we hid behind a brick wall as the bullets went off. It was still a thrill for a ten year old.

We also found a stash of grenades and decided to go fishing. The Lahn River flows through Wetzlar and was right next to the camp, a good place to test our theory. We went to a bend in the river, pulled the pin and threw a grenade into the water as far as we could. Soon there was a muffled boom followed by a geyser of water as the fish floated belly up. We ran to the bend of the river and picked them up as they floated by. When I brought the fish home for Mama to cook and told her how we fished them up, she said that she was not going to eat any more fish that I brought home; but she did fry them that night. Too bad we didn't have any butter to fry them in. From then on grenade fishing was forbidden.

I also learned to ride a bicycle in Wetzlar. Bicycles were taken from the town residents, however they were usually without tires. The owners removed them in hopes that no one would take a bicycle without tires. They were wrong. One of the older boys in our barracks had "acquired" such a bicycle and was trading rides with anyone who had something of value to offer. I had a peanut butter sandwich which gave me a half-hour experience. It took me about ten minutes to learn balance, it was easier than with tires since the rims were square. We had to ride on the road but there was no concern for traffic, there was none, only people were in the way. The bicycle bell and our yelling scattered them very quickly. The major problem in riding a bicycle without tires on a hard surface is the lack of traction. When one starts, the rear wheel just spins and you can't get going. Once you were riding and had to apply brakes, you skidded. Eventually I learned that to get moving, I had to walk the bike and then, very slowly, apply pressure to the pedals. Several falls and skinned knees later, I was able to stay up and go about one hundred feet. Steering was also difficult because the square rim tended to send one in a straight line. Curbs were a real problem. However, these difficulties were of lesser concern than having the opportunity to ride a bicycle. Later in life I finally got a bicycle, with tires.

One of my less fortunate experiences occurred in Wetzlar during our first winter in the Displaced Persons (DP) camp, as the new collection points for former slave laborers were called. A fellow acquired a pair of ice skates of the type that could be clamped onto the sole of a shoe. They were great skates since they could be used by anyone, for a "price", at least by those who had a pair of shoes with soles. I was lucky, I had my army boots, they even supported the ankle. A small pond just outside the camp gates, which froze very quickly, became the arena for our games. We played hockey with sticks made from limbs of a tree. The puck was usually a flattened tin can. The goal was an open space between two stones. Starting and stopping on ice in shoes was very difficult and many a time we slid across half the pond, scoring, when both the player and the puck went through the goal.

Those who could skate bartered something for a few minutes on skates. Once they were attached, we raced like demons around the pond making the most of the allotted time.

I had learned to skate in Mariupol and, for a chocolate bar, had the skates for a half hour. I raced around and around not noticing that my time was up. The owner of the skates kept strict time of the "rentals" and pulled me off the ice when my time was up, saying, "If you want to skate more, it'll cost you." Not having anything more of value that he wanted, I had to return the skates and sat down on the bank to rest. I was all sweated up but wanted to watch others skate. I don't know how long I sat on the ground, but it was getting dark and I promised Mama that I would not stay out after dark. That night I slept like a log. In the morning when I awoke, I felt chills all over my body and told Mama about it. She, in her usual way, pressed her lips against my forehead to see if I had a fever, and stepping back said, "You have a high fever. Stay in bed.," and went looking for a thermometer which she kept in a very safe place. When she found it, she placed it under my left arm pit and told me to lie still. Thermometers in Russia were of this type, at least I never saw any of the mouth or the rectal kind. After a few minutes she came back and checked the reading. It read 102 degrees. She cried out, *Boze Moy!"* (Oh my God!) and called Papa. I had not been ill in the camps throughout our ordeals. Mama ran to the bathroom, soaked a kerchief in water and placed it on my forehead. Waiting a few seconds, she flipped the cloth over and continued to repeat the process. The fever was not dropping. She took my shirt off and started rubbing me down with water and alcohol. After a while the fever dropped, but within an hour it was up to 103.5. Mama and Papa wrapped me in a blanket and ran to the infirmary, which was just around the corner. Apparently there were many others with high fevers, the room was packed. Medical help at the camp was minimal, it provided care for cuts and bruises but anything more complex had to be attended to at the hospital in Wetzlar. People were overwhelming the small staff of medical workers; whether there was a doctor available we could not tell, most of those helping were nurses. Then Papa saw a man from our barracks whom he knew to be a dentist; he had seen the doctor pull a tooth for one of Papa's friends.

Papa pushed his way to him and asked for help. The doctor took out a wooden stethoscope and listened to my chest, placing the large end on the chest while listening through the smaller end. He said: "The boy has pneumonia. Here, give him this medicine and I will stop by your room this afternoon." Relieved that some help was available we went back to the barracks. After a few hours the fever dropped to 101, but after a few hours it spiked to 104 degrees. Once more the water and alcohol compresses were applied; this time with little help, the fever was not dropping.

At the age of two, in Mariupol, I had double pneumonia and almost died. I was their last child, what were they to do? *Banki* saved me the last time. *Banki* are placed on the back and draw additional blood supply to the affected area. Papa went scurrying around to see if anyone had *banki*. After a while, he returned with a woman who said she could apply them. I was stripped down to the waist, turned on my stomach and the procedure began. Each *banka* was about the size of a small fruit juice glass with the lip of the glass being heavier than the rest. A wick made from of a piece of wood was wrapped with cotton, dipped in alcohol and lighted. The burning wick was inserted into the empty *banka* consuming the air. Then the wick was quickly removed and the cupping glass pressed against the flesh. The vacuum created by absence of air held the banka in place drawing additional blood supply to the area.

I do not know how many *banki* were placed on my back but I looked like a porcupine. Mama covered me with a blanket and I fell asleep. I awoke the next morning as the dentist doctor was removing the *banki* from my back. Apparently they helped, but my fever was not coming down sufficiently and further help was needed.

He sat me up in bed and started thumping my back with his finger. The sounds returning to him apparently showed that I had contracted pleurisy. Pleurisy is the accumulation of fluid around the lung reducing its ability to exchange oxygen in the blood. In extreme cases, if not treated quickly, the lung would "drown." The doctor asked me some questions and I told him of my skating experience on the previous day. This convinced him that it was pleurisy, and there was no time to waste since my breathing was becoming labored and I felt faint.

He gave some instructions to Mama and Papa and left the room to get his medical bag. When he returned, he explained to me that he was going to get the fluid out of my lungs, and that I would feel very little pain from the procedure. Then, he pulled out two syringes from his bag. One was the normal size I remember when I got the rabies shots, while the other was huge, topped by the longest and thickest needle I had ever seen. He then asked Papa to hold me in his lap as I faced him. I began to cry and Papa tried to console me. First the lower part of my back, on the right side, was swabbed with iodine and an anesthetic was injected in several places. I winced with every shot but Papa held me tight in his strong arms. After each shot the doctor massaged each injected area, and gave me another shot. Then he picked up the huge syringe and told Papa to hold me even tighter. I felt pressure in my side and heard a crunching sound as the large needle penetrated my flesh between the ribs. Papa gave me his watch to hold during the process asking me to listen to the tic-toc, tic-toc, and hoping that it would distract me from the procedure; it didn't. I felt no pain but the crunching sound bothered me so much that to this day I cannot have anyone touch me in that area, without jumping.

Then, the pumping procedure began. The syringe was attached to the needle, and the plunger retracted, filling the cavity with a greenish fluid. When the syringe was full, it was detached from the needle and the fluid emptied into a flask. Then it was reattached and the procedure repeated. I wanted to keep count of how many times the syringe was filled but could not. At the end of the procedure Dr. Tadjayev showed me a liter of the fluorescent greenish liquid he removed from the lung cavity. He was a Chechen by origin and looked oriental. After the procedure, he gave me some medicine to drink and I fell asleep. The next day I had almost no fever and was up and about within two days. Dr. Tadjayev saved my life and I was strongly admonished by Papa not to "rent" the skates again.

World War II was winding down, allied leaders in the persons of President Truman, Prime Minister Churchill and the Soviet Generalissimo Joseph Visarionovich Stalin met in Potsdam and Yalta to discuss steps to be taken in dealing with the slave labor and concentration camp victims who were presently in the various Displaced Persons camps. It was agreed that the people would be returned to their country of origin, with the processing costs to be borne by the receiving nation. When this became known in Wetzlar and other camps, many Russians knew what awaited them if they returned, execution or exile in Siberia, just for having seen what life was like outside the Iron Curtain. Many began making plans to hide, escape or fight to the death, rather than return.

Four young Russian people lived on our floor and could not wait to "go home." Papa and two other families who had suffered under communism tried to persuade them not to return but were unsuccessful. The call of the homeland and family was too strong. They said they would go home at the next opportunity. Papa decided that for us it was better to fight, and possibly die, rather than return, and began to make preparations for that eventuality.

After the war there was enough equipment and ammunition around to start World War III. All we had to do was to pick it up, hide it in a safe place, and then use it to defend ourselves. Papa and his "non-returning" friends found a bunker in the forest just outside the camp and started hauling "defense equipment" to the site. When they were finished, we had two fifty caliber machine guns with ten belts of ammunition, three grenade launchers, six boxes of grenades and a number of rifles in working order. They also stashed food and water sufficient for the twelve people who would fight and occupy the bunker. All were families with children.

To confuse and divert any Soviet troops who came looking for us in the barracks, Papa made arrangements with some former Polish citizens to occupy our room if we had to run. One morning we were awakened by one of the men who told us: "The camp is surrounded by American tanks and Soviet soldiers you had better run to the "shelter!" We had practiced the escape a number of times and knew just how and where to go.

As we followed the escape route we could see Russian soldiers coming into the camp followed by American MP's. That spurred us on and we reached the shelter unnoticed within a few minutes. The men set up the machine guns at the entrance while the women readied the grenade launchers. We stayed on alert for four hours, shivering and waiting for the inevitable. Then we heard someone approaching on foot, It was one of the Polish men who came to tell us it was safe to return. When we got back, our Polish room "residents" were still in our room and told us how they got rid of the Soviets.

Apparently the Soviets had obtained a list of former Russians in the camp from the registrar and the unsuspecting Americans. "Uncle Joe Stalin" was an ally of America and according to the agreements in place, former Russians had to return home. Why would anyone not want to return home? Some time later Papa met an American officer who spoke Russian and told him of what was awaiting the returnees. The officer did not believe him and threatened to deliver Papa to the Soviets on their next visit. This was 1945, and Papa asked the officer to remember their conversation in the future, when the Americans will be fighting the communist threat. The officer laughed. How could we fight our friends? The Korean War began in 1950.

Unbeknownst to us, there was a group of Russian men in the

camp who were part of the Vlassow army. These soldiers fought on the German side against Communism. When it was evident that Hitler was going to lose the war, most of them ran trying to save themselves. Many were captured and held by the Americans in prison camps, but quite a few escaped and attempted to hide among the people in DP camps. In Wetzlar they, like us, found support among the Poles when the Soviets came to search for "their citizens."

However, many of them were caught unawares during the last raid and only a few escaped. Those who could not escape, when they saw the Soviet uniforms, committed suicide by jumping from the roofs of three-story buildings, cutting their own throats with tin cans or falling on grenades, rather than be taken back. Those who were captured, rather than return, threw themselves under the wheels of trucks as they were being driven to the waiting train which would take them "home." They knew, that as soon as they left the American or English Zones, the best they could expect was a firing squad, the worst they could only imagine. Those committing suicide were not only the former Vlassow men but also people like Papa and Mama who had endured Soviet oppression. They had tasted freedom, outside of the Soviet Union and nothing would make them return.

After this frightening experience Papa and his friends began to make plans to escape deeper into the American Zone, towards Bavaria. We were almost on the border of the English and American Zones; the Russian Zone was not far away and who knew if the Americans would be with the Soviets during the next search for Russian citizens.

Chapter 13

The "DP" Camps
Searching for Aunt Mary

Places to which the former slave labor and concentration camp inmates were resettled became known as Displaced Persons (DP) Camps. The facilities usually were former German army training barracks and Wetzlar was one of the largest.

Because of the post World War II agreements by the allies these camps were being set up by nationality, making it easier to gather and return people to their country of origin. Wetzlar was to become a Polish and Hungarian camp. We did not speak Polish but felt that we could easily hide there. However, there were Poles who resented us because of the atrocities committed by the Soviet Union against the Polish nation during division of their land and agreements between Hitler and Stalin, before the start of World War II.

We knew that should another "search mission" by the Soviets occur, these people would inform on us. Twice before, the Soviets came to find "their Russians," but each time we were able to escape to our shelter as our Polish friends occupied our room. The four young Russian people who lived with us ached to return home. Mama tried to convince the young girls that they would be returning to hell and told them her and Papa's story. They did not want to believe what Mama was saying, calling it propaganda. The young men said that after the war, life would be different and better in the USSR. There would be more freedom to do what one wanted.

One young man named Fyodor and a young lady named Liuba were madly in love and wanted to marry before returning home. They felt it would be better if they returned as a married couple. Getting married was simple, all you needed was a priest to say a few words and then follow it with a party. Fyodor had two very close friends with whom he survived the labor camps. One

The Pugatchev, Feodor and Liuba's Wedding
Wetzlar 1945

Front row: Sergei's date, Liuba, Fyodor and Anatole
Back row: Sergei snd Jan

was a Russian named Sergei, and the other a tall Polish fellow named Jan. I was asked to be part of the wedding party. Fyodor was a wheeler-dealer and could get almost anything. What they needed was wine. He and Papa went to the Rhine River where the shores bristled with grape fields and vineyards. This was the heart of the German wine country, famous for its Rhine Wines. They took several five gallon gasoline cans, which Jan stole from an American jeep, and proceeded to the Rhine. While they were away Jan "found" a piglet at a nearby farm. He said the pig cost him only one bullet.

The wedding took place the following Saturday. Mama and the girls prepared the meat, making sausages and hams which they cooked on an open fire. The whole pig had to be cooked since there was no refrigeration. Mama and the women made several types of sausages sprinkling them liberally with salt to preserve the meat. The party was held in our room. Beds were moved against the walls and a makeshift table was set up in the middleof the room. Wine flowed like water and soon all the men were drunk. Jan said that a wedding was not official unless the whole neighborhood knew about it, and proceeded to run up the stairs to the roof of the building. When he got there he pulled out a handgun out of his jacket, which looked more like a sawed off shotgun, and proceeded to fire tracer bullets into the sky. He then reloaded a Mauser pistol, and repeated the process. Then he sat down and waving the gun about, as men ducked, proceeded to tell us his own story.

Jan came from Krakow in Poland. When the Germans occupied the town, someone told them that Jan's family were Jewish. No one bothered to investigate the allegation and the family was executed. Jan was in another town when the SS came and took his mother, father, brother and two sisters. They were thrown on a truck, taken away and shot that same afternoon. Jan was seventeen at the time and swore that when the time came, he would avenge the deaths of his family, ten for one. Ten Germans for each member of his family and very proudly told us that as of that day his count stood at thirty two.

The next time the Soviets came to the camp looking for Russians, Fyodor, Liuba, Irina and Sergei went to meet them and boarded the trucks "taking them home." On the way they sang patriotic songs while sharing a bottle of Russian vodka. Once more, this time with Jan in our group, we ran to our shelter in the woods.

The Wetzlar DP camp was getting organized. A catholic "church" was established in one of the barrack halls and priests were looking for altar boys. One of the major Polish/Catholic holidays was coming up, the celebration of the Holy Mother of Czestohowa. The icon of the holiday is also known as the black Madonna and Child and is credited with many miracles. One of my new Polish friends was going to be an altar boy, I told him that I also believed in God, and we both went to be trained. I didn't say anything about this to Mama.

When the holiday came, the priest made cassocks for us out of bed sheets and each of us was given a candle to carry. The procession started at the church and proceeded around the parade grounds returning to the church where a High Mass was to be celebrated. As we came past our barracks, I saw Mama, and she saw me. She crossed herself and shook a finger at me, indicating that she was not very pleased. When I returned to the room, she informed me that I was not to participate in any more Catholic services, we were Russian Orthodox. So ended my Catholic education, but I learned enough Polish to hold a conversation and attend the third grade of the camp school. It was my first formal education experience and my third language.

We had been in Wetzlar about three months when Papa and Jan decided to go and visit the Dynamitfabrik slave labor camp in Wurgendorf. Papa said he had to go back and dig up some papers which he buried and could not get to before being brought to Wetzlar.

The war in Europe was over and railroads were beginning to run again. Papa purchased the tickets using money he made selling wine, for which he traded with the German vineyard growers for cigarettes. Cigarettes were the currency of the day, Camels, Lucky Strike, Chesterfield and Pall Mall being the most popular. Papa said that they would be away a maximum of two days. Mama was against it, but Papa persevered. "What if the Soviets come while you are away," she lamented. "Don't worry," he said, "Our friends will take care of you just like before." The next day I walked to the train with them. I wanted to go but Papa said Mama would crucify him if he took me and besides it was my responsibility to take care of her. Jan was all for me going because he wanted to see how a five-foot Mama would handle the six-foot-two Papa. I waved good-bye as they left on the 9:00 a.m. train from the Wetzlar Bahnhoff. Several of my friends came with me and we were going to have an adventure rummaging through the bombed out buildings on the way back to the camp.

As we scampered over the fallen walls and windows near the center of Wetzlar, my eye caught something bright blue in the rubble. I climbed down and began to remove the debris from something that looked like a book. As I uncovered it and cleaned off the dust, it was a book, with very thick pages. Opening it up, I discovered that it was a stamp album filled with many beautiful stamps. I yelled to my friends and showed them my find, they all said that I had to share it, but I reminded them that as we had no such agreement before we left, it was finders' keepers. This small find, started me on a lifelong hobby of philately, stamp collecting.

Papa and Jan kept their word returning the next day and ex-plained that while in Wurgendorf they went to our former camp and found it to be just about demolished by the last ditch shelling of the Wehrmacht. Papa was able to find the papers he buried and brought them with him.

On their return to the railroad station he spied a familiar fig-ure. It was the former camp commandant. When Papa and Jan approached him, he recognized Papa and started to run. Jan pulled out his pistol and without taking proper aim, fired. The bullet missed the commandant but he fell to his knees. As Papa approached him, he began to beg and scream: "*Hilfe!*" (Help!) Jan still had the pistol in his hand and was ready to fire but Papa stopped him. He took the pistol from Jan's hand, walked over to the kneeling whin-ing, begging, and trembling figure and grabbing him by the neck, yanked him up, then slammed the pistol butt across his face. As the commandant went down once more, Papa kicked him in the groin saying: "Remember when you did this to me? I will not kill you now, but remember your life is mine!" Then with years of pent-up rage and frustration, he slammed his fist into the commandant's face and kicked him in the butt. Jan insisted on killing him right then and there so that he could add to his total, but Papa said "No, let him think about when I will be coming back." They left the squirming and moaning figure in the street and walked on to the station. No one came out to help him.

The allies were still working on establishing the various military zones of occupation. Wetzlar was in the American zone but very close to the proposed Russian zone border. This meant that the visits from the Soviets could be ongoing. Running and hiding each time was not only unsettling but the probability of us of being captured and sent back was real. One Pole even threatened to call the Russians to get us out. Staying in Wetzlar was getting chancy.

Papa heard of a DP camp established in Mainz/Kastel, Bavaria where the Rhine and Main rivers met. This camp was in the American Zone and promised to be a safer place. We packed up our few belongings ready to take the train to Mainz. Just before we were to leave, Papa was called to the camp office and informed that our valise had been found. The only reason we were called was because Papa had carved our name in the plywood case. We were overjoyed to have it since it held our only change of clothes and some personal items. That morning we walked to the Wetzlar train station and took the train to Mainz. We didn't know the actual location of the camp but after some inquiries learned that it was in Mainz/Kastel, 10 kilometers from Mainz. Just then a trolley pulled up across the street and I went to ask the conductor if there was a trolley to Mainz/Kastel. He said, "Certainly. Get on this trolley and I'll tell you where to get off. At that point walk across the street and take Trolley No. 10, it will say Wiesbaden/Kastel." We got on, paid our fare, and waited for the conductor's signal. After riding for about fifteen minutes, he motioned for us to get off at the next stop, and right there, as if waiting for us, was trolley No. 10.

The conductor gave us a transfer and we didn't have to pay an additional fare. I told the conductor on No. 10 that we wanted to get to the DP camp and he said that it was one of the stops on the line; we would get there in about twenty minutes. Sure enough there was a stop. We got off and walked toward another DP Camp, it was just like Wetzlar, only smaller.

The gate was manned by two civilians in makeshift uniforms with a blue and yellow armband, the colors of a Ukrainian flag. As we came up to the booth, Papa recognized their speech as Ukranian and began to speak in their own language. One of the guards walked us over to the camp office. The documents we had from Wurgendorf and Wetzlar were accepted and we were added to the camp rolls settling in a room with another couple who spoke broken Ukrainian. Later we learned that they were actually Russian who lived in Kiev and were pretending to be Ukrainian.

We moved in and while Mama started making supper, Papa and I decided to become familiar with the camp. One of the first people we met was Konstantin Us. He told us he was a former Cossack from the river Don, not far from where we had lived and was familiar with Mariupol. He was a very outgoing man and quickly guided us to the various places where we would get food and medical attention. Konstantin told us that we were fortunate to have arrived just then, since several days earlier they had a visit from the Soviets who were taking people back to Russia. However, men in this camp had been anticipating such a raid and were organized to deal with it. They jumped the Soviets, beat them up, and chased them out of the camp and pushed their trucks into the river. Apparently by now the Americans were familiar with why people were refusing to return and did little to prevent the beatings. On one of the previous visits by the Soviets, a man took his wife and children to the steps of the camp office, pulled out a knife, slit the throats of his wife and family, and before committing suicide screamed, "I would rather that we die in freedom than once more suffer under Communism!"

His sacrifice made a tremendous impact on the American forces and their commanders. In accordance with the Potsdam agreement, they were required to assist the Soviets. Now they turned their heads and did little or nothing to help. Well, perhaps we were not much safer than in Wetzlar, but at least there was a unified effort to stop forced repatriation and we were deeper in the American zone.

We picked up our rations from the food distribution center and returned to our room. The man and woman living with us were very quiet and didn't bother with us. That evening Papa and I went for a walk around the camp. In front of the camp office was a large bulletin board with all kinds of camp information posted. One corner of the boards was devoted to announcements of people looking for relatives or friends. Many of them were from America. One of the announcements caught Papa's eye, I didn't know why, but he got out a pencil and wrote something down in his little brown calendar book which he always carried with him. When we got back, Mama had some food prepared. At this camp each barracks had a cooking area with a stove and running water. We had wonderful soup that night. After finishing the meal, Papa pulled out the small book from his pocket and told us that a person from New York was looking for her brother somewhere in Germany. Why this was so important I did not understand. He, however, proceeded to remind Mama that he had a first cousin named Mary and her husband Kuzma who lived in New York. Papa had written several letters to her after their escape from Siberia, begging Mary for help, and if it was at all possible, to bring them to America.

By 1926, the Soviet government suspended all immigration and canceled all visas to America. Later, when the Iron Curtain came down, all correspondence with anyone outside of the Soviet Union was forbidden, punishable by imprisonment. Even possession of an address of anyone behind the Iron Curtain was a reason for arrest. Therefore Papa had destroyed all the letters and envelopes he received from Mary in America. That very evening he wrote to the person with the New York address explaining our situation and asking for any help they could possibly provide in locating Aunt Mary. This was to be the first of over 100 letters he was to write to anyone in America with a New York return address.

Almost every day, Papa and I continued to look at the bulletin board in search for additional people with a New York return address to contact. He was a man who could not sit idle and always wanted something meaningful to do. An opportunity arose at the American Red cross in Wiesbaden, only a fifteen minute trolley ride from the camp. He applied for and got a job as a janitor. It did not pay very much but provided additional opportunity to search for Aunt Mary. Most of all, it gave him access to the latest news and information via "Life" and "Time" magazines which he was allowed to bring home. We could not read English, but the pictures usually conveyed the story. Papa was sure that someday we would go to America and started me on an arduous process of learning the English language.

Every week he selected several photographs in "Life" and I would have to translate the inscription using the English/Russian dictionary by Alexandroff. I would look up every word in the inscription then select the appropriate meaning and write it in Russian. When Papa returned from work, he would judiciously review my progress for that day, grading my efforts and encouraging me to work hard at it. When the complete inscription was translated and copied into a notebook, he would give me a new assignment. An additional notebook was maintained for the entry of every new English word; we devoted two pages for each letter of the alphabet. Inasmuch as we did not know any English, the book filled up very quickly. Each entry was made in accordance with the schema in the dictionary and the word entered was checked off in the dictionary. The dictionary pages were becoming frayed from use not only by us but by others who wanted to find an "American" word. Due to the age of the book, some of the pages began to crumble. To preserve it, Papa decided that a book binder had to be found; this book was too important to lose. He found one in Wiesbaden who said he could restore it and told Papa that it would cost a carton of American cigarettes. It was not an easy or quick task and would take at least a month of effort to complete. One carton of American cigarettes was a high price to pay but Papa felt it was a

Mainz / Kastel D.P. Camp - Germany - 1946

Jacob A. Kurdsjuk

Writing one of over 100 letters to people in the United States with a "New York" return address, who were searching for their relatives in the DP camps asking them to help him find his sister Mary in New York with whom he last corresponded in 1930.

necessary investment.

While the dictionary was being repaired, my daily transla-tions were put on hold allowing me more time for other young boy's activities. I made friends with two boys approximately my age. One was named Yurko and the other Vasily Basansky. Yurko's father was a priest and Mama considered him to be the "right kind of friend" to have.

Mainz/Kastel is located at the juncture of the Rhine and Main rivers. Not far from the camp flowed a canal which pro-vided access to Wiesbaden and became our favorite place to play. It was summer when we arrived at Mainz-Kastel, and the canal became our swimming hole. We also tried to catch fish with a string, a pole and a safety pin. However our efforts seldom succeeded since there was no barb to hold the fish once hooked, and we usually lost it. Frustrated, we searched for other solutions. Our new friend Konstantin came to the rescue. He was a very inventive fellow and loved to spend time with us boys. In Russia he was a mechanical engineer and a mathematics and physics teacher. His family was killed during the war and he loved every opportunity to be with children. He showed us how to make a hook with a barb and fashioned holding sticks for our poles so that we could play and explore while waiting for the fish to bite. Often he would come with us on our expeditions and teach us how the principles of phys-ics applied to ships, bridges and other structures. His explanations were never beyond our comprehension and we enjoyed learning everything he told us. He had a way with words and made every-thing so interesting.

Some DP camps attempted to organize schools, but the eth-nic conflicts and the lack of paper, books and pencils made it an extremely difficult task. As a matter of fact, most of the teaching occurred extemporaneously on the parade ground/football field. The dust became our notebook and any handy stick a pencil. I learned my multiplication table in this manner. There were many educated people in the camps; professors, teachers, jurists, au-thors, poets and members in every field of academia. They were anxious to convey what they knew to the eager young minds around them and did so at every opportunity. Their tales were so interesting that we often stopped playing football to listen. We heard a great deal of history and poetry, told from memory, and any available book was read aloud. It was too precious to be passed around. I was now almost eleven years old and had never attended a formal school for any length of time. I was to start first grade in Mariupol in 1941, but the Second World War and German occupation interfered.

The camp at Mainz/Kastel consisted primarily of Ukrainians, who were very chauvinistic and detested anyone who identified himself as Russian. They called us *Moscali* (Moscovites), a term coined in the seventeenth and eighteenth centuries when the princes of Moscow, together with king of Poland, occupied the territory known as Ukraine. At every opportunity the *Moscali* were given a "stick in the spokes." A Ukrainian Orthodox Church was established in the camp and used Pure Ukrainian Language - all of the prayers were translated into Ukrainian. To me they sounded very strange from those I learned in Russian and Mama said that they had "corrupted" the Slavonic Prayers and hymns. So, we went looking for a Russian Orthodox Church and once again Konstantin came to our aid.

During the Czar's time, Wiesbaden was a spa for the monarchs and intelligentsia of Europe, where "cures" were taken in mineral baths. On the outskirts of Wiesbaden stood a magnificent Russian Orthodox Cathedral of gray and pink marble with beautiful gold onion domes. It was only a tram ride away and two kilometers walk up the hill where services were conducted in pure Slavonic by the Very Reverend Paul and Bishop Filofey. It had a beautiful choir and next to the church was an expansive cemetery where a number of Russia's nobility and military officers were buried. The church has a very interesting history. It was said that it was built by a German prince who married a Russian princess during the time of the czars. They were so completely in love, that when the princess died giving birth to their first child, the prince vowed that she would never be forgotten and spent his entire fortune building the cathedral as a memorial to their love. Many train-loads of Russian soil were brought to the site creating a large mound for the church and cemetery. Artists, architects and sculptors were selected with great care and created a monument worthy of their love.

Interior walls are covered with magnificent frescoes and icons of Christ, His apostles and many Orthodox Saints. The iconostasis, which separates the altar from the congregation, was also gilded, similar to the cupolas, and the cathedral had two areas for worship. The ground level was used during summer and the subterranean level, to conserve heat, during winter. Entering the church, on the left one is immediately greeted by a sculptured bier of the princess in her sleep. The sculptor selected a piece of marble with white, gray and pink tints. The sleeping princess' exposed flesh has a definite shade of pink, almost lifelike, while the robes are pure white lying on a bier of gray. Directly below, in the subterranean level, is her actual grave.

The cemetery next to the church is the last resting place of many Russian nobles and generals who left Russia before the revolution. As one walks through this graveyard, he is surrounded by the history of Russia. Our family became ardent members of the church community and attended every Sunday and holiday, making many lifelong friends. Because of the church's history, many Russians came to pray on "The Russian Soil," some even took a handful of earth to be sprinkled over their grave when they died, to symbolize that they were sleeping on Russian Soil.

In addition to Most Reverend Paul, the church was the official see of Bishop Filofey who was a brilliant theologian and a powerful speaker. Every time he gave a sermon there was hardly a dry eye in the place. We were faithful attendees and inasmuch as there were very few boys or young men to assist the bishop during services, I was asked to begin training as an altar boy and acolyte to the bishop. Konstantin Us was also an ardent supporter of the church and steered many Russian Orthodox believers to it.

About two months after we settled in the Mainz/Kastel we had unexpected visitors, Fyodor and Liuba, whose wedding we celebrated in Wetzlar and who joyfully had returned to the "homeland" appeared at our door. They looked gaunt, tired and worn.

Russian Orthodox Cathedral-Wiesbaden

Princess' Burial Site Inside The Cathedral

Mama embraced them as if they were her own children. Had my brothers and sister survived the Siberian exile, they would have been approximately the same age. We hugged and cried together, as they told us of their ordeals during the past three months.

Everything was songs, vodka and slaps on the back as they boarded the "Train Home." As soon as they crossed the Polish border into Russia, things turned one hundred and eighty degrees. No longer were they welcomed as the returning sons and daughters to their Motherland but became the country's enemies, collaborators with Hitler. They were summarily kicked out of the train and lined up as a group of Soviet officers with guns drawn began to look over the assemblage. Every so often they grabbed someone from the line, kicking them toward a group of stout soldiers who packed them into the waiting trucks as they repeated, "We will teach you how to collaborate, a few years in Siberia will cleanse your thoughts!"

When the trucks pulled away, the "returnees" began to scatter, seeking refuge and escape wherever they could. Fyodor and Liuba escaped into a nearby thicket as the familiar staccato of machine guns reverberated in their ears. There was no need to question the sound, those taken away were being executed. Thus ended the glorious welcome of its children by "Mother Russia." Fyodor and Liuba walked, ran, and did whatever they could to get back to Germany and made it!

Fyodor was originally from Poltava, a city in the heart of the Ukraine, and had no problem being accepted at the DP camp in Mainz/Kastel. However our family was beginning to feel the animosity from the *Shchiry Ukraintsy*, the ardent Ukrainians. We were shunned in everything, beginning with food distribution and in all other services. The only time we were called first was when there was a dirty job to be done. Every time we boarded the tram to go to the church in Wiesbaden, there was always a loud "*Moscali*" call from somewhere. It was time to move on, but to where? Maybe some day we will find a place of rest and be accepted.

Papa began to ask the Red Cross people in Wiesbaden for such a haven and was told of DP camps in Aschaffenburg, in the

219

province of Bavaria. In several days the Red Cross was sending a truck to the Hanau depot which was only twenty kilometers from Aschaffenburg and we could be on it.

While we were waiting, we received the most incredible news of our lives, a telegram from America. It was from Aunt Mary and Uncle George/Kuzma Karol, informing us that they saw our ad in the Russian paper *"Novoye Russkoye Slovo"* and were following up with a letter. We almost could not believe our good fortune and gave thanks to God for His help and mercy. That Sunday we celebrated with *Molyeben,* a Prayer of Thanksgiving, at the Wiesbaden Cathedral. Our hope for life shone once again. Papa immediately wrote a letter to Aunt Mary, outlining our history since he last wrote to her in 1930. He took the letter to the Red Cross in Wiesbaden and had it mailed through the American Military Post, in hopes that it would get to Mary quicker and not get lost. Much of the mail in post war Germany was getting lost. The Director of the Red Cross office also had Papa prepare a telegram and sent it to Aunt Mary at the expense of The Red Cross. As it turned out he was from the same area of Queens, New York and knew where Aunt Mary and Uncle George lived. What is the probability of that?

God, indeed works in His mysterious ways and will never leave us or forsake us.

In subsequent letters we learned of the manner in which Mary heard of our search for them. It was another of God's miracles. Our plans to go to Aschaffenburg were postponed as we awaited for the letter from America.

Most of the people in our barracks were excited and happy at our news. However others were jealous of the *Moskali* and Papa became concerned as to whether the letter we were so eagerly waiting for would reach us. The mail process was in the hands of the Ukrainian administration but telegrams were delivered directly to the recipient by the German Post. Papa went to the post office in town, sought out the postmaster and gave him two packs of Pall Mall cigarettes, asking him to be on the lookout for our letter from America. The postmaster promised that when it arrived, it would be delivered directly to us and not the camp post office. He was true to his word, two weeks later the letter from America was delivered into our hands.

Chapter 14

Once More Struggling to Escape

When we received the letter from Aunt Mary, Papa answered it immediately, indicating our potentially precarious situation at the Mainz/Kastel DP Camp. He asked her not to send anything else through the mail, until we were able to give them a new and a more secure address. Next day he began to make arrangements for a ride to Aschaffenburg through the American Red Cross. The following week a truck would be going to Hanau and possibly we could get a ride. We didn't share our plans with anyone, including the couple who lived in the same room with us. The only person we trusted was Konstantin Us. Prior to departure, in order not to raise any suspicion in the camp, Papa, each time he went to work that week, took a small bundle to the Red Cross office in Wiesbaden. Konstantin agreed to smuggle out the big valise. He traded with the locals and was often seen with a variety of bags and would not arouse any suspicion. The office manager at the Wiesbaden Red Cross agreed to store the bundles in a janitorial closet and gave Papa a key. On a Thursday, in September of 1946, we said good-bye to Mainz/Kastel and on the ruse that it was a Russian Orthodox Church Holiday took the trolley to Wiesbaden. No one suspected anything since we often went to church. As we walked to the tram, the *"Moscali"* call was heard several times and we prayed that we were leaving this DP camp for the last time.

Konstantin met us at the Red Cross office where we said good-bye and agreed to stay in touch, promising to let him know of the conditions in Aschaffenburg when we settled. He also was uncomfortable in the Ukrainian camp and wanted to relocate to a place where he felt more secure and at ease. That afternoon we boarded the Red Cross truck to Hanau. Mama and I rode in the cab, while Papa curled up in the cargo compartment. Luckily, they were transporting blankets and Papa was able to make himself a bed, falling asleep as soon as the truck started rolling down the

Autobahn. He was exhausted, both physically and emotionally. The truck driver spoke German and some Polish and we had a wonderful conversation along the way. It was my first ride in a cab of a truck and I was full of questions. I wanted to know what all the gauges were about and how the gears shifted. During the drive, we stopped several times to check on Papa and make sure he was not affected by the exhaust fumes which may have leaked through the floor boards.

When we were nearing Hanau, the driver pulled off the road and asked Papa to get into the cab with us and get our travel papers from the Red Cross ready. Hanau was the warehousing area for the American Army and the Red Cross. When we pulled into the depot, the driver asked us to stay in the truck while he went in to report his arrival to the dispatcher and to find out if there was a truck going to Aschaffenburg that afternoon. He returned very quickly and the dispatcher wanted to know which of the four camps we were going to. We didn't know which of the four camps would be the best place for us, our papers just said Aschaffenburg. He went back to the office and soon returned followed by a huge man with a pleasant face who was completely bald, introducing him as Igor. Igor made daily runs to Aschaffenburg and was just about ready to leave. Igor quickly extended the largest hand I had ever seen to Papa. Papa was not a small man but his hand seemed childlike next to Igor's. Greeting us, Igor said *Zdravstvujte*/Hello. Igor was Russian! At first Papa thought Igor was from the Soviet army but quickly learned that he also was a DP and worked for the Red Cross as a driver. It turned out that he was from Vitebsk in Beloruss and this established an instant friendship. Igor was Papa's *zemlyak*, a clansman from the same area of Beloruss that Papa was born in. Papa knew the city well and through continuing conversation learned that Igor was telling the truth. At this point in our life we didn't trust anyone.

It was a two hour ride to Aschaffenburg and Igor wanted to get started right away in order to deliver the truck to the depot on time. He explained that he and his family were living at the Artilerie Kaserne, one of the four DP camps in town. Their camp was a mixture of nationalities, mostly Russian, Belorussian and some Ukrainians and thought that there would be no problem for us to be added to the camp rolls. Besides, he knew the police chief of the camp. When we arrived, Igor helped us carry our few belongings into the room where he and his family lived.

The room was quite large and his family was the only one in it. Apparently Igor had some pull to have a room all to themselves. He introduced us to his wife Anfisa, daughters, Lily and Helen, and a young son, Alexander. As we were getting acquainted, Igor left the room and soon returned with three folding army cots. We had a place to sleep and Anfisa shared some of their food with us. With the three of us added to the room, it was somewhat crowded but we slept peacefully that night .

In the morning Igor took Papa to the camp office and got us registered. Our papers from Wetzlar, Mainz/Kastel and Papa's ID from the Red Cross in Wiesbaden were sufficient documents to enable us to be accepted at the Artilerie Kasserne DP Camp. We could not stay in Igor's room and were assigned to another building. When we came into the room, there was a family of five already living in it. Their name was Zelezniak. Initially they were not too happy to share the room, since they had two grown sons and a daughter about my age named, Zina. After finding out that Mama and Papa were from Beloruss, and they were from Minsk, we were accepted, and began settling in on the left side of the room. Igor had already marshaled two beds with mattresses and pillows for us. He would bring some blankets that evening when he returned from Hanau. That afternoon Papa wrote a letter to Aunt Mary giving her our new address.

On the following day we received our meal cards and were officially added to the roster of the camp. This camp was similar to the one we were at in Wetzlar consisting of ten to twelve three story buildings each designated with a letter of the alphabet, our building was "B" and our room number was 17. Anton, the older of the Zelezniak boys, showed us around the camp pointing out the location for food distribution, medical, and work assignment areas. Each day one of the buildings in the camp was assigned to perform the necessary camp maintenance, cleaning and food distribution duties. We learned that at this camp most of the food was being provided by the German merchants and only a small amount by IRO, the International Relief Organization. It was primarily grains, vegetables and once a week four ounces of meat per person. The DP's, as we were called, supplemented their diets with what they were able to trade with the local German residents and what they gathered in the fields and forest.

It was the month of September and mushrooms, berries and nuts were plentiful in the forest. We learned that in a nearby village called Schweinheim, a company was trading one liter of oil for ten kilos of hazel or beech nuts. Any kind of oil, lard or fat was precious, since it was rarely available and only a small portion of our diet. Once in a while there was horse meat at the butchers, but we could not afford it.

The next day, Zina, her father, Mama and I went into the forest to gather hazel nuts and mushrooms. It was a very good day. We collected over twenty kilos of nuts, a basket of mushrooms and some wild berries. We took the hazelnuts to Schweinheim, exchanging them for two liters of oil. That evening we had a feast with the Zelezniaks.

This camp was also attempting to establish a school for the children, but nothing was in the offing for several months. However, the German school in Schweinheim was accepting children who spoke German for regular classes. I spoke almost fluent German and Papa said; "It is time that you started school." I was not very happy about it because this camp had many children my age and there was always a soccer game or some other activity on the former parade ground. Who wants to be in school when one can play? However, the following week I was registered in the sixth grade.

In one of the barracks, the camp had established a Russian Orthodox Church where services were held almost every day. One of the boys I met was Nikolai Sobolev who lived in the next building and was an altar boy. I told him that I had served at the church in Wiesbaden and he said he would introduce me to Father Yurij Turzansky, the priest of the church. The next Saturday I served at

Aschaffenburg Artilerie Kasserne DP Camp, Germany

*Camp to which the Kurdsjuk family escaped from Mainz/
Kastel. Photo shows Block "B".
Their room was on the second floor,
third window from the left.*

Aschaffenburg DP Camp Church
*Anatole, Rev. Yuri Turzansky, and
Nikolai Sobolev*

the vespers services and was accepted by Father Yurij. He was Ukrainian, but had been trained in a Russian Orthodox Seminary and said the prayers in Slavonic, not Ukrainian. Mama was overjoyed, there was a church so close and I was an altar boy.

The next time we went to look for mushrooms and hazel nuts, Nikolai and I had an additional task, it was to look for pine trees and gather the hardened sap to be used as incense in the censer at the church. Nikolai was my age and we became friends, doing everything together. Nearby there was an abandoned rock quarry where we went swimming and an apple orchard right next to it. We scrambled over the fence and stole apples. The orchard however was guarded by a great big police dog and we had to be careful but, a few well aimed rocks gave us sufficient time to stuff our shirts with apples and run. With all these fun things to do who wanted to go to a stuffy school. Besides, there were so many former educators in the camp who loved to instruct the children in their specific subjects that it was more interesting to listen to them, especially if one of them would read us a book. To be taught by the Catholic nuns at the German school was not a happy prospect. I got Papa to relent and let me be taught by the local intelligentsia, but he insisted that I practice calligraphy.

Several weeks after we settled in Aschaffenburg, we received a letter from America. Aunt Mary wrote that they were able to obtain a guarantee of work for us from a florist and a visa allowing us to come to America would arrive soon. What happiness, we were going to America! But, before this could happen, we had to go through a very intense physical exams at the American Consulate in Frankfurt. We also had to declare our intentions as to why we were going to America and not returning to our country of origin. Declaring our intentions was simple. We considered ourselves to be stateless, political immigrants. Papa was labeled "Enemy of the people by USSR" and did not adhere to any specific national regime. This made our acceptance under America's Immigration rules quite simple and made us exempt from specific national quotas.

I could not contain my happiness and told everyone I knew

that we were going to America. At that time everybody in the camps was trying to get out of the war torn Germany by any means possible and America was the ultimate choice. In Germany there was no meaningful work except in the demolition of bombed out buildings, chipping concrete from bricks. It didn't pay much, but even this work was allocated only to the German population as part of the *Wiedraufbau*, (rebuilding of Germany). Some countries, namely Australia, Venezuela, Brazil, Belgium and Canada were opening their doors to immigrants. One could go to America only if one had relatives who were willing to sponsor them. We were lucky, we had Aunt Mary and Uncle George in Jamaica, Queens, New York. Maybe, God had finally heard our prayers and would give us an opportunity for a new life.

We could hardly wait for the visa to arrive and checked the post office daily but it didn't come. Every week Papa wrote letters to Aunt Mary hoping to get some information. She told us that her son-in-law, James, had personally carried the request to Washington, DC and was assured by the Immigration and Naturalization Service that it was sent out several weeks ago to our address in Aschaffenburg via the American Consulate in Frankfurt. We waited several weeks more, but to no avail. Finally, Papa and I decided that we should go to the American Consulate in Frankfurt and make inquiries in person. I would go because I spoke German and Papa could share his thoughts with me.

We took the train to Frankfurt. Then we walked to the consulate building where we learned that in order to speak with someone at the consulate we had to make an appointment. All appointments had to be made in person. The appointments line extended over several floors and one had to remain in line. Otherwise, we would lose our place and attempts to get back in line at his previous place resulted in fisticuffs; people thought you were cutting in. What were we to do? Everyone wanted to go to America and would wait in line for any opportunity, no matter how remote, to apply and possibly be accepted.

We stayed in line until the consulate closed at the end of the business day. Before closing, an MP came around with a consulate official and handed out tickets with a sequential number indicating your place in line. The next day we had to line up according to the numbers issued. After we received our ticket, and on our way out of the consulate, we were accosted by a countless number of people who offered considerable money for a ticket. Our ticket was priceless.

Papa said we would go and see if his friend, Peter, who lived on the outskirts of Frankfurt/Hochst, and who could possibly put us up for the night. He opened his little brown book and found Peter's address. Peter lived in a private German home. It took us quite a while to find it, but when we arrived, Peter Polikarpenko was happy to put us up for the night. He told us that he had an American soldier friend working at the consulate who helped him to work through the quagmire of the visa process. He also told us that we should make sure the visa is not mailed, but handed directly to the recipient, us. Peter also had a relative in America and was waiting for a visa. We were very grateful for the lodging and the information and decided to follow his advice. The next day we returned to the consulate and spent the day waiting in line, chit number in hand.

It was Friday and the consulate was closing for the weekend. The MP started to hand out chits to those who did not have them and told us to return on Monday. We still had our chit from the previous day and were about twentieth in line from the Appointment window. Surely Monday would bring us success in locating our visa or at least find out its status.

Before returning to the camp in Aschaffenburg we made plans to stay with Peter in Frankfurt/Hochst. During the weekend we learned that Igor was making a run to Frankfurt and would be leaving very early on Monday morning. We gratefully accepted the ride since it would not only save us money, but would bring us there early to get in line.

When we arrived, the consulate doors were still closed, but people were already in line. Thank God, the Americans had several MP's controlling the crowd. Our chit number put us at the front of the line. By the time the doors opened the other ten people ahead of us showed up and we were still twentieth in line. That morning the consulate opened two additional windows so the line moved quickly. Soon we were at the Appointment window.

A very pleasant lady took our information and sent someone to check on our visa and asked us to sit on one of the benches beyond a wooden screen. We were making progress. We were inside the consulate and in an area where only the potential immigrants to America were allowed. Not much later she called us back and told us that indeed, several weeks ago, the visa was received and forwarded by mail to our address in Aschaffenburg. In all likelyhood, it was being held at the post office since a signature from the addressee was required. Papa and I explained that we had been asking at the post office daily, but were told that it had not come. The lady said we would have to go back to the camp post office and get a certified copy of the signed receipt and bring it to her for verification. That afternoon we ran to the train station and took the next train back to Aschaffenburg. We arrived in time to check with the German Post Office and were told that the visa indeed was delivered a week ago to the Artelerie Kasserne Post Distribution point. We ran the three kilometers to the camp, but were not in time, the Post window was closed and everything locked up. We would have to wait until the next day to pursue our quest.

That night we couldn't sleep and the morning could not come soon enough. At first light, we were at the office. Of course no one was there at that time and we had to wait an hour before a clerk showed up. We told him our story but he said he could do nothing for us and we had to wait for the Director to arrive and explain things to him. An hour later the Director finally showed up and once more we repeated our story. He went to a locked cabinet and came back with a ledger. It showed that the visa was delivered to: Block "B" and signed for, but the signature was not Papa's or Mama's. Someone else had taken our visa! The signature was so illegible that one could not decipher any of the letters. The Director said it would require police work to investigate. Since so many DP's were constantly moving in and out of the camp, records of movements were either unavailable or so out of date that it would be almost impossible to find the culprit who took our visa.

In the evening, when Igor returned from work, Papa went to see him and asked for help from his friend, the Police Chief. The Chief listened to our story but felt that there was little he could do. It was evident to Papa that the police chief's title was mostly ceremonial and he did not have any investigative or authoritative powers. A title was very important in the camp but had no meaning with anyone except the inmates. The visa wasn't lost - "Someone had stolen our visa!" Someone else was going to America instead of us. We got a copy of the signed ledger from the Director and prepared on the following day to return to the American Consulate in Frankfurt.

Apparently there was a lucrative black market for American visas. If one had gold a visa "could be found" and many visas were being "lost" all the time. We had no more gold ruble buttons, they had been long ago spent to purchase an extension for our lives. The only possible alternative was to go to Peter in Frankfurt/Hochst and see if his American Soldier Friend could help. First we had to tell aunt Mary that the address she had for us was "not safe" and that any future communications with us should be sent to Peter's address because he lived not in a camp but was renting a room in a regular home where the mail was delivered by the German Post Office, this would help insure that no one at the Artelerie Kasserne camp could intercept our mail. Peter would notify us when any mail came.

This time Peter went with us to the consulate and introduced us to his American friend who in turn brought us to an officer and explained our plight. The officer could do little to get another copy of our visa, it had to come through the official channels from America. He did place a note in our file stating that any documents, relevant to our immigration to the USA should not be mailed but handed only to a member of our family. Thus began our long wait in the corridors of the American Consulate in Frankfurt.

We returned to the camp devastated. That evening we went to church and prayed. Mama prayed that we could forgive the person who "stole our life"; but most of all, she prayed that God would take away the hatred from our hearts. There had to be a reason for this, only God knew why.

Letters from Papa kept streaming to Aunt Mary. Finally her son-in-law, once more traveled to Washington and persuaded the consulate to issue a new visa which was being sent via the diplomatic pouch to the consulate in Frankfurt and it should arrive within a week. During the wait, one of us was on the "consulate bench" daily awaiting the call: "Your visa has arrived!"

Papa and I were sitting on the bench when the call came. Hallelujah! We are on our way! But first, there was a requirement to pass a stringent American Health Commission exam.

A consulate person who had seen us on the bench for the past weeks helped us to be placed on the examination list for the following week. All of us had to go through a thorough medical evaluation. There were many communicable diseases in the camps; and who knew what other factors could possibly exclude us from reaching our dream of entering the United States. We were not overly concerned, except for Papa's heart condition, but having survived Siberia, KGB interrogations, the Dynamitfabrik, and the DP camps, his heart had to be in acceptable shape.

First we had to obtain certificates of chest X-rays, blood work, and medical history, from German doctors. It seemed that our concern was for naught, it was a breeze and we returned to Aschaffenburg that evening with a promise from the doctor that we would hear from the consulate within a week. We didn't trust anyone at the camp with such information and gave the consulate Peter's address. The following week we received a message from Peter that there was a letter for us from the American Consulate.

Papa took the next train to Frankfurt to retrieve it. It stated that Papa and I passed but Mama had to return for another X-ray. A spot was found on her lungs and it could possibly be tuberculosis. The disease was prevalent in the camps and many were infected.

Tuberculosis was rampant after the war due to the horrible conditions in the concentration and slave labor camps and was a definite reason for exclusion from entering America. Our hopes again were dashed. Mama remembered that she had pleurisy when she was a child and that there remained a scar on her lungs. She knew the scar was there from X-rays taken when she was hospitalized in Mariupol, but we had no copies of those films and the American doctors would not accept our word. The Medical Commission had to have proof positive. They would only accept X-rays taken within six months and had to compare the results. If there was no change, Mama could come to America. Mama could not believe that she was holding us back, and for the first time I thought she was angry at God as she prayed and cried uncontrollably.

This was late 1948 and another ominous cloud appeared on the horizon. Disputes over the military zones between the allies were raising fear of another conflict. Berlin was in the Soviet Occupation Zone and the Soviets were refusing access to the allies. The only access was by air; thus began the Berlin Airlift and the Cold War.

Mama was adamant about Papa and I going to America now while she remained to await results of the new tests. Papa and I refused. We had stayed together for so long and would not be separated now. They discussed another alternative; it was to send me to America first and they would follow once Mama passed the medical exams. I refused to go alone. It was only six months and I was sure that God would not separate our family. Look at what He has brought us through so far. There were three of us and I was their only child. Papa still had concerns about the possibility of war because of Berlin, but agreed to wait. He sent a telegram to Aunt Mary through the consulate informing her of the reason for our delay and asking if she could possibly send us a food parcel with meat and fats so that Mama's health could improve. Within a month we received a package at Peter's address. What bounty: hard salami, Crisco, chocolate, flour, rice, real butter in a can, and enclosed in an envelope was a twenty dollar bill. It was manna from heaven, we would make it!

Many months earlier Papa wrote Konstantin in Mainz/Kastel telling him that our camp was better, with minimal ethnic clashes or differences, and that he should come. After two weeks Konstantin arrived but could not get into our camp, settling in the adjoining camp called Bois-Brule. That camp had many Cossacks and Konstantin even found someone from his village.

During our six month wait, Papa insisted that I go to the German school in Schweinheim. I had no choice this time. At first it was difficult for me to adjust, even though by this time I spoke fluent German. But I was still an *Asulender*, a foreigner. Many of the children spoke Plat-Deutch, a dialect of the Bavarian region, rather than Hoch-Deutch I learned in Westphalen, but soon I was accepted and began to make friends. The schoolwork was easy, mostly reading and arithmetic and the notes the teacher sent home to my parents said I was doing well.

I was doubly blessed when I met Pavel Nikolayevich Glagolsky and his wife Anna Efimovna. They were former professors at universities in Russia, he a professor of literature and she of history. They were both in their late fifties and loved to share their knowledge with children. Pavel Nikolayevich became my tutor in Russian. In addition to the school work from the German school, I had Russian lessons. Pavel Nikolayevich loved poetry and recited Pushkin and Lermontov all the time. He was also writing poetry. He showed me how rich the Russian language was and how masterfully Pushkin used it to convey the deepest human feelings. My favorite Lermontov story was the *Mednyj Vsadnik* (Copper Knight). Pavel Nikolayevich had a book of this tale and made me memorize many passages and then recite them. Pushkin and Lermontov are the authors who raised the Russian language to its zenith.

Anna Efimovna told me stories of Old Russia when *Rytzari*, Knights, ruled the land. The most famous were named Rurik and Illya Murametz, both of whom defended Russia from the invading hordes. History was like a fairy tale and I loved it. It is because of these two wonderful people that I have retained my love for Russia, its people and the language.

The humdrum, uneventful life of the DP camp continued. The only excitement came when we learned that Belgium needed men for the coal mines and was accepting new immigrants.

Igor and his family were among the first to go, but he promised to stay in touch with Papa in case things did not work out. He wanted to come to America, but for now getting out of Germany was the first priority. Also, Australia was accepting people. Fyodor and Liuba Pugatchev decided that they would go to Australia together with Dr. Tadjayev and his wife. He was the one who performed pleurisy surgery on me in Wetzlar.

The six-month wait was finally over and we took Mama to be re-examined. Once more we traveled to Frankfurt where X-rays were taken as we awaited the results with fear and trepidation.

Again God was good, and after an hour or so the American doctor came out and said that there was no change in the size or location of the spot on Mama's lungs. In fact, it was most likely an old pleurisy scar. Mama could go to America! There were no words for the joy we felt as we danced in the halls of the American Consulate. The person in charge told us that soon we would be getting notification to prepare for immigration. All our papers were in order and they received a letter from the Church World Service stating that it would pay for our transportation. Our miracle of miracles had arrived!

As we walked, or rather floated, out of the consulate building, the sun was shining and at the bottom of the steps a vendor was selling the first flowers of spring, lilies of the valley.
I bought a bunch for Mama. Their aroma was so wonderful that it heightened our joy even more. From that time on, lilies of the valley became my favorite spring flower.

Our euphoria could not be contained as I shouted and danced down the street...

"We are going to America ! We are going to America!"

Chapter 15

We Are Going To America!

The train which brought us back to Aschaffenburg seemed like it had the best first class accommodations. When we arrived, we could not walk but ran to the DP camp wanting to share our good news with all we met. It took us several days to come down from our euphoria.

When Konstantin heard our good news, he was on our doorstep in a flash with a bottle of Schnaps and some sausages; where he got them we did not know. It is a Russian tradition that good news is celebrated with a party called *Zamochit/* Wet it down. We had one that afternoon but Mama sternly reminded us that we should thank God first. That evening Father Yurij celebrated a Thanksgiving *Molieben* at the Artelerie Kasserne Russian Orthodox Church with many of our friends attending.

It was also a wonderful day for our roommates. The Zelezniak family. They completed their papers to immigrate to Australia and received a notice to meet with the Medical Commission. It would most likely take six months or more, but they too, were on their way.

My teacher, Pavel Nikolayevich Glagolsky and his wife Anna Efimovna, were happy for us while troubled at the same time. We had become their family and now we would be leaving. Pavel Nikolayevich sat on our bed with his head bowed as tears streamed down his face. They had lost two sons during the war, and at their advanced age, would have difficulty getting out of Germany. He said to Papa: "Please do not forget us." Papa, in turn, promised that at the earliest opportunity, once we got settled, he would do everything in his power to bring them to America. Pavel and Anna's faces brightened as hope for life was renewed with that promise.

The Sobolev family was also happy for us and sad at the same time. They knew that their chances to get out of Germany were slim. Their daughter was a semi-invalid and they also had an

237

aged mother, not the best criteria for any nation looking for immigrant labor. We had many friends in similar situations and Papa promised he would work diligently to bring as many of them to America as he could. But first there was much to do to get ready for our trip of a lifetime.

We did not have much to take, just a change of clothes, several sweaters, uncle Boris' *kazukh*, two of Mama's dresses and some linens, but there was enough that Papa decided we must get a suitcase for each of us. We could not go to America with bags over our shoulders, we should have proper suitcases. Since immigration was in full swing, an entrepreneur in Aschaffenburg established a suitcase manufacturing business. The cases were built on wooden frames, covered with cardboard and gray print cloth. The hinges and locks were nickel-plated, and when assembled, resulted in an acceptable looking suitcase, even the closing clasps had locks. Papa ordered three; two large, one each for Mama and himself and a smaller one for me. They would be ready in a week, just in time for us to pack for Schweinfurt, the assembly point for immigrants going to America. We prayed it would be our last DP camp.

We didn't realize how much more remained to be done before leaving. I had to get a certificate that I attended a formal school for six months in Schweinheim. Papa said that his first priority, when we arrived in America, was to get me started in school. I was already fourteen years old and had no formal education. I didn't even speak English. From that day on our Russian/English dictionary got a lot of use. We had to learn at least a few words. We got additional help from the "Conversational English" book by Shidlovsky which was a best seller in the camps.

There were also countless DP camp bureaucratic procedures one had to go through before leaving the camp rolls. Most important was the return of "equipment" supplied to the DP's upon their arrival. Igor had been our supply and now he was in Belgium. It seemed more difficult to return items than to get them in the first place. We also had a constant stream of visitors, anxious to learn how we were so lucky to be approved for immigration to America.

My friends, who gathered at the football field where we were taught by the professors, already started to call me "The American." That moniker, although somewhat premature, made me feel proud. I was no longer an *Untermensch*, but would soon be an American, a real person.

One of our teachers was a man named Shirokov, an economist by profession. His son, Yurij, was a linguist and taught Russian at the Army Special Officers School in Hanau. Shirokov said to me, "Anatole, America is a wonderful land with many opportunities. But you must remember this, it is ruled by the dollar. Therefore learn how to make the most dollars and you will become a success, at least by American standards"

On the day we were leaving for Schweinfurt, it seemed that the whole camp turned out to say good-bye. I am sure it was not just for us; one other family was also leaving. Most likely it was to look at the transport that was provided by the Church World Service (CWS). It was a beautiful bus with padded seats. Our meager luggage was loaded into the compartments under the bus but there was a problem with our trunk. It was too big but we could not leave it behind; it had so many memories. The *kazukh,* would not fit into the trunk. Someone said they don't wear that type of coat in America. Papa gave it to Konstantin. Tearful and sorrowful good-byes were said because most likely we would not see most of our friends again. But there were also teras of joy, since we were a step closer to freedom and a chance for a new life.

On the way to Schweinfurt, the bus stopped at several other DP camps and by nightfall we arrived at our processing point. Before we disembarked a CWS representative came in with "The List," and called off our names. As we left the bus we were given a tag which was attached to our outside garment. This tag identified us as being sponsored by CWS and the control number was our pass to board the ship for America. It was not an OST patch, which we hated, but a ticket to freedom. It also gave us lodging and meal tickets while at the processing center. Our quarters were similar to the Kasserne we lived in at the other DP camps but here we had a room to ourselves and our own bathroom. What luxury!

We had to pass one last medical check before boarding the ship. It seemed like only a formality since we had passed the Medical Commission in Frankfurt only a month ago. However this final check was to make sure that we had not picked up any stray infections in the meantime. Two days before we were scheduled to go for the exam, Papa's face broke out in boils. Not just one or two small zitts but over eight "beauties" the size of a nickel or dime. Some began to "ripen" showing yellowish infection in the center. We knew that this malady would certainly delay us and we would not pass, hopefully not cancelled, but for how long? The Berlin blockade was still on, allied rhetoric was angry and who knows, any spat between them could turn into a deeper conflict, even a war. What would happen to us then?

Mama began scouring the place for a special brown ointment known to soften the boils, making them dissipate and heal. She found some, and smeared Papa's face with the smelly brown salve. Thank God we had a room to ourselves and Papa did not have to go outdoors. He looked awful and would frighten anyone who saw him. The ointment helped but some of the boils were still protruding enough to be noticed. We were scheduled to see the Medical Commission in a few days and prayed harder than ever before, wondering, why this trial was upon us when we were so close to freedom? Our bodies were still weak because of the a meager diet in the camps and it seems we were succeptible to every disease.

On the day before our scheduled final medical exam, Papa did one of the bravest things I ever saw or could imagine a man do. He took his straight razor, went into the bathroom and shaved off the boils. The pain he endured must have been horrendous. Then using an astringent bar, which he bought from a barber, he stemmed the flow of blood and carefully applied powder to his face. No matter how he tried to hide the boils, even to a nonmedical person it was evident that there was a skin problem; to a doctor it would be obvious.

The next day as we entered the examination room we continued praying that God would do something and let Papa pass the medical exam. The American doctor who examined Mama and me just listened to our chest, took the blood pressure and pulse, looked in our mouth and then stamped our documents "PASSED." When it came to Papa, he immediately noticed the face and before examining him put on rubber gloves and started to feel the bumps. Taking out a magnifying glass he examined the bumps more closely. Then, shaking his head, he said, "Anyone who can endure such pain deserves to go to America!" and stamped Papa's file "PASSED."

Thank You Lord! Tears filled Papa's and our eyes as Papa shook and kissed the doctor's hand uttering his first American words,"Thank you, thank you!"

Two days later we were told to get ready for the train trip to Bremerhaffen where the ship for America was waiting. It was a day's journey and we would go directly from the train onto the ship. Everyone was required to display their CWS tags and number. There was joy as we boarded the third class coaches. Everyone was so polite and smiling; something we had not seen for quite a while. The train rumbled north but this time it was not going to dump us on the snow or into a concentration camp. By evening, we pulled in right next to the harbor and for the first time since Mariupol smelled the salt air. Many memories and emotions came floating back. We were going farther and farther away from our original home. Would we ever see it again? As we started to board the ship, we heard many different languages and recognized many nationalities, but most of the passengers were Jewish. We recognized them by their long beards and curled locks on the sideburns; they were from the Orthodox side of Judaism.

Once more we were being separated. Men were going topside to the bow and stern of the ship while the women were sent to the center. We were told that the women were being placed in the center of the ship because there was less motion and would prevent sea sickness. Although we were being separated, we knew we were together and would be permitted to visit the womens' quarters once everyone got settled. We got the number of Mama's cabin and her berth, promising to return as soon as we settled. Papa and I were placed in the forward part of the ship.

Our ship was named SS General Black, a former troop carrier. The sleeping area was a large space filled with bunks one above the other. The bed was actually a hammock with a tarp stretched over it. Papa and I took the lower two berths and stuffed our suitcases under the lower one. The cacophony of speech in the area sounded like the Tower of Babel, so many different languages! The man who took the berth above us spoke Polish and we made our acquaintances. Before long there was an announcement over the loudspeakers in German, Polish and other languages which I did not understand, basically saying that we would be leaving in about two hours and those who wished to say good-bye to Germany could go top side.

Yes, we wanted to say good-bye to this continent and mainly this country which had put us through so much hardship and sorrow. The ship's horn gave several toots just when we came on deck. People were leaning on the rails waving handkerchiefs, but whom were they waving to? There were no relatives or friends at the pier. I guess it was good-bye to a life that was ending. Someone started a song with a Russian sounding melody but it was in the Jewish language. It was picked up by other voices and seemed like the whole ship was singing. The melody was both sad and joyous at the same time and I am sorry that I never found out what it was. We all just hummed in unison, each with our individual thoughts and apprehensions as to what lay ahead. Nothing could be worse than what we had endured.. Anything would be better than that . The Berlin Air Lift was still on but there was no war, and we were on our way to America, another blessing from the Lord.

It was 3:00 P.M. March 29, 1949 when we departed from shore! That afternoon we had our first meal on board ship. The dining hall was filled with people. As we passed through the line I said: "Thank You" to every sailor who served us and didn't refuse anything offered. Beef sausages, fresh vegetables, mashed potatoes, white bread, milk among other things, there was food we had not seen in years. The aromas were so delicious that everyone ate more than they should have. The salt air was invigorating and almost everyone went on the deck before returning to his bunk. The ship was slowly moving forward without any rocking motion, we were still in the estuary and had not reached the ocean. Mama said she was a little nauseated and wanted to go and lie down. The day had been too much for her. On the way down to the bunks I stopped by the dining hall in hopes of getting something else to eat. I wasn't hungry but everything had tasted so good. One of the sailors was cleaning up the serving trays and dropped several on the floor. I ran over and said, "I help you, Joe. OK?" He looked at me and said, "Sure." Then calling over to one of the other men in the galley he said, "Hey you guys, there's a kid here who speaks English!" The other sailor said, "Great, he can help me with the pots!" That is how I got my first job in America. He put me to work scrubbing pots in soapy hot water and I was happy to help these wonderful sailors.

Everyone went to bed right after the meal. As the evening and night progressed, the ship started pitching and rolling to the motion of the waves and many passengers began finding out that what they ate that afternoon was on the way out. *Mal-de-mare* began. The man above our bunk started just about after midnight and was followed by our neighbors. The acrid odor in the cabin was getting bad, to say nothing of the slippery floor beneath our feet. Cleanup groups were being organized but many of them added to what they were cleaning up, it seemed that this was a job that would never end. Papa and I were okay but how was Mama surviving?

When we finally slipped and slid to the womens' area, we found Mama green and pale. She was not tolerating the "sea voyage" well. Someone said that sour pickles settled the stomach. I ran to the galley to get some but there were many before me. However, I got two pickles and brought them to Mama. At first she turned away but then, when her neighbor ate one, she took a bite. It seemed to make her feel better. Papa and I stayed for a while to clean up around her area but soon desperately needed a breath of fresh air.

On deck the wind was blowing and the ship was pitching and

rolling making it difficult to keep balance without holding on to something. The fresh air felt good and it was warm enough that we decided to walk to the bow where the spray was churning. There were others at the bow, one of them said that he heard one of the sailors say that we were heading into a typical Spring Atlantic storm and that it might last for some time. I had heard and read about storms in the Atlantic and now would have a chance to experience one. Great! Papa and I were hungry and decided to go to the galley. This time there were only a few men in the line. Very soon we were enjoying a breakfast of sausages, eggs, ham and bacon with juice, toast and jelly. I did not know anything about the juice, but it smelled like a tangerine which I had tasted before, so it had to be good. I saved it for desert. We finished our breakfast and on the way out I took an orange for Mama and some dry toast. When we dropped off our trays my sailor from the previous day yelled over, "Hi! You gonna help?" I told Papa about the previous evening and he agreed that it was okay for me to help. I went over and was given an apron and brushes to scrub the pots and pans and felt like part of the crew. The hot water and soap wrinkled my fingers, but who cared, I was helping the sailors taking us to America.

The next day the storm got worse as the ship began really pitching and rolling so that we had problems keeping our footing. More and more people were getting severely ill but Papa and I were still all right, while Mama was not at all well. There was little that anyone could do, the ship's medical staff distributed some pills, but they would not stay down long enough to help. The nurse said, "We have never lost anyone because of sea sickness. Besides being miserable, everyone will survive." This gave us hope with Mama. After all she had suffered to lose her on the way to freedom, would be unimaginable. We prayed harder, once more asking God's help.

The storm lasted five days. On the fifth day as I was getting to be an old hand at pots and pans, one of the sailors gave me a banana. I had never seen a banana, much less tasted one. My only acquaintance with the fruit was from Daniel Defoe's epic Robinson Crusoe. I hungrily consumed the fruit and asked for some more. It was too much of a good thing and for the first time I began to experience the illness that was all around me. I got seasick and readily understood why some people said they wanted to die. Thank God, it only lasted one day. The following morning I had no ill effects from the bananas, but we also apparently outran the storm and the sea was calmer. Soon more and more people began to appear on the deck, and the chow line was getting longer. On the sixth day we were able to carry Mama on deck to give her some air. I do not know how much more she could have lasted. I had begun to think that the nurse's comment about not losing anyone to *Mal-de-mare* was about to be proven false. The fresh air rejuvenated her and for the first time in many days her face began to look normal, not green.

At the end of the seventh day, an announcement over the speakers told us that we would be sailing into New York harbor that evening. We were almost there! I wanted to be one of the first to see those blessed shores. America and the Statue of Liberty! My sailor friend in the kitchen told me in broken German that we would enter the harbor probably at night and would moor the following morning. I asked where would be the best place for me to to see America first, he said: "On the bow of the ship." That night I got some additional blankets and nestled myself on the bow lines. As we were getting closer and closer, fog started to roll in. Soon we could not see anything, but the captain continued on his course with frequent blasts on the fog horn. Soon the ship stopped and I heard the anchor drop. Strain as I might, I could not see anything through the fog. My eyes got so tired from the strain that I fell asleep.

I woke suddenly. It was still night and the fog was almost gone. On my right side I saw the most awesome sight. Lights were blazing in the darkness and there was the longest trail of blinking lights, very similar to the conveyor belts at the Dynamitfabrik. For a moment, I thought we were back in Wurgendorf and a chill ran down my spine. But the fresh salt air and the ship's surroundings brought me back to reality. A sailor passed by and I asked, "What is the name of the factory on our right?" He laughed and said, "Factory? That's no factory, that's Brooklyn." We were in the Verazzano

Narrows and the blinking lights were those of automobiles on the Belt Parkway.

When the sun rose, I spied the Statue of Liberty on our left. It stood out so majestically against the morning sky that my eyes filled with tears. I ran to get Mama and the three of us stumbled up the stairs to be welcomed by a beautiful lady in green. Our hearts almost burst with joy as we remembered reading the poem in "Life" magazine...

> "Give me your tired, your poor,
> Your huddled masses yearning to breathe free...
> Send these, the homeless tempest tossed, to me
> I lift my lamp beside the golden door."

Those words certainly applied to us and to the hundreds of others on the SS General Black.

We docked in New York at Pier 43 and were transferred to a ferry which took us to Ellis Island for processing. We were once more counted, examined, registered and returned back to the ferry. The process took no more than four hours and within minutes we were back at Pier 43. And when we docked at the pier, the sailor, whom I helped wash the pots and pans, gave me two dollars. My first, American earnings!

As we left the ferry, CWS personnel directed us to specific spots according to the first letter of our last name. "K" was right up front by the separating fence. We were told that those of us who had relatives meeting us would be processed first others who were continuing to other destinations in America would be handled separately. When we reached the square marked "K" we spotted our luggage including the trunk. We had no idea of what Aunt Mary and uncle Kuzma/George looked like, since our only photograph was over twenty years old. As we searched the faces of those beyond the fence, we heard, "Yasha! Yasha!," and spotted a little lady jumping up and down. Papa recognized her right away. We ran to the fence and started hugging each other without really knowing who was who. But before we were to be released to freedom, there was

246

one more process we had to complete. We had to sign the arrival forms for CWS.

The line was long and we were getting hungry. While Mama stayed by the fence with Aunt Mary, Papa and I took a place in line. It was moving very slowly and right in the middle of the whole crowd was a man with a wagon covered by a striped umbrella, who was chanting...

> "Get your hot dogs while they're hot,
> Some with mustard some with not
> Some with kraut and some with peppers,
> You can't get it any better!

His sing-song promotional chant did not seem to repeat, and has stayed with me all these years. I went to the wagon and ordered three hot dogs and two Coca Colas. Proudly, I gave him one of the dollar bills the sailor bestowed on me. The vendor, gave me two coins change.

Mama, Papa, and I shared our first truly "All-American meal."

Epilogue

Papa was true to his word. Two weeks after arriving in the United States, I was enrolled in school, without knowing English. Here also God's hand was with us. When I was brought to the North Bellmore Public School by Aunt Mary's daughter, Nina, we learned that the principal of the school spoke German, and I was able to answer his questions on a variety of subjects. According to his evaluation, I was enrolled in the seventh grade at the age of fourteen.

Papa and Mama began working at Dauernheim Florist for $.75 and $.50 per hour, respectively. After we applied for and received our First Papers, showing the intention of becoming American Citizens, Papa immediately began the process of getting visa applications for those of our friends still in Germany's Displaced Persons Camps.

Following are the families Mama and Papa helped bring to America:

First to arrive was Konstantin Us, followed by Pavel Nikolayevich and Anna Ewfimovna Glagolsky, then Dr. Stephan Shpikalov and his wife, Olga.

Six months later Igor Gousseff and his family of five arrived from Belgium followed by the Sobolev and Stolarenko families. The last group was the Iwanov family also from Belgium, where Ivan worked in the coal mines.

In total, Papa and Mama sponsored twenty five people to the United States, providing commitment for work and housing without any encumbrance on the American government. We received our United States Citizenship in November of 1954 at Ebbets Field in Brooklyn, sworn in by the Secretary of State.

Papa could not work in his profession as an engineer and chose to become a carpenter. Mama worked for four years, until November, 1953 when, while walking home from work at 6:30 PM, she was struck by a car driving without headlights, sustaining major injuries.

For a year and a half, we continued living in the house we rented from Adam Bidzukiewicz in North Bellmore, Long Island, New York. When the Stolarenko family arrived, it became necessary for us to look for a home of our own. We didn't have much in the bank and had to borrow five hundred dollars from a lady who lived just down the street for a down payment on a four room bungalow in Bellmore. We moved to our house on the fourth of July 1951. Once more we had a home of our own and felt certain that it would not be taken from us, as we began a new life.

Most of the people Papa and Mama brought to USA settled in the area of East Meadow, Long Island and I can remember only a few weekends when we didn't have gatherings at the Kurdsjuk home at 702 Swenson Place under the maple tree. Much of what is contained in this book came from my recollection of Papa's discussions with those gathered around the table, after many *Na Zdorovyas*! and has been my most valuable resource.

If the reader has an opportunity to visit the Ellis Island or the Statue of Liberty National Parks Monument, in New York, he can find the Kurdsjuk Family names inscribed on "The Wall Of Honor" on Panel Number 530 as:

Jacob A. Kurdsjuk, Olga Makarenko Kurdsjuk
and Anatole Kurdsjuk

Jacob Zacharyevich Kurdsjuk/Papa died on October 22, 1972 and is buried at St. Vladimir Russian Orthodox Cemetery in Jackson, New Jersey. After Jacob's death, Olga/Mama made a trip to Russia with her cousin Anne in 1975 and was able to see many of her siblings and relatives. She died on January 16, 1991, just at the start of the conflict with Iraq, and sleeps next to the love of her life. A family monument was erected at the burial site and lists the names and dates of their deceased children and Jacob's parents, Zachary and Yelena. Our life, after arrival in America, was also full of miracles, but that's another story.

The saviors of the Kurdsjuk Family

Front - Jacob Kurdsjuk, Mary and Mike Wroblewski.
Back - Olga Kurdsjuk, Mary and Kuzma (George) Carol
The people who brought us to America.

Mary Wroblewski was searching for her brother in Germany. Jacob wrote to her because she had a "New York" return address and Jacob knew his sister Mary lived in New York.

It was another miracle of how Mary learned that Jacob was searching for her. When Mike Wroblewski placed the ad in *Novoye Russkoye Slovo,* Uncle George was a subscriber to the paper but, he did not see the ad. A friend of his went fishing and, after cleaning the catch, was wrapping the remnants in the newsprint, when he noticed the ad and called Uncle George.

APPENDIX

Letters

Glossary

Notes

Bibliography

Letters

Note of Clarification:

The original letters were saved by Jacob's cousin Mary Karol in the USA. Jacob wrote them while hiding after his last escape from Siberia and Mary gave him these letters upon his arrival in the United States in April, 1949.

During this time period, the Russian style of correspondence began with extensive and effusive greetings and best wishes. I have removed these lengthy salutations from all but the first letter for brevity. Each individual was addressed by his first name and the patronymic - Jacob father's name was Zachary, hence he is addressed as: Yakov Zacharyevich, Jacob son of Zachary. In addition, a first cousin was considered to be a sister once removed, that is why Jacob often refers to Mary as "Dear sister," or Maria Andreyevna, since her father's name was Andrey.

The following letters are included:

June 27, 1930
August 17, 1930
September 7, 1930
September 12, 1930
January 19, 1947

Jacob's letters are a call for help, during the most difficult time of his life, and show his continuous desire to come to America.

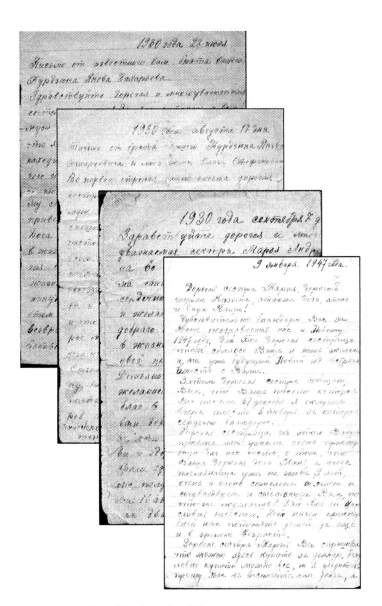

Jacob's Original Letters To Mary

First Letter Dated June 27, 1930

This letter is from your brother Kurdsjuk, Jacov Zaharyevich. Greetings my dearest and respected sister Maria Andreyevna, your husband Kuzma Demyanovich and your children. I wish to inform you that I and my wife Olga and brother Alesha (Alexei) are well thanks be to God and wish the same for you, good health to you and your family . We send you our heart-felt greetings and best wishes in your life.

Now I want to fill you in, my dear Sister Maria Andreyevna about our life, and specifically about my existence. My life is good for nothing and I am living like a rabbit under a bush. On the tenth of May I was arrested in Moscow when I escaped from the North (Siberia) on my way home in the attempt to obtain the return of our property, for three days I was without food or water, or any other human considerations.

I was detained three plus months in prison from May 10 to July 1, almost two months, then once again I was returned to Siberia but not to the same place where we were initially sent. Thieves robbed me of everything I had and I was left with only what I was wearing, a shirt, a coat, my trousers and boots. Thank God I did not take off the boots to sleep.

After all of this I decided I had only two choices, die or try and get back home. On the first of July I stepped out into the woods and took off on foot. I walked, hopped freight trains and walked some more. I did not have any money for the ticket, but I also did not have any papers and somehow got to my brother Boris where I spent three days. From there I took off for the homeland. (Our papers were confiscated by the government when we were first exiled as kulaks). Thanks to Boris, he bought me a ticket and gave me some money for the trip and I arrived home on the seventeenth of July. Here I am persecuted and am afraid to see even my oldest and best friends.

Well my dear sister, when I get hungry, I go and knock on the door of people who know our fate. Most of them ask you in and are happy to feed and water you, then once more I run and hide from the bad people. One can not live in this manner for long, but where does one go. God knows.

This is why my dear sister Maria Andreyevna I ask you to help me in my grief, if it is at all possible to get me to America, please do not deny me and I will be forever grateful and will never forget you, once again I beg you, help me, because I can not live this way for long. My conscience does not allow me to go and beg .

You ask me what is our life like. This is a brief history of my life. My wife is living with her brothers. I had two children, a girl 5 years of age and a boy one year three months . They died in Siberia a week and a half from each other, one right after the other. The girl (Anastasia) on April 13th and my son (Sergei) on the 23rd of April. My brother Alexei is living with uncle Stephan and Sergei is still in the same camp in Siberia, God knows how he and my parents are.

It has been a month and a half since we had any news written or otherwise. Where they are today I do not know. Are they still alive or have they died? We know nothing about them.

You, my dear sister, ask about Boris. He left home before we were exiled and is living in Ural where he is working as a laborer. I was where he lives and to the best of my knowledge he is all right and has no urgent needs. The work is hard and the food is insufficient, but what can one do? Most importantly, there is little meat or fat, butter or oil but he is surviving. He misses the family very much; you remember what a soft heart he had and cried all the time. When I arrived at his

257

place from that point on he didn't stop crying as he looked at me and remembered our life back home and my children.

You also say that you can not understand the suffering, and what have we done against the government ? I will tell you, we did not do anything bad, we just worked hard. Before exile we had horses and cattle, probably the best of anyone around. On our Khutor (the land allotted them) we dug canals and drained the swamp, the land became very productive. There are people amongst us who are jealous of us, we even made the swamp productive. Because of the jealousy they informed the government that we were hiring people. As you know we ourselves hired out with papa and wanted to earn some money. The government put heavy taxes on us 450 rubles and demanded 250 pud of grain (Pud is an old Russian weight measure, 1 pud = 36 pounds), All this on four desiatyns of land (Desiatyna is a land measure, one (1) desiatyna = 2.7 acres). As you remember there were nine members in our family and we needed grain for the horses and cattle. Then on the 7th of March we were exiled from our homeland as kulaks (See description in Chapter 4) and are threatening us with starvation in exile. People are escaping to where ever one can.

This is our situation, therefore once more I beg you, help us. Our address is as follows:

Slutsk, Bobrujsk Area, Sobornyj Pereulok No. 7, Meyer Zelagin, for Makarenko.

With greetings, your brother Jacob, my wife Olga and brother Alexei. Awaiting your reply.

Letter Dated August 17, 1930

We received your letter. Thank you for not forgetting us. Uncle Stephan also received a postcard from my parents in which my father is begging all of the relatives and friends for help. He is asking them for bread and fat, he didn't say anything else about their lives, who is still alive and how their health is. Are the three of them still together? Were they able to get work? We know nothing about their life or health, but since we ourselves were there and experienced similar circumstances, we believe things have not improved.

My dear sister Maria Andreyevna, you say to my wife that it is fortunate she escaped this bottomless pit and that I have returned to her. Yes, thanks be to God I have returned home, but what I had to endure during the months of incarceration is difficult to write in a letter. After my three months in jail, I was once again returned north, but not to the same area from where I escaped, saw my brother Boris, then returned to our homeland. Here we live like rabbits, afraid of every sound in the bush. They have started capturing people like us and are sending them to God knows where. This is where Alesha is today. As you know he was living with your sister Nastia, when some people from the collective deceived her husband, and said that Alexei had to register with the police, where he was arrested and has been in Slutsk prison for two weeks. Uncle Stephan got Alexei's school papers, and went to Minsk in attempts of getting him released, but we will not hold our breath for the success of his endeavor, since people like us are treated worse than dogs, we have no place to go, just suffer and die.

Well my dear sister Maria Andreyevna, here is the address of my dear parents, and I am asking you to help these poor folks. In May when I ran away and saw them for the last time, papa was skinny and all gray, if you saw him you would not recognize him. Mama has also aged a great deal, as you may recall she has always been sickly and the northern climate is aggravating the situation, medical help is nonexistent. This is their address:

Severovodsky Okrug, Toymushka Rayon, Pochtovyj Otdel "T" Village of Toymushka, Kurdsjuk Zachary, F.(edorovich).

You also ask Olga if I know that the children died. My dearest I now, and how I loved them! They are gone from me! When I was working in the forest, Olga sent me a note that the children were ill. I immediately ran from the work site to Kotlas, but when I got there, my daughter had died just a few minutes before, Nastia was no longer there, my son was sick but I was still able to see him alive; he died the following week in my arms. May God remember them in His Kingdom, and may their memory be eternal! "Vechnaya Pamyat". They may be fortunate that they did not survive. Had they lived, they would have had to endure persecution by the plagued police for the rest of their lives. I wanted to let you know that when I arrived home, I sent you a letter in which I described our life after exile, and why we were exiled. I hope you received it, and learned that in Russia truth does not exist, and people have no love within them. Goodbye for now, greetings to all. Yakov and Olga Kurds. We beg your help. We beg your help, and will be forever thankful. Write to previous address, via Meyer.

September 7, 1930 - Bondary Beloruss

First of all my dear sister Maria Andrejevna, I want to let you know that my wife and I are alive, and wish you the same, good health etc...

We received your letter, written August 18, on September 4, 1930 which contained two dollars, we thank you for both of them, and again thank you for not forgetting us.

I want to let you know that I have been home since July 17. Life is totally boring and grim. My wife since the 4th of August is hiding in the forest, and we do not know how we can survive a life like this? We must hide so that even our neighbors should not see us.
When I first arrived I wrote you about our life. On the 10th of August we received your letter and responded immediately, in which we described the life of my father and mother.

You ask Olga, how were we transported to the North, and what kind of life greeted us there? I will describe it to you. We were taken to Slutsk on the 7th of March, to the railroad station, where we were immediately loaded into freight cars, 40 -50 people per car. There was no place to sit, saying little of laying down. The children were exhausted. During our trip of seven days, we were not allowed to exit the freight cars, even if you were dying. Finally on the 15th of March we arrived in Kotlas where we were settled in earthen barracks without heat. The barracks were worse than the cattle cars, each of them housed about two hundred people. After several days, children started dying, more than one hundred per day, and we were powerless to help them, there was no medicine.

When we left Slutsk it was spring and warm, when we arrived in Kotlas we were greeted by severe winter with temperatures of minus twenty degrees and barracks without heat, this is

261

what greeted us upon arrival. In addition, we did not get any bread or food, and little by little children began dying, including our children, Nastia 5 years old and Sereza one year and three months.

We received a letter from father in which he is begging us to send him sukhari(dried bread), since they are dying of hunger. Although we ourselves are in dire circumstances, we were able to send them a small package, but do not know if they received it. You are asking for their address, it is as follows: Severodvizinski Okrug, Toymskij Rayon, "T" Pochtovyj Otdyel, Derevnya Toymushka, poluchit K. Z. F.

Please help us and my parents, the unfortunate, in whatever way you can my dear sister.
As I wrote you before they are starving and we in our circumstances cannot help.

NOTE: The last page of this letter was lost, all efforts to find it failed.

Letter Dated September 12, 1930

I wish to inform you that my wife and I are well, and wish you the same. We received the letter written by your husband, thank you for not forgetting us. Two days prior we received your letter and the enclosed gift, thank you again. I am glad that my letters are getting to you and that you learned of our unfortunate life and our conditions, we do not know when and if it will change in the future, therefore my dear sister and Kuzma Demyanovich I once more ask for your help to get us to America. Dear Kuzma you write that it will take some time to accomplish my request and that you must find a farmer who can guarantee work. It matters not if it takes a year, two or more just that we can escape this life which we are enduring today, all for our hard work and calluses on our hands. My dear sister you know of our hard work and all of a sudden we are labeled kulaks and cannot get work anywhere, how does one deal with such untruth and lies, all that is left to us is to die. Once more dear Kuzma Demyanovich, if at all possible please help us to escape from this horrible chasm, even if it takes some time, just as long as we can escape this lying environment. I visited Andrej and read your letter to him. He said that it is possible to cross the border but I am afraid to try it since I have no papers, mine were taken in Slutsk when we were first exiled and I can't even get a certificate of any kind even that I am a farmer. Without it I do not know how we can survive in the future, therefore once more I beg you Kuzma Demyanovich please try as hard as you can to help us and I will never forget you or your efforts in the future. Good-bye for now yours J.Z. Kurdsjuk

Letter dated January 9, 1947
Written from Aschaffenburg D.P. Camp

This letter defines the correspondence process to be used in sending the Affidavit for immigration to America and asks help with a food package.

Dear Sister Mary and brother-in-law Kuzma thank you for your New Year's greetings for 1947. I pray the Lord will hear your prayer and your daughter, son-in-law and your grandchildren! From the bottom of my heart I pray that the next year we will be celebrating with you. I want to tell you that your letter which you mailed on Dec. 27, I received yesterday, that is on the 8th of January, thank you from the bottom of my heart.

Dear sister from this letter we learned the very sad news of your eldest daughter Mary's death almost nine years ago, our deepest condolences to you both. But what is one to do? May the Lord grant her Eternal Life. There is nothing more painful than the loss of a child, especially a mature one.

My dear sister, you ask what can be purchased here for dollars, anything can be bought, but I sincerely ask you, please do not send us any money, but save the money for the expenses to bring us to you, for this kindness we will never forget you and be forever thankful.

Today, my dear sister, our life is worse than it was in Kastel-Wiesbaden, because UNRA, the United Nations Refugee Association, is providing less food, we receive primarily the German residents' allocation which has very little fat in it, and for us (as you know) who have suffered so much in the concentration camp, much more substantial food is needed, if we are to regain at least some of our strength. It is difficult to live like this, although UNRA is helping but still, it is hard. Once more I ask you my sister, do not send money. If it is possible for you to send us a food parcel, we will not refuse it, this will be substantial help to us. Most importantly include foods with more fats and oils. We will be eternally grateful for any help you can provide.

Dear sister, your last letter I received via my friend Peter Polikarpenko. He is my dearest friend and is recommending that I send you the address of his best friend, a former American soldier, who lives in New York and who can help you to obtain the affidavit.
His address is: Edward Mamchur, 425 East 6th Street, New York, New York. Sincerely I beg you to visit him, he speaks Russian and Ukrainian very well, is a wonderful person, and can possibly help you with the affidavit procedures since he knows how we unfortunate "DPs" live. He has also visited my friend Peter at his place of residence at Frankfurt-Hochst.

Also, my dear sister, in this letter I enclose (already for the fourth time) another application. The errors were mine, since in your last letter you needed information about my wife. She was born in the village of Bondary, her father was Stephan Makarenko and her mother was named Mary, this makes her Maiden Name: Olga Stepanovna Makarenko.

Dear sister Mary and brother-in-law Kuzma, since the time we transferred from Kastel-Wiesbaden, I have written you many letters, I am once again asking you to respond to the address shown on the envelope, that is to the address of my best friend Peter Polikarpenko, who will get the letters to me.

Now my dear sister, if you or the organizations which are involved in processing the paperwork, need my address, please give them the address shown on the enclosed forms : Frankfurt-Main-Hochst, Arbeitheim, 110 (bei Frau Voland) fur Kurdsjuk, your letters should be sent to the name whose address is shown on the letters they send to you for me. Now then, my dear sister, I did not fill in my citizenship on the forms, for me it makes no difference, whether I am a Russian or Polish citizen, what is most important, is for us to get to you as quickly as possible; fill in whatever you think will speed up the process.

For now good-bye with kisses your brother J. Kurdsjuk. Greetings from my wife and son, who wish you the best in your life.

Now, I think the time has come for me to be known by my given name, Jacob. It has been seventeen years that I have had to live as someone else. Let us forget the past and begin anew. Wishing you the best and awaiting your response from the New World.

Glossary

Achtung (Ger.) Attention!

Alexander II Czar of Russia (1881 - 1894) sometimes called czar the liberator, associated with many reforms of 1880 -1890, including the emancipation of the serfs; assassinated by a "revolutionary". Father of the last Russian czar Nicholai II.

Alexandra of Hesse the czarina, wife of czar Nikolai II, the last czar of Russia. The whole family was executed by the Bolsheviks in 1918.

Anastasia daughter of Jacob and Olga. She died at the age of five in Kotlas, Siberia, a GULAG to which the Kurdsjuk family was exiled as kulaks.

Antonescu, General assigned by Hitler to head the Romanian armed forces which fortified the Wehrmacht in Nazi occupied zones.

Aranets town in the Northern part of Siberia, in the Urals and the location of the second GULAG, to which Jacob Kurdsjuk was exiled.

Arbeit Macht Frei (Ger.) - "Work shall make you free." A slogan used by the Nazis in Slave labor and concentration camps to induce inmates to work. A metal banner of the slogan hung over the main entrance at the Auschwitz Extermination Camp.

Article 58 Portion of the 1926 Bolshevik Legal Code which defined the rules of law for the Soviet population, and the rule under which millions of Russians were exiled and died.

Azov, The Sea of A body of water located in the southern part of Russia/Ukraine connecting to the Black Sea, near the Crimean Peninsula.

Azov Stal (Steel) Steel production facility in Mariupol which Jacob helped build, and where he worked from 1933 to 1943.

Babushka (Rus.) grandmother

Banki (Rus.) a glass cup used in helping to cure respiratory infections by drawing blood to the infected area.

Banja (Rus.) communal bath, used by workers.

Batyushka (Rus.) father (used in addressing a priest) or any male in high esteem.

Bedarka a Ukrainian two wheeled horse drawn cart.

Behi (Rus.) meaning run

Berezniki Town in Ural Mts.where Boris lived, and to which Jacob ran after his escape from the GULAG in Aranets.

Blatnyje (Rus.) members of the criminal underworld in Russia.

Blitzkrieg (Ger.) the Lighting War, as described by the SS and the Wehrmacht

Blokha (Rus.) "the Flea," Anatole's next door neighbor. The name children called Pavlik Yudin because of his small size.

Bobik Name of the Kurdsjuk family's guard dog in Mariupol.

Boris, Zacharyevich Jacob's' younger brother who escaped to the Urals before the family was exiled to Kotlas, Siberia in 1929.

Bolshaya Sliva A Village in Beloruss near the town of Slutsk, and the birthplace of Zachary and Jacob Kurdsjuk.

Bondary Village in Beloruss near Slutsk, and the birthplace of Olga Stepanovna Makarenko, wife of Jacob Kurds-juk.

Bolshevik Segment of the revolutionary cadres in Russia ascribing to itself the larger contingent in the communist party.

Boris Godunov Czar, who in 1580 issued a decree to control the serf's movements.

Boze Moi (Rus.) Exclamation!" Oh My God!"

Burgemeister (Ger.) mayor or head of a city.

Borovik (Rus.) an aromatic wild mushroom prized by the serfs. It represented a large portion of flavoring for soups and grain dishes; eaten fresh, fried, boiled, pickled or dried during the winter months.

Bosenky (Rus.) barefoot

Bozenka (Rus.) a child's affectionate name for God.

Budienovka A peaked hat worn by the Bolshevik cadres during the 1917 Revolution in Russia with a large red star on the front and ear flaps on the sides.

Buryak, Ivan Name on the papers found on the corpse Jacob stumbled upon in the Taiga while escaping from the Aranets GULAG.

Caftan (Rus.) a man's warm three quarter length coat.

Chabak (Rus.) type of fish found in the Sea of Azov, and the workers favorite zakuska, an antipasto.

Chernyj Voron (Rus.) the "Black Maria" used by the secret police to transport prisoners for interrogation.

Collective (Rus.) Stalin's attempt to compete in the international markets, forced the farmers to "join" the *kolhoz*, which became the basis of the USSR agronomy and economy in which all were supposed to work toward the same goal, and help the growth of International Communism. It never worked because there were no incentives for the participants.

Comendatura (Rus.) A District ruling body responsible for enforcement of laws.

Commissar (Rus.) A Title given to the head of the local communist organization.

Crazy Zachary nickname given to Zachary Filipovich Kurdsjuk, Jacob's' father, after he chose the swamp for his khutor.

Dedushka (Rus.) grandfather, also a term ascribed to any elderly male.

Desiatina Russian land measure; 1 desiatyna = 2.7 acres.

Detka (Rus.) affectionate, my child.

Dosvidanye standard Russian parting greeting, good-bye or rather au revoir, "till we meet again."

Duma (Rus.) the Russian senate under the czars. The name has also been appropriated by the current, post-Glasnost, Russian government.

Dwoskin, David cousin of Dr. Zelagin who helped Jacob get established in Mariupol after his last escape from Siberia,

Dvorianie (Rus.) Russian nobility or gentry. A post established by the czar after defeat of the Tatar hordes in the 1400's who were given extensive powers in control and ownership of serfs.

Ersatz brot (Ger.) false or manufactured bread, served in slave labor camps and made from ingredients in which flour was the lowest component, with sawdust being the main ingredient. Combined with water It filled the belly but provided minimal nutrients.

Ersatz caffee (Ger.)"false/manufactured" coffee usually made from molded grains which were roasted or rather burned and then ground to make "coffee."

Etap (Rus.) a column of prisoners traveling under guard.

Fialka (Rus.) tender night blooming violet flower with an enthralling aroma..

Ferdinand, Grand Duke of Austria assassinated in 1914 in Sarayevo, Serbia, whose death is said to have caused the beginning of World War I.

Five Year Plan The quotas developed by the Politbureau for production in all industries in Stalin's attempt to increase production in order to break into International commerce. None of the set objectives were ever achieved.

Gogol, Nikolaj A Russian humorist and author of "Dead Souls," a novel about the sale of a village with an inflated count of serfs.

GPU (Rus.) Gosudarstvenoye Politicheskoye Upravlenie, the name ascribed to the Soviet Secret Police in the 1930's.

Gubermeister (Ger.) The person in charge.

GULAG Glavnoye Upravlenie Lagerei - The Main Camp Administration. A name given to the camps for exiles during the Stalinist period in the USSR.

NOTE: In 1929 Stalin decided to speed up the Soviet Union Industrialization and used forced labor to do it. At the same time the Secret Police began to take control of the penal system, taking it away from the Judicial System. By 1930 camps could be found in every part ofthe Soviet Union and over 15 million individuals passed through this horror.

Hauptfuhrer German term given to "The Head Man".

Hero the name Boris gave to his pet bull .

Henka Anatole's friend in Mariupol, the biggest boy on the street.

Hilfarbeiter (Ger.) volunteer worker, a false term the Nazis assigned to the forced labor camp inmates, implying that they volunteered for work, thereby attempting to obfuscate the term "Slave Laborer".

Holtzshuhe (Ger.) shoes made from sail cloth with wooden soles issued to slave labor inmates.

Imenye (Rus.) an estate, usually of nobility

Irina Olga's younger sister.

IRO International Refugee Organization, it provided food to the people in the Displaced Persons Camps in Germany after World War II.

Intelligentsia (Rus.) term used for the educated population who were the guiding light in development of the Russian nation under the czars.

Kaluzin, Anatoly Author's friend on Vishnevyj Pereulok with whom he endured the 500 km forced march to Kirovgrad in 1943.

Kapusta (Rus.) cabbage, sauerkraut.

Kalka A River near Mariupol, said to be the site of a great Tatar Victory Feast over the Russian Rytzari in the 15th century.

Kasha (Rus.) grain gruel made from grouts, corn or wheat, and the main portion of the peasants diet.

Kazukh (Rus.) sheep skin coat, similar to the one given to Jacob by his brother Boris.

KGB (Rus.) Name of the Soviet Secret Police after WW II.

Khata (Rus./Ukr.) a serf's domicile, a bungalow

Knut (Rus.) a horse whip, also used for punishment of the peasants for any infraction or disobeyed order during czar's time.

Khutor (Rus.) a piece of land allotted to the serf by his pomeshchik/land owner.

Kirov Town in North-eastern part of European Russia, in the Ural Mts.

Kolkhoz (Rus.) a collective of peasant farmers, the mainstay of the Soviet agronomy.

Kotlas City in Siberia near the Arctic Circle, and a camp for exiled *kulaks*.

Kulak (Rus.) A Term assigned to anyone who posses more than the average farmer, anyone who hired workers to assist in any endeavor. In 1930 all peasants strong in management, work or conviction were so called and the term was used to smash the strength of the peasantry.

LCHD (Rus.) radio "call letters" coined by Soviet citizens for any broadcasts of propaganda. The initials in Russian/Cyrilic alphabet stand for : Lopaj Chto Dayut, Eat What You are Fed.

Lenin, Vladimir Ilych A Russian revolutionary who together with Trotsky led the Russian revolution in 1917, which brought the Bolsheviks to power establishing the communist regime in Russia.

Leonid Kurdsjuk the name under which Jacob's younger brother Sergei was buried after he was killed by a jealous lover of a girl Sergei was dating.

Liuba Olga's niece with whom Anatoley fell in love at the age of five.

Liturgy The High Mass in the Orthodox Church.

Lubyanka Headquarters of the Soviet Secret police in Moscow, infamous for its brutal interrogation of inmates and political prisoners.

Luftwaffe The German Air Force.

Makuha (Ukr.) remnants of the sun flower seeds after it has been pressed into oil, a very nutritious additive to many dishes in the Ukraine.

Makarenko, Stephan father of Olga Kurdsjuk, nee Makarenko, his oldest daughter.

Makhorka (Rus.) chopped stem of the tobacco plant and the only affordable 'smoke' to a Soviet worker. The chopped stem is rolled in a pieces of newsprint then smoked.

Mamalyga Romanian, corn bread

Mamochka a Russian term of endearment for mother.

Murka Anatole's pet cat in Mariupol.

Mariupol city in the Donbas region of Ukraine located on the Sea of Azov and the site of Azov Stal (Steel). During WW II it was renamed Zdanov in honor of a communist leader, after the war the name was changed to the original.

Maya, Auntie a nurse who was Anatole's baby sitter whenever his mother Olga had to run any errands. Maya told wonderful stories to Anatole and his friend Yulja.

Meyer Zelagin, Dr. A Jewish doctor in Slutsk, Beloruss who diagnosed Jacob's heart condition and helped him to escape and settle in Mariupol through his cousin David Dvoskin.

Michael The first child of Jacob and Olga. Born in 1924 who died of pneumonia at the age of one.

Minsk Capital city of Beloruss.

Nary (Rus.) board shelves attached to sides of freight cars or barracks, used for sleeping.

Narzan (Rus.) Mineral waters said to help heart patients.

Nastia an affectionate name for Anastasia, Olga and Jacob's second child.

Na Zdorovye (Rus.) A toast "To your health", whenever a glass is raised during a celebration.

NEP New Economic Policy, a period after the Russian revolution of 1917 when the Soviet Union was being established. The process provided for land distribution to the peasants based on the "number of mouths" in the family.

Neizvestnost (Rus.) uncertainty.

Nach West (Ger.) An expression: "To the West".

Nikolai II The last Czar of Russia and a member of the
Romanov Dynasty which ruled Russia for over three
hundred years. He and his family were executed by
the Bolsheviks after the October Revolution of 1917.

Novosyelovka Ouskirts of Mariupol, where Jacob built his
house and where Anatole lived until the age of eight.

Novushka (Rus.) A prison term for a new inmate brought
into a communal cell.

Obrok (Rus.) a tax paid by the serf to his owner for permission to work outside the estate. Also, after the revolution, the tax paid by the former serf to the state for
the land allotted to him.

Okroshka (Rus.) cold cucumber soup.

Ostcommendature (Ger.) the German occupation forces
governing body for the Eastern territories.

Parasha (Rus.) a prison term for a bucket or a barrel used as
a latrine in a cell or railroad car transporting exiles.

Partianky (Rus.) cloth wraps used instead of socks to
provide additional warmth.

Partisan (Rus.) a guerilla, not part of a regular army.

Pascha The Resurrection of Christ. This is the highest
Orthodox Holy Day of the year, celebrated after the
Jewish Passover.

Patronymik - Father's name appended to the first name of a person, i.e. Jacob son of Zachary, would be Yakov Zacharyevich

Pavlik author's next door boyhood friend, nicknamed Blokha - the flea.

Peter III czar in 1600 who issued the "Manifesto on the Freedom of Nobility" further restraining serf's rights of movement or relocation..

Plague term ascribed to the kulaks by their guards while transporting them into exile.

Proletariat (Rus.) a term used to identify the lowest level of the working class whose members depended on the sale of their daily labor for subsistence. Karl Marx considered them a class of virtual slavery whose productivity exceeded the wages they were paid. The mainstay of communism.

Pokazukha (Rus.) "just for show", window dressing, a term used by the Soviet workers who did not believe that something was "for real", or "too good to be true."

Politburo (Rus.) the highest ruling body of the Soviet Union government.

Pomeschik (Rus.) landowner, who controlled the lives of the serfs.

Pushka Romanian, for gun or rifle

Pzemysl, Poland an eastern region assembly point for persons being shipped to various German forced labor and concentration camps such as Dachau, Buchenwald, Treblinka, Wurgendorf and others.

Romanovs The ruling dynasty of Russian czars from 1613 - 1917.

SS (Ger.) A notoriously viscious segment of the German army, known for their atrocities during WW II.

Salo (Rus.) bacon.

Samohonka (Rus.) home-brewed vodka.

Samanka a peasant's hut in the Ukraine, built of handmade mud and straw bricks.

Severnaya Dvina River in northern Russia which empties into the Arctic Sea. The site of Kulaks exile camp in Kotlas, Siberia.

Shalom (Jew.) standard Jewish greeting, meaning peace.

Shapka (Rus.) a hat, but usually refers to a hat with ear flaps.

Shchavel (Rus.) a leafy sour grass, also known as sorrel, used in salad or soup.

Siberia The northern region of Russia above the Latitude of 75 degrees stretching across the whole continent. A name associated with the coldest region of the USSR, and a place of exile.

Slutsk A town in central Beloruss.

Solzenitsyn, Alexander Dissident Russian author of many books on the Stalinist GULAG camps, i.e., "GULAG Archipelago". "One day in the Life of Ivan Denisovich", was his first novel, smuggled out of USSR published in the West, describing the life of exiles in the GULAGs.

Stalin, Iosif Visarionovich Dictator of Russia, who succeeded Lenin as the General Secretary of the Communist Party, under whose rule Russia became the Union of Soviet Socialist Republics (USSR). Stalin's purges of friends, kulaks and imagined foes is said to be responsible for deaths of over thirty million Russians.

Stuka German dive bomber in WW II.

Stolypin, Pyotr Arkadyevich A czarist statesman who served as the minister of interior after 1906 and was the proponent of new agrarian reforms which involved the resettlement of poor peasants to Siberia.

Sukhari (Rus.) dried bread, used by travelers in Russia, and the basic bread in prisons.

Svjatodukhow, Dedushka The elder who taught Anatole to pray, and told him of God.

Swaty (Rus.) honorable members of the groom who negotiated with the bride's father for the hand in marriage and establishment of the dowry.

Taiga (Rus.) a primeval forest in the northern regions of Russia or Siberia

Three fifteen (Rus.) a small bottle of vodka. A size popular with workers, since it handily fit into any pocket, and cost only 3 rubles and 15 kopeks.

Toymushka Village in Siberia near Kotlas to which Zachary, his wife, and son Sergei were exiled.

Tovarishch (Rus.) comrade, a pal, and the common name for the Proletariat in USSR.

Troika (Rus.) a team of three horses pulling a wagon or a sleigh, often used as a symbol for "Russia."

Troitsa the Orthodox Holy Day of Pentecost, celebrated in May or June, and dependent on the date of Pascha, Easter.

Trotsky An early revolutionary leader in Russia and associate of Lenin, who split with Lenin, establishing the Menshevik Party

Tsar/Czar (Rus.) Term ascribed to the Russian ruler before the revolution, a diminutive of Caesar.

Tsurki a game children play in Russia and Ukraine, whose rules are similar to those of baseball, but played with sticks rather than bat and ball.

Turgenev, Ivan Russian writer of "Notes of the Hunter", "Fathers and Sons" and other novels dealing with life in Russia during the 1800's.

Tundra (Rus.) a desolate northern region of Russia with little or no vegetation.

Ukase (Rus.) decrees issued by the czar or local nobility to control the movement of the serf population.

UNRA - United Nations Refugee Asssociation. This organization provided food and shelter for the Displaced Persons in Germany and assisted with immigration.

Valeryanka (Rus.) sedative derived from a local herb and the source of valium, usually prescribed for heart condition.

Vera One of the "girls" who always wanted to play with the boys on Vishnyevyj Pereulok.

Vishnevyj Pereulok a street where Anatole lived in Mariupol

Volksdeutch German citizens who migrated out of Germany to any territory in the hands of the Nazis during WW II in preparation of building Hitler's Third Reich.

Volodya Jacob's boyhood friend in Bolshaya Sliva

Vykhodnoy (Rus.) "the day off", a day of rest provided to Soviet workers.
Wehrmacht the German infantry during WW II.

Wetzlar Town in northwestern Germany to which Jacob and Olga were relocated after being rescued from the Wurgendorf slave labor camp, and where they were reunited with Anatole.

Wurgendorf a town in the Westphalen region of northern Germany where the Alfred E. Nobel Dynamitfabrik was located and the area for the forced slave labor camp No.4939 where the Kurdsjuk family worked from 1943 to 1945, making dynamite.

Yanka Kupala A pagan holiday, honoring a superstitious spirit which was said to help young girls find out who their husband might be.

Yasha an endearing name for Jacob

Yevangelie (Rus.) The Holy Gospel which is read by a priest during the Orthodox Liturgy and contains the books of the New Testament.

Yesip, Makarenko younger brother of Olga and Jacob's best friend.

Yulja, Kalivanow Anatole's childhood friend in Mariupol.

Zak car (Rus.) a railroad car specifically designed to transport exiles to their place of internment. The name stems from the Russian word zakliuchenyje, prisoners.

Zakuska (Rus.) any appetizer served with a drink.

Zamolchi (Rus.) shut up !

Zaklyuchennye (Rus.) persons who have been arrested and imprisoned.

Zelagin, Dr. Meyer Physician who treated Jacob after his heart attack in the Lubianka KGB prison.

Zemlyak (Rus.) fellow countryman, or person from the same region.

Notes

Notes

Notes

Bibliogrqaphy

Ellis Island Immigrants - (Photo) National Parks Service: Statue of Liberty National Monument. Used with permission, Photo EI20

Archipelag Gulag - 1919 - 1956 (in original Russian) Alexander Solzhenitsyn Experience of Artistic Research, YMCA PRESS - 1974

One Day in the Life of Ivan Denisovich - Alexander Solzhenitsyn, Lancer Books Inc. 26 W. 47th St. New York, New York -1963

Russian Writers and Society 1825 - 1904 by Ronald Hingley World University Library, McGraw-Hill Book Company

Rasputin by Brian Moynihan, The Saint who Sinned, Random House - 1997

The Blessed Surgeon - The Life of Saint Luke, Archbishop of Simferopol by Archdeacon Vassiliy Marushchak Divine Press - Point Reyes Station, California

Echoes of a Native Land - by Serge Schmeman, Two Centuries of a Russian Village, Alfred A. Knopf, New York, 1997

History of Russia Vol. III Reforms, Reaction, Revolutions By Paul Miliukov, Funk and Wagnals, New York

The Russians - by Hedrick Smith - New York Times Moscow Bureau Chief, 1971 - 1974 Quadrangle/the New York Times Book Co.

English-Russian/Russian English Dictionary
by Kenneth Katzner, Revised and Expanded Edition,
John Wiley & Sons, Inc., 1994

The Origins of WW II - by Igor Ovsyany, Novosti Press
Agency Publishing House - 1989

The Summer of 1941- An Anatomy of the Tragedy
Novosti. Moscow 1991

The Great Exploit of the People - Novosti Press Agency
Publishing House - Moscow 1990

The Holy Bible -King Jamess Version
Thomas Nelson, Inc., Camden, New Jersey